OLD ENGLISH TOWNS

ANDREWS & LANG

OLD ENGLISH TOWNS

BY

WILLIAM ANDREWS AND ELSIE M. LANG

"The Feathers Hotel," Ludlow

Bracken Books
LONDON

First published 1931
by T. Werner Laurie Ltd, London.

This edition published 1985 by Bracken Books,
a division of Bestseller Publications Limited, Brent House,
24 Friern Park, London N12 9DA, England.

ISBN 0 946495 64 5

Printed and bound by
Mackays of Chatham Ltd., England

FOREWORD

An attempt is made in this work to give descriptive and historical accounts of the more important of our "Old English Towns." Their rise and the chief buildings of past ages, remarkable episodes and phases of old-time social life, receive consideration. It will be shown how towns have risen under the protection of castles, how others have grown under the care of religious houses, while others have advanced under royal patronage. Old customs linked with the lives of the people receive attention. The Cathedrals of the country are fully dealt with in other volumes in this series, and are, therefore, not described at length.

CONTENTS

Part I

By William Andrews

PART II

BY ELSIE M. LANG

ILLUSTRATIONS

Part I

Part II

† From a Drawing by W. Dacres-Adams.
‡ From Drawings by Myra K. Hughes.

OLD ENGLISH TOWNS

WILLIAM ANDREWS

(PART I.)

WINCHESTER.

"A CITY of historical memories" is a modern designation often applied to Winchester, once the capital of England. It is one of the most delightfully interesting places in the country, and when once seen can never be forgotten. Here the past and present meet without spoiling each other. The city is famous alike for its cathedral, college, castle, and other buildings of bygone times.

It is pleasantly situated on the Itchen, and is only sixty miles west-south-west of London. In far distant times, it was a tribal settlement on the summit of the hill which overlooks the Winchester of to-day. As the early settlers grew in strength, they left St. Catherine's Hill for the more convenient plain below. When the invading Romans became a power in the land the ancient Britons were driven from their strongholds, and the strangers occupied their chief towns. The settlement of the British at Winchester was not given up without battle and bloodshed; but they had not the power to withstand the superior numbers of the highly trained Roman men-at-arms.

The invaders reached the town by the river, and recognised the advantages of its site. They planned the place in a rectangular form, the chief street corresponding with the High Street of the present time. Around the town was built a wall for protection. Within were evidences of southern civilisation, and temples were raised to Apollo and Concord. Many of the remains of the Roman occupation of the city may be inspected in the local museum; they consist of tesselated pavements and other objects, and in the ruins of Wolvesey are examples of Roman bricks.

One is tempted to linger over the legendary lore of pagan times, and the early dawn of religious life in the remote past. We should, however, deal with doubtful topics, which, though not difficult to state, are not easy to prove. Modern research has proved that many of the older historians often substituted fiction for fact in their works. The chief interest of the city belongs to the five hundred years when it disputed with London the claim to be the capital of England. The period covered the last three Saxon and first two Norman centuries.

Early in the seventh century an Italian monk, Birinus, converted King Kynegils to Christianity. It was the King's intention to build a large new church at Winchester, then a Royal city. Within six years of his conversion the King passed away, and was laid to rest before the altar of the church which was being erected. Kynewald, his son, completed the building. All land within seven miles round the city was given for its endowment. Part of the land belonging to the early sanctuary is still held by the Dean and Chapter. Birinus fixed his see at Dorchester, but it was transferred to Winchester in 676. Little is known of the Saxon structure, but within its walls the Saxon kings were crowned. William the Conqueror, it is true, was first crowned at Westminster Abbey, but on the arrival of his Queen in this country he was again crowned with greater ceremonial display in Winchester Cathedral. It was at the banquet which followed that the Champion first comes on the scene. He rode into the hall, and challenged anyone to mortal combat who denied the right of the King to the throne.

Wolvesey, near the cathedral, had long been a Royal residence. Here lived the kings of Wessex. Alfred the Great was educated at the Prior's school, his tutor being St. Swithun, a native of the place, and who in later years became the Bishop of Winchester. It was at Wolvesey that the first English prose book was compiled—the "Anglo-Saxon Chronicle." The scribes were assisted in their work by King Alfred, and he directed that the volume should be kept there, but in later times it was removed. In this chronicle was given an annual record of the country from the invasion of Cæsar down to the accession of Henry II. in the year 1154. The Winchester copy of this great year book, by order of Alfred, was fastened to a chain, so that all who wished might read it.

St. Swithun was the King's Counsellor, and it was he who recommended the erection of a strong wall round the precincts of the cathedral. It saved the building when the Danes burnt Canterbury, and in vain attempted to destroy Winchester. St. Swithun played an important part in Saxon life, and the story of his career is full of interest. He presided over the see for eleven years with holiness and humility. He was of noble parentage. He was buried, we read, according to his own request, in a humble grave outside the cathedral, where the feet of the passers-by might tread and the rain of heaven fall. According to the common legend, the monks afterwards tried to remove his bones to a more fitting tomb for such a great and good man, but it rained so incessantly for forty days that, taking such a visitation as a mark of the saint's displeasure, they were obliged to desist and allow his remains to continue in their humble resting-place. Such is the story of the popular superstition of rain on St. Swithun's Day. Other legends of Saxon times are linked with the cathedral, and have come down through the ages, but their interest is not sufficient to induce us to linger over them.

The present cathedral was begun during the episcopate of Bishop Walkelin in 1079, and is a fine monument of the skill of the earlier Norman architects. Within the fane are the tombs of many who have added to England's greatness, kings and princes, bishops, soldiers, men of science, literature, and art. To this cathedral the remains of William II. were brought in a charcoal cart from the New Forest, where he had met with a violent death. He was buried under the tower; the record adds—"many looking on and few grieving." A number of mortuary chests contain the remains of Canute and other monarchs, and form a curious feature in the church. There are some chantries; the one of William of Wykeham, who impressed on his countrymen for all time that "Manners Makyth Man," is of considerable interest. The greater part of a day might be spent inspecting the monuments and their inscriptions. Not only are they graven in memory of famous men and women, but often expressed in excellent English. Izaac Walton, the "Prince of Fishermen," is commemorated by a memorial slab in the Silkstone Chapel. He spent the last twenty years of his life at the city, first with his friend Bishop Morley at Wolvesey Palace and later with his son-in-law Prebendary Hawkins, in the Close. Walton died during a great frost, and over his remains is an inscription as follows:

Here resteth the body of
MR. IZAAK WALTON,
Who died the 15th of December, 1683.

Alas! He's gone before,
Gone to return noe more;
Our panting Breasts aspire
After their aged Sire,
Whose well-spent life did last
Full ninety Years, and past.
But now he hath begun
That which will nere be done,
Crown'd with eternal Blisse,
We wish our Souls with his.
Votis modestis sic flerunt liberi.
Thus with modest vows his children wept.

The foregoing is ascribed to Bishop Ken. An inscription of more modern interest is one near the unusually curious font; it is to the memory of Mrs. Montagu, the founder of the Blue Stocking

Club, a student of Shakespeare and the Chimney Sweepers' Friend:

> Here lies the body of ELIZBETH MONTAGU, daughter of Matthew Robinson, Esq., of West Layton, in the County of York, who, possessing the united advantages of beauty, wit, judgment, reputation, and riches, and employing her talents most uniformly for the benefit of mankind, might be justly deemed an ornament to her country. She died on the 25th of August, 1800, aged 81.

The greatest of English women novelists, Jane Austen, passed away in a small house not far distant from the cathedral and near to the college. A memorial window and underneath it a ledger stone bearing the following inscription will be found in the north aisle:

> In memory of JANE AUSTEN, youngest daughter of the late Rev. George Austen, formerly Rector of Steventon, in this County. She departed this life on the 18th of July, 1817, aged 41, after a long illness supported with patience and the hope of a Christian. The benevolence of her heart, the sweetness of her temper, and the extraordinary endowments of her mind obtained the regard of all who knew her, and the warmest love of her intimate connexions. Their grief is in proportion to their affection : they know their loss to be irreparable, but in their deep affection they are consoled by a firm, though humble hope, that her charity, devotion, faith, and purity have rendered her soul acceptable in the sight of her Redeemer.

This gifted authoress whose name stands so high in the annals of literature had a struggle to get her books published. She sold "Northanger Abbey" to a Bath bookseller for the insignificant sum of ten pounds. The manuscript remained for some time in his possession without being printed, he fearing that if published it would prove a failure. He was, however, at length induced to give it to the world, and its merits caused it to be extensively read.

In the popular mind these inscriptions wane in interest before one in the beautifully kept burial ground around the cathedral. It reads as follows:

In Memory of
THOMAS THETCHER,
A Grenadier of the North Reg't of the Hants Militia,
who died of a violent Fever contracted by drinking
Small Beer when hot the 12th of May, 1761,
Aged 26 Years.

In grateful remembrance of whose universal goodwill towards his Comrades this Stone is placed at their expense as a small testimony of their regard and concern.

Here sleeps in peace a Hampshire Grenadier,
Who caught his death by drinking cold small beer;
Soldiers, be wise from his untimely fall,
And when ye're hot, drink strong or none at all.

This memorial being decayed was restored by the Officers of the Garrison, A.D. 1781.

An honest soldier never is forgot,
Whether he die by musket or by hot.

This stone was placed by the North Hants Militia, when disembodied at Winchester on 26th April, 1802, in consequence of the original stone being destroyed.

It was at Winchester that the curfew bell was first rung at eight o'clock at night by order of William I. This was the signal for putting out lights and fires. Not until four next morning, when another bell was sounded, could the fires be rekindled. For more than eight centuries the curfew bell has been heard, and it is still rung at the present time, but the practice has long been sentimental. Another curious bell-ringing custom was instituted by Richard Budd. He was a native of Winchester, and in 1630 left to the Dean and

Chapter £40 on condition that the great bell of the cathedral be tolled for condemned criminals before their execution, and that certain prayers be read on their behalf. The usage was in course of time discontinued, and the money devoted to other charitable objects.

Not far distant from the cathedral is Winchester College. The charter of William of Wykeham incorporating this school bears the date of October 20th, 1382, and may still be seen in the Muniment-room. Long prior to the Conquest the city had its grammar school, in which it is asserted that King Ethelwulf and King Alfred were educated, and the present college is a continuation of the earlier school. The school is a noble pile, and has undergone many changes as time has run its course, but has ever held its reputation for scholarship. In one of the old schoolrooms on the western side are inscriptions with emblems:

> AUT DISCE—A mitre and crosier, as the expected reward of learning.
>
> AUT DISCEDE—An inkhorn and sword, the emblems of the civil and military professions.
>
> MANET SORS TERTIA CAEDI—A rod.

The first sentence may be translated Either learn, and the second, Or depart hence, and the third, Or remain and be whipped. A good free translation of the whole is:—Learn, leave or be licked. Until modern days the drink at meals was ale, but in a great measure tea and coffee have taken its place. The visitor is shown as relics of other days ancient leathern jacks, mugs, trenchers, and candlesticks which were in use long before gas and electric light were thought about, and when the candle shed its feeble light. To-day the buildings remain about the same as when erected by William of Wykeham at a cost of £1,014, equal in modern money to £20,000. They are more solid in appearance than rich in detail.

At Hyde Abbey there is little to arrest attention, but it calls for inspection more for its associations than its remains of the past. It was here that Alfred the Great was buried, but the site of his grave is lost.

The castle at Winchester, built by William the Conqueror, has been swept away. It was here that the "Domesday Book" was kept for some years. During a banquet at the castle Earl Godwin died, and his end was regarded as a judgment for his evil life. In later times another castle was built. It was here Henry III., "of Winchester," was born and resided. It is rich in history. On its walls have been spiked the heads of warlike men, and within its stately rooms parliaments were held. Here Raleigh was imprisoned. In the hall may be seen what is called Arthur's Round Table, but most probably it is part of a gaming table.

Not far from the castle stood the brick palace of Charles II., which is now used as a barracks. Considerably further away is the City Cross in High Street. It dates back to the reign of Henry VI., and it is believed to have been built by Cardinal Beaufort, on the site of an ancient market cross. The present cross was repaired in 1835, and was restored by Gilbert Scott in 1865. It is enriched with saints and notable men. The principal figures are:

William of Wykeham, with his book of statutes of his College and Pastoral Staff.

Laurence de Anne, Mayor of Winchester.

King Alfred the Great.

St. John the Evangelist, said to be the only old figure remaining.

In the top niches are eight figures as follow:

SS. Thomas, Maurice, John, Peter, Laurence, Bartholomew, Swithin, and the Blessed Virgin.

The cross is a reminder of olden days and olden ways. We find it stated in a volume of "Transcripts from the Municipal Archives of Winchester," Compiled by Charles Bailey, Town Clerk, 1856, "By an Ordinance of the 4th of August, in the twenty-eight year of the reign of Elizabeth, bull-dogs were prohibited running through the city unmuzzled."

Itm.—That noe person within this citie shall suffer or permit any of theire Mastife Doggs to goe unmusselled upon paine of everie defalte herein of 3*s.* 4*d.* to be levied by distresse, to the use of the Poore people of the citie.

The records contain many items on the baiting of animals. It is stated that certain butchers were ordered to find bulls to be baited, and the other butchers were directed to pay sixpence each yearly towards maintaining the custom. The mayors appear to have transferred the site of the baiting from the bull-ring of the city to the vicinity of their

WINCHESTER. The High Street, 1838.

own houses. The citizens felt that this was an infringement of their rights, and finally, on the 19th November, 30th Henry VIII., the Corporation made an order:

That from henceforthe ther shal be no bulstake set before any Mayor's doore to bayte any bull, but onlie at the bull-ringe within the said cytie.

Like other old towns Winchester attempted to gain favours by bribing the palate of those in high places. The local records include particulars of many presents of sugar loaves and other gifts. On March 24th, 1592, it was decided at a meeting of the municipal authorities to present the Lord Marquis of Winchester with a sugar loaf weighing five pounds and a gallon of sack on his coming to the Lent Assizes. The accounts of the city at this period contain entries of payments for sugar loaves given to the Recorder for a New Year's present and for pottles of wine bestowed on distinguished visitors.

The fair at Winchester was held on St. Giles's Downs, and for centuries it was the great event of the year. It ranked among the largest fairs of Europe. It is about a thousand years since Alfred the Great instituted fairs in England. They were popular among the Saxons, and our first Norman king recognised their value as a means of extending commerce. He framed Acts for conducting trade, etc. William the Conqueror established the great fair here. Its jurisdiction, we gather from Brand's "Popular Antiquities," extended seven miles round, and comprehended even Southampton, then a trading town. If a merchant sold wares in the circuit during the fair he forfeited them to the bishop. Officers were placed at a considerable distance, at bridges and other avenues of access to the fair, to extract toll of all merchandise passing their way. In the meantime, all the shops in the city were closed. A court called the Pavilion, composed of the bishop's justiciaries and other officers, had power to try causes of various sorts for seven miles round. The bishop had toll of every load or parcel of goods passing through the gates of the city.

On the Eve of St. Giles, the mayor, bailiffs, and citizens of Winchester delivered the keys of the four gates to the bishop's officers. Numerous foreign merchants attended this fair, and several streets were formed in it, and assigned to the sale of different commodities. The surrounding monasteries had shops or houses in the streets, used only at the fair, and held under the bishop, by whom they were let for a term of years.

When the fair was first established it only lasted three days. It was in the reign of Henry III. prolonged to sixteen days. Brand says in the days of William I., the tolls were given as a kind of revenue to the Bishop of Winchester. He strongly enforced his privileges, in such a manner as to obstruct local trade and oppress the people.

Of the old gates of the city Westgate is the only one left, and an interesting monument it is of the olden time. The date of the exterior of this gate dates back to the fourteenth century. It forms a pleasing entrance to the city, and in the past was a strong means of protection. In 1558 it was converted into a prison. Alderman William Henry Jacob, in his account of "The Ancient West Gate," gives several interesting details drawn from the city records of some of the prisoners. We reproduce three entries:

1615.—Robt. Payne, a prisoner for debt in Westgate, in consideration of his decayed state, being a freeman and one of the twenty-four (the Corporation), and of good behaviour and carriage, received a compromise with his creditors, £6.13.4.

1723.—Thos. Elton, a prisoner, died of small pox in the Gate.

1724.—A poor woman confined for debt, and likely to perish, released with 15*s*.

There are many charges in the old accounts for persons being whipped. Here was the old whipping post. Some of the entries are as follow:

1555-6.—Whipcord, to whip two vagabonds beyond the city - - - -	ii*d*.
1556-7.—Whipcord, to whip vagabonds twice -	iij*d*.
1653.—Thos. Stone, punishing beggars at Westgate - - - - - - -	1*l*. 11*s*. 8*d*.

To-day in this gate is a small museum of local antiquities, mainly relating to bygone punishments.

Just beyond the gate is a reminder of the city when in sorrow. Winchester suffered much from the plague of 1666. On the neighbouring downs are numerous curiously-shaped mounds, which are said to cover the pits into which the dead were cast. When the pestilence raged a primitive kind of quarantine was practised. The county folk supplied food, which was placed on a stone outside the city, and in exchange citizens placed money in a bowl of water. The old plague stone remains, built into a memorial which bears the following inscription:

This monument is erected by the Society of Natives on the very spot of ground to which the markets were removed, and whose basis is the very stone on which exchanges were made whilst the city lay under the scourge of the destroying pestilence in the year sixteen hundred and sixty-six. The Society of Natives was founded on the 26th August, 1669, for the relief of the widows and orphans of their fellow citizens who died of the great plague.

The old churches in the city, and some of the modern buildings, will repay inspection: such are the Guildhall, the Museum, and a striking statue of Alfred the Great by Thorneycroft, unveiled September 20th, 1901.

About a mile distant from the city is the Hospital of St. Cross, where is still maintained a curious charity, which was founded by Henry de Blois, Bishop of Winchester, in the year 1136. This institution was established for housing, clothing, and feeding thirteen poor men, "feeble and so reduced in strength that they can hardly support themselves without another's aid." In addition rooms were provided for chaplains and attendants, and suitable apartments for the master. The thirteen poor men on the foundation had a daily allowance of three and a half pounds of bread, a gallon and a half of beer, a modicum of mortrel (a sort of egg flip made with milk), and wastel bread. Twice a day, at dinner and at supper, flesh or fish was allowed, and dessert followed the former meal. It has been truly said the appetites of the fortunate thirteen were certainly not stinted. In addition, the charity provided food for a hundred of the poorest men of good character in Winchester. Each man, it is stated, was allowed two messes of flesh or fish, according as the day was a fast or not, a loaf of bread, and three quarts of beer; and if a man could not consume his allowance he might take it home; indeed it is suggested that the lavish quantity was provided so that the poor man's family might share in it. The beer in these remote times was very light and not of an intoxicating character.

The founder placed his hospital under the general supervision of the Hospitallers of St. John of Jerusalem, an order that had been established in 1100, but the arrangement did not long survive its originator. Henry de Blois was succeeded in his bishopric in 1174 by Richard Tochyve, and he and the military knights disagreed over the administration. The second Henry was called upon to act as mediator in the quarrel, with the result that the Hospitallers retired and the control passed into the hands of the bishop, who, in gratitude, endowed dinners for another hundred men. Scandals in the management were rife when William of Wykeham came to the episcopal throne in 1367, and he corrected the abuses. In 1405, Henry, Cardinal Beaufort, thoroughly restored order, and greatly enriched the charity. Extensive enlargements were undertaken, and provision was made for thirty-five more inmates and for additional priests. Rooms were built for three nuns to attend to the sick in the infirmary.

It had now attained a large measure of usefulness, and the name given to it was the "Almshouse of Noble Poverty," but the older title of St. Cross is the one that remains. Henry VIII., at the Reformation, made no formal attack on this house, but it is said he considerably reduced its revenues.

From the reign of King Stephen down to the days of Edward VII., this charity has remained, and still follows in many respects the regulations and aims of its founder. The residents have sunk to the original number of thirteen, the daily dinners for 200 poor men have ceased, but a tradition of it still survives in the Wayfarer's Dole—a slice of bread and a horn of ale given to anyone who knocks at the porter's lodge and asks at reasonable hours.

When Emerson was in England he called at St. Cross and received the wayfarer's dole. He triumphantly related the circumstance as a proof of the majestic stability of English institutions. When the late King Edward was the Prince of Wales he made application and obtained the bread and beer. American visitors on repairing to this place usually ask for the royal horn. You have only to ask and receive, no questions are put.

CANTERBURY.

In distant times a pilgrimage to Canterbury delighted our ancestors, and to-day a visit to the ancient city is equally enjoyable. It is delightfully situated in a district known as the "Garden of England." It is a city full of interest to the student of religion, history, architecture, literature, and kindred subjects. From the dawn of the history of this country Canterbury appears to have been a place of importance. Under the Britons it was known as Dur-whern, and it is supposed that Dane John mound was one of their works. Lucius, a mythical British king, is credited with building the first Christian church, A.D. 187, on or about the site of the present cathedral.

The Roman name was Durovenum, and is specially marked on the Itinerary of Antoninus, and its importance may be realised from the fact that the two great military roads, Watling Street and Stone Street, met here.

By the Saxons it was designated Cantwars-byrig, the fortress of the men of Kent. When Ethelbert, in 597, was converted to Christianity, this town was the capital. It was in the Saxon era that St. Augustine and his faithful companions, bearing a silver cross and chanting songs of praise, entered the city; they found the teaching of the Christian religion recognised. Queen Bertha worshipped in the church of St. Martin, which belongs to Roman times, and it was here that St. Augustine started his teaching. Another fane known later as St. Pancras' Church, which had previously been used as a place of pagan worship, was given to the Christian Church. Other favours were granted by the King; certain lands were given, and he even retired from his palace and presented it to the Church. Thus arose the new Archbishopric of Canterbury, and the first union of Church and State.

We cannot linger over the first cathedral, and its romantic history, the story of its pillage by the Danes, and its almost complete destruction by fire. The glory and chief attraction of the city is the cathedral. It and its surroundings are a history of England in stone. "There is no church or place in the kingdom," says Dean Stanley, "with the exception of Westminster Abbey, that is so closely connected with the history of our country as Canterbury Cathedral. It is not too much to say that if anyone were to go through the various spots of interest in and around and asked—What happened here? Who was the man whose tomb we see? Why was he buried here? What effect did his life or his death have on the world?—a real knowledge of the history of England would be obtained, such as the mere reading of books or hearing lectures would utterly fail to supply." The present building comes down to us from 1070 to 1495. It is made up of the various styles of architecture which prevailed between the times named. The north-west tower is modern, and was completed in 1840, replacing a

CANTERBURY. Westgate, 1828.

Norman tower, which was so much decayed that it could no longer be preserved.

It was within the walls of this cathedral that Becket was murdered. The tragedy was the outcome of a contest between Church and Crown. An overture was made in 1170 by Henry II. for the banished prelate to return to England. He came back to his diocese, and one of his first acts was to suspend the Archbishop of York, and excommunicate two bishops who had taken the King's side. His Majesty was in France when the news reached him, and without deliberate thinking asked if someone would not rid him of the pestilent Becket. Four knights took up the challenge, and made their way to his palace at Canterbury. They obtained an interview with him in his residence; it was of a stormy character, but happily their weapons were left outside the house. He was not dismayed, and boldly said, "You threaten me in vain. Were all the swords of England hanging over my head you could not terrify me from obedience to God, and my lord the Pope."

A terrible scene followed. The monks closed the doors of the cathedral, where the Archbishop had repaired to evening prayers, but he bade them open the doors, saying, "The church must not be turned into a castle." The knights entered and slew Becket. Still is pointed out the site of the murder, but the shrine—one of the most famous in the Middle Ages—was completely demolished by Henry VIII.

Of the many interesting tombs, that of Edward, the Black Prince, receives the greatest attention.

It is covered with a canopy which was once richly painted; above it, suspended on a beam, are his helmet, shield, gauntlets, surcoat, and the scabbard for his sword. It is said that the sword was there until the time of Cromwell, and that he took it away.

Another important memorial of the past is a stone seat called St. Augustine's Chair, on which have been enthroned all the Archbishops of Canterbury.

The crypt is large, and has a history of interest, the more important part of which relates to the French and Flemish refugees. Queen Elizabeth, in 1568, gave them the use of the crypt for their religious services, conducted by their own preachers, and in which to set up their silk-looms, and to use as a residence. Sunday services in French are still held here for the descendants of the Protestant exiles.

Both the inside and outside of the cathedral are extremely majestic, but the building forms only a part of the original monastic establishment. It is difficult to leave the cathedral with its many charms, but we must remember that the old city has many buildings of great interest which may be seen in almost every direction.

It is especially rich in churches. St. Martin's is the mother church of England, and draws many people to it on account of its remote antiquity, while others have special points of interest. There are the remains of several monastic houses, which are replete with historic stories of the olden time. The ancient city gates are very fine, more especially the West Gate. Some of the old city walls are near to the famous gate. The Royal Museum should be visited, as it contains numerous objects of local antiquarian interest, including the Burghmote horn, with which the Corporation was called together, down to 1835.

The old-time records of Canterbury throw much light on the social and domestic life of the city. A quaint note about lighting the place occurs in 1544. We find that it was decided "that during the winter, every dark night the aldermen, common council, and inn-holders are to find one candle, with light, at their doors, and the other inhabitants are to do in like fashion upon request, and if any lantern be stolen, the offender shall be set in the pillory at the mayor's discretion; the candles are to be lighted at six, and continued until burnt out." It will be noticed that there is an allusion to the pillory. At Canterbury and elsewhere it was a custom to punish people at the time of public market. Here, in the year 1524, a man was set up in the pillory, which was in the Market Place, bearing a paper on his head inscribed: "This is a false, perjured, and forsworn man." He was confined in the pillory until the market was over, and then led to the West Gate and thrust out of the city wearing the paper. "If he be proud," says an old writer, "he may go home and show himself among his neighbours." The ducking stool was frequently in use for curing scolding women and others guilty of breaches of the national and local laws.

Henry VIII., in 1535, ordered courtiers to "poll their hair," and permit the crisp beard to grow. Taxing the beard followed. In 1549 the Sheriff of the city paid a fine of 3*s*. 4*d*. for wearing his beard.

Another quaint item in the records under the year 1556, is an order directing the Mayor every year before Christmas to provide for the Mayoress, his wife, to wear one scarlet gown and a bonnet of velvet. If the Mayor failed to procure the foregoing he was liable to be fined £10.

During the Commonwealth, when attempts were made to stop the celebrations of Christmas, Canterbury was one of the cities where rioting took place. Those in authority directed the holding of a market on Christmas Day, and some dozen shopkeepers opened their premises. The populace, supported by some of the "classes," requested the tradesmen to close their establishments, and on their refusing, broke the windows, scattered the goods, and roughly treated the shopkeepers. The leading citizens did their utmost to stop the riot, promising that if the people would disperse no further notice would be taken of the proceedings, but the authorities would not accept those conditions, and attempted to punish the ringleaders. This action gave rise to more rioting, but the Government ultimately dropped the matter, fearing that the rioting might be taken up in London.

There are several fine monuments in the city. One is to Marlowe, a native of Canterbury, and another is to the memory of the Kentish martyrs (thirty men and eleven women), who suffered death under Queen Mary. The old streets with their quaint houses afford pleasure to many, and there are the usual public buildings of an old city full of importance, but too numerous to notice at length. Canterbury has only to be seen to be appreciated.

BATH.

THE delightfully situated and well-built city of Bath has many charms. It is famous in legendary lore, history, literature, and fashion.

We may regard it as second to no other place in the country for chalybeate springs. Prosperity has been obtained from them for the inhabitants from an early period.

Some writers relate that here, 800 years before the birth of Christ, Prince Bladud was cured of leprosy. He was the son of the ancient British king, Lud Hudibras, and father of Shakespeare's King Lear. The historian is on far safer ground when he starts with the Romans, for it is quite certain that in early Roman times Bath was a place ot importance, and that the conquerors fully recognised the healing properties of its waters. It was a Roman station called *Aquæ Solis*, and it was here that their great roads from London and from Lincoln to the south coast intersected.

The site of the forum is known, and from time to time the remains of temples, altars, and pavements have been discovered. In 1882 a large Roman bath was laid bare. This and others were founded by Vespasian, or his son and successor, Titus, between the years A.D. 69 and 81. The site was covered with houses and forgotten, and it was quite by accident that it was found, yet the large bath, in which the Romans bathed in luxury, is 82 feet long, 40 feet wide, and 4½ feet in depth. Now it forms one of the chief points of interest in the place. Some Roman baths were found in 1755. It is most surprising that such important and large baths should be so long lost to sight.

The Abbey Church has a long and interesting and curious history. The building, as we see it to-day, is the latest example of any magnitude erected in this country in the purely Gothic style. On account of numerous and splendid windows it has been called the "Lantern of England." On a cross the story of the church is told in outline, and reads as follows:

In 775 the first Cathedral was built by King Offa.
In 973 King Edgar was crowned therein.
About 1010 the church was destroyed by Sweyne, the Dane.
And rebuilt by John de Villula, 1018–1122.
In 1137 partly destroyed by fire, it was subsequently restored by Bishop Robert, 1136–1166.
In 1499 the Cathedral, then in a ruinous state, was taken down, and Bishop King and Prior Bird began to build the present structure, which was not completed for public worship until 1616.
In 1834 the Corporation of Bath carried out extensive repairs, and removed adjoining buildings which for many years had disfigured the church.
In 1864 the Rev. Charles Kemble, aided by public subscriptions, began the work of restoration under the direction of Sir Gilbert Scott, R.A

The measurements of Bath Abbey Church are less than half those of York Minster, with which it disputes for the title of the "Lantern of England." Both the exterior and interior of the church of Bath are deeply interesting, and the windows and many

BATH. The Pump Room, 1801.

monuments are extremely fine. As we inspect the monuments we are reminded of a well-known couplet:

> These walls, so full of monument and bust,
> Show how Bath waters serve to lay the dust.

The poet and the sculptor have united in lifting the memorials out of the commonplace. One of the best epitaphs is on Quin, the actor, who died in 1766, at the age of 73. It was written by David Garrick:

> The tongue, which set the table on a roar,
> And charmed the public ear, is heard no more;
> Closed are those eyes, the harbingers of wit,
> Which spake before the tongue what Shakespeare writ.
> Cold is the hand, which living was stretched forth
> At friendship's call to succour modest worth.
> Here lies James Quin; deign reader to be taught,
> Whate'er thy strength of body, force or thought,
> In Nature's happiest mould however cast,
> To this complexion thou must come at last.

Quin was a somewhat wayward man, and had a misunderstanding with Rich, the manager of Covent Garden Theatre, which resulted in the former leaving in an unceremonious manner. He soon regretted the step that he had taken, and wrote to his old friend and manager:

I am at Bath.—QUIN.

Rich did not deem such a letter a sufficient apology for his unwarrantable conduct, and replied:

Stay there and be hanged.—RICH.

There is a monument to Beau Nash, the master of ceremonies at fashionable Bath in his day. In Latin prose and English verse, we are told the virtues and power of the man. As we read the pompous inscription, we recall his encounter with John Wesley. "Early in 1739," we read, Wesley "was bold enough to visit Bath and brave the scorn of Beau Nash's fashionable throng. Nash, whose orders were obeyed by aristocrats, was not afraid to rebuke the humble preacher, and in Avon Street, in the hearing of the crowd, he plainly told him that street preaching was contrary to the law, 'Besides,' he added, 'your words frighten people out of their wits.' 'Sir,' said Wesley, 'did you ever hear me preach?' 'No,' said the Master of Ceremonies. 'How then can you judge of what you never heard?' 'By common report,' said Nash stoutly. 'Common report is not enough. Give me leave, sir, to ask, is not your name Nash?' 'My name is Nash.' 'Sir,' replied Wesley, 'I dare not judge of you by common report.'"

The witty retort greatly amused the crowd, and Nash beat a silent retreat to the Pump Room.

As we read the inscriptions we are impressed by the fact that within the walls of the abbey many find a resting-place far from their homes situated in distant parts of the country. It is asserted that no other church, save Westminster Abbey, has so many memorials of the dead as Bath Abbey Church, which, it is said, has more than six hundred. There are other interesting churches in the city which will well repay a visit. Some of the Nonconformist churches are rich in associations as well as attractive. The name of Jay, of Bath, is important in the annals of the Free Church, and there are others still remembered.

Many of the baths and public buildings which meet the eye as we wander through the streets are of considerable interest, and display taste and wealth. In recent times a most important addition has been made to the attractions of the town by the Holbourne Museum, which was presented to Bath by Sir Thomas Holbourne, Bart., and contains a fine collection of pictures, china, and porcelain and other artistic treasures. The Royal Literary and Scientific Institution has also a museum, especially rich in geological specimens and in examples of birds, and eggs, and other natural history objects. The gardens of the institution are pleasant, and extend to the Avon, a river which adds to the charms of the city. The parks and gardens of Bath are pleasantly situated and well laid out. The Victoria Park, which was opened in 1830 by the late Queen, when Princess Victoria, is the chief in the city, and contains memorials of her Majesty.

The Botanical Gardens are a favourite haunt of the world of fashion. The best of music adds to the attractions of Bath, and there are so many forms of diversion that one thinks that here pleasure is the only object of life.

The literary annals of Bath include the names of leading men-of-letters of the past. Jane Austen is in several ways associated with the city. She made it her home in the earlier years of the nineteenth century. Fanny Burney resided in the city for eight years, in Gay Street. Sir Walter Scott and Southey spent some years of their youth here. Landor, Wordsworth, Dickens, Macaulay, Lord Lytton, Goldsmith, Sheridan, Dr. Johnson, James

Boswell, and many others have been residents or visitors, and linked their names with the literature relating to Bath. In many directions you see their names on the houses they occupied, or find them mentioned in the local guides. That benefactor to the journalistic profession, Sir Isaac Pitman, inventor of shorthand, carried on for many years his useful work in the city. When Pitman was knighted he was wont to say the title was a white elephant, but the stabling did not cost much!

GLOUCESTER.

THE city of Gloucester occupies a bold and pleasant situation on the left bank of the Severn. It is a place of great antiquity, and during British and Roman ages was of some importance, while Bede asserts that in the Saxon era, when it was in the kingdom of Mercia, it was one of the noblest cities in the kingdom. The lives of some of the more notable Saxons are associated with Gloucester. Here in 896 Alfred the Great held a Witenagemot. A few years later, if we follow the stream of history as it flows through the ages, we must record that the Danes made an attack on the city, but were routed. Coming down to 940, we find death closing the career of Athelstan. He had, it has often been stated, a claim to be called the King of England. His reputation reached far beyond his native shores, for no fewer than five of his sisters were united in marriage to Continental princes. Mr. F. A. Hyett, B.A., the author of a capital little volume, "Gloucester in National History" (1896), dismisses as fiction a statement which has found its way into local history. "The story of the mutilation and murder," says Mr. Hyett, "of Queen Ælgifu at Gloucester, about the year 958, because she had contracted an uncanonical marriage with King Eadwig, was coined in the brain of a monkish writer, and must be dismissed as legendary." Some ten years later King Edgar made his home in the city, but not for an extended period. Early in the latter half of the tenth century the Danes were spreading terror and committing slaughter in the locality. They sailed up the Severn in 977. It is recorded that they attacked the city, which they ravaged, and it was almost consumed by fire.

Christianity was introduced into Gloucester before the seventh century, and has since retained its hold on the people through the changes of centuries. It has found its way into proverbial lore. "As sure as God's in Gloucester," is an old saying, and gave rise to Oliver Cromwell's retort that "it had more churches than godliness." Here monasteries and other sanctuaries arose in Saxon times for praise and prayer. In 1022 an important Benedictine Abbey was erected, and remained an important religious house until its suppression in 1539.

Our early Norman kings were often at Gloucester. William I. and II. frequently kept their Christmases at the abbey. The tables groaned under the profuse fare provided for the feast. These ancient and splendid celebrations of the olden time have passed into history. It is pleasant to recall an agreement of peace at Gloucester at one of the Christmas festivals. In 1098 the second William entertained Malcolm, King of Scotland, and at the high revels settled a treaty. Another king of the House of Normandy met his death here, not on the field of battle, but from feasting at the table. Henry I., during his residence in the city, acquired

GLOUCESTER. The Old County Gaol and part of the Ancient Castle, 1819.

a passion for lampreys, and died of a surfeit of them in 1135. We must not forget that he had attained the age of sixty-seven, and had reigned thirty-five years, much longer than any other Norman king.

The Empress Maud found support in her troubled career from the citizens of Gloucester. When she escaped from the castle of Winchester she found shelter and assistance at Gloucester. The first of the Plantagenet line, Henry II., called together a great council to this city in 1175. King John was frequently in residence at the castle in the city, and keenly enjoyed hunting expeditions in the neighbouring forest. In the Abbey of Gloucester was crowned Henry III., in 1216, at the tender age of ten years. His crown was merely a chaplet of gold, for his father, King John, had lost the original crown of the country when crossing the Wash. The third Henry's was one of the longest and most inglorious reigns in the annals of England. He was a weak and vacillating king, and a mere puppet of powerful barons. It is asserted that he loved Gloucester better than London. When defeated at Lewes by his brother-in-law, Simon de Montfort, and taken prisoner, he passed his confinement in Gloucester.

It has been an important place of Parliaments, and among the monarchs who have held them here were Edward I., Richard II., Henry IV., and Henry V., and even to-day some of the statutes passed are still in force, and are known as "the Statutes of Gloucester." In 1327, that weak monarch Edward II. was barbarously murdered at Berkeley Castle, and his remains were interred in the cathedral. Richard the Third granted the city a charter, but his name does not win any local esteem, for it was from Gloucester that he wrote the order to Brackenbury for the murder of the princes in the Tower. A warmer welcome was given to Henry VII. when on his way to Bosworth Field in 1485, where Richard, the last of the House of York, was slain. It is generally recorded that Henry VII., the first of the long line of Tudors to occupy the throne, was crowned on the battlefield with Richard's diadem, which was found in a hawthorn bush near the spot.

Henry VIII. and James I., during their progresses through the land, were warmly welcomed at Gloucester. James I. lodged at the Deanery, and during his stay touched for king's evil. The service for this superstitious rite remained in the "Book of Common Prayer" as late as 1719. The ceremony had been dropped five years earlier by George I.

When the Civil War divided the households of England in twain, when even father and son belonged to different parties, and brothers fought under different banners, the city which had so often basked in the sunshine of monarchs threw in its lot with Parliament. This was mainly brought about by the proceedings of the Star Chamber and by Archbishop Laud, who had been an unpopular Dean of Gloucester. Charles besieged the city, and reduced the inhabitants to great straits, but they were relieved by Lord Essex. The Royalists lost a thousand men, while only fifty citizens were slain.

When the Stuarts came to their own again, Charles II. had some of the gates and walls razed to the ground, and does not appear to have had any friendly feelings to the city; yet the citizens sent him warm congratulations on his safe return to the throne of his country. In later times other royal visits have been paid to the city, but these do not relate so much to the shaping of the history of England as those of far distant times.

The chief building in the city is the cathedral, which has a long and interesting history. It is the outcome of a religious house founded in 681, but went through many changes down to 1541, in which year the See of Gloucester was founded, and the then abbey church became a cathedral. The tower is very fine, and a beautiful example of fifteenth century work. The whole of the exterior is pleasing, and the interior is of great interest, and includes many important monuments. The one raised over the remains of the murdered King Edward II. brought much wealth to the church. It was visited by pilgrims, who gave freely of their substance. They lodged at the New Inn, in Northgate Street, one of the oldest houses in the city, dating back to 1450. It is strong and massive, and timber was largely used in its construction. It has external galleries and courtyard, and we get from it a good idea of an old-time hostelry. There is a curious monument, of Irish oak, of a chest on wheels, with an effigy (carved on top) of Robert Curthose, eldest son of William the Conqueror. He was a great benefactor to the church, and when his career ended after being a prisoner in Cardiff

Castle, he was brought here for interment before the high altar. Numerous other monuments will arrest the attention of the visitor, of men and women who in their day played an important part in the drama of life. Of those belonging to recent times is a monument in memory of a famous Gloucestershire man, Dr. Edward Jenner (1749—1823), discoverer of vaccination. The stained glass windows are much admired.

Just outside the abbey gate is St. Mary's Square, the scene of the martyrdom of Bishop Hooper. A Gothic cross contains his statue. It was erected by public subscription in 1864. This memorial recalls the days of Queen Mary, when an attempt was made to re-establish the Roman Catholic power in England, and when the faithful would rather suffer death than give up the religion they believed to be true.

A half-timbered house is still standing where Robert Raikes was born in 1735. He established the earliest Sunday school, which was conducted in St. Catherine Street, Gloucester. His father was a printer, and published the first newspaper issued in the city.

Like all old towns, the city has its quaint and narrow streets, but generally speaking the thoroughfares are broad and well kept. The streets are busy, and prosperity prevails. It is by no means a sleepy city. There are the usual public buildings, some of which are imposing, for conducting the business of the city and county.

A progressive spirit prevails in every direction. There is a capital public library, well abreast of the times. It has a good special collection of books relating to Gloucestershire. Near it is a museum and school of art, which, combined, must greatly add to the improvement of popular education in the city. The Gloucester schools are both numerous and excellent.

Gloucester is noted for its love of music. Alternately with Worcester and Hereford a triennial musical festival is held in the city. It is an inland port of sea-going ships. It was declared a port in 1882, and the Severn is reached by a ship canal.

It has been the birthplace of many notable men, and among the number George Whitfield, the popular preacher. It is situated in a charming district, making a good headquarters for a holiday.

HEREFORD.

THIS city has a quiet charm of its own, which few, if any, English cities can surpass. One, it is true, notices a lack of the wealth which prevails in a great northern city. There is not the rank and fashion which makes an inland spa so popular. Matters are made lively by the motor-car coming along at a rapid rate, but it does not improve the scenery. It merely leaves a dust and smell behind. The shops are well stocked, and give an indication that the citizens have money and taste. There are good examples of architecture and important antiquarian remains, while the annals are replete with historical interest; and a rich profusion of flowers in every direction adds to the beauty of the celebrated city on the Wye. It has numerous quaint alleys; but, speaking generally, the streets are wide, and the public buildings are seen to advantage.

The first view of Hereford, if it is obtained from the railway station, is by no means pleasing, but as one proceeds to the main part of the city, having passed the grim-looking county prison, and reached High Town, the attractiveness of the place is apparent.

Doubtful legends go back to an early period, but it is not until the Saxon era that the annals take authentic form. It was the capital of Mercia. Queen Ethelfreda, daughter of Alfred the Great, directed, it is recorded, that a castle and city walls be built for the protection of the inhabitants against the inroads of the Welsh. The walls were raised round three sides of the city, and the Wye afforded a natural protection from the enemy on the fourth. Only a small portion of the ancient walls remains, and the six gates which gave ingress and exit to the town have long been swept away.

When Edward the Confessor occupied the throne, history relates that within the walls there were only 103 families, and each citizen who took up a plot of land had to pay a tax of 7½*d.* per head, and an annual payment of 4*d.* for the hiring of horses for general use. He had to perform certain personal services such as the sheriff might fix. Three days' reaping in August was one of the services he had to render. Mr. Richard Johnson, a former Town Clerk, compiled a valuable volume on "The Ancient Customs of the City of Hereford," which presents a storehouse of local information. From its pages we draw a few items of forgotten lore. Every man's wife, it appears, who brewed either within or without the city, had to pay a tax of 10*d.* Brewing is one of the most ancient trades, but has long been regarded as an inferior calling, and on this account in bygone times was usually conducted by women. Tradesmen groaned under taxes in the past as they do in the present. The city in early times had six blacksmiths, and each had to pay a penny for the use of his forge, besides making 120 nails for the King. William I. established a mint in the city, and the inhabitants had to pay him £60 a year in silver money for the privilege of coining. Every house in the city was taxed at the rate of a pound a year. In the every-day life of the people bells played an important part. The ringing of the bell was the intimation that vagrants and night-walkers must leave the city. When a fire broke out of a terrible character, or when a coming enemy was announced, a bell was rung which brought together the citizens. In the event of a fire, each man came with a leather bucket to throw water on the flames; but if foes were approaching he responded to the call armed with weapons as fitted his degree. Scolding women could not be tolerated, and were made to suffer degrading forms of punishment.

Nearly all roads at Hereford lead to the cathedral, and the visitor experiences little trouble in getting there. Its beautiful and massive tower at once arrests attention from different parts of the city. It may not be so striking as the tall and graceful spire of All Saints', Hereford, but it is far more impressive, and when seen from the riverside at some little distance, a picture is presented which cannot be forgotten. The cathedral is not a large one, but it is full of architectural features of the greatest possible interest. It is built of a reddish-coloured stone, which gives it a warm and pleasing appearance. Hereford is one of the oldest sees in England, dating from the seventh century. There can be little doubt that the oldest church was a rude structure of wood. We know that the erection of a stone church was started in 830 A.D., in honour of Saint Ethelbert, the King of East Anglia, who was murdered by Offa near Hereford. Miracles were

HEREFORD.

North Transept and Tower
of the Cathedral.

said to have been wrought at the King's shrine. During the reign of Edward the Confessor the church was re-built, but it did not remain long a house of prayer, as the Irish and Welsh plundered it and set it on fire.

The present cathedral was begun by Robert de Losing, who was consecrated bishop in 1079 A.D., and in 1110 A.D. the church was consecrated. Many important additions were made, but prayer and praise of holy men were heard within the sanctuary, while the sound of the trowel, hammer, and chisel was heard without. We have here good examples of Norman, Early English, Decorated, Perpendicular, and modern architecture. A large profusion of ball flower ornaments will be noticed. The outer part of the north porch is the latest addition to the mediæval church. On Easter Monday, 1786, the west end of the cathedral fell, carrying away a tower and part of the nave. Wyatt was employed to repair the church, and his extensive alterations did not improve it; indeed, his work may be called vandalism. Happily under Cottingham and Sir Gilbert Scott many improvements have been effected.

The interior contains many interesting objects which charm and detain the visitor. Chantries, shrines, monuments, crosses, stained glass windows, a remarkable crypt, and other features arrest attention. The organ was built in 1686, and was a present to the faithful city by Charles II., in gratitude for the aid of the citizens to the Stuart cause in the time of war. In recent times it has been rebuilt at a considerable cost. We cannot profess to describe at length the many objects of interest in the cathedral, volumes would be required for that purpose; but we must not pass a curious map of the world without reproducing a short notice of it, for it proves of interest to most visitors. For a long period it was lost, but was afterwards discovered under the floor of Bishop Audley's Chapel. It is believed to date back to 1314 A.D., and was designed by Richard of Holdingham and of Lafford (Holdingham and Sleaford, Lincolnshire). "It is believed," says Prebendary Havergal, "to be one of the oldest maps in the world; and it is full of the deepest interest. It is founded on the cosmographical treatises of the time, which generally commence by stating that Augustus Cæsar sent out three philosophers, Nichodoxus, Theodotus, and Polictitus, to measure and survey the world, and all geographical knowledge was the result. In the left-hand corner of the map the Emperor is delivering to the philosophers written orders, confirmed by a handsome mediæval seal. The world is here represented as round, surrounded by the ocean. At the top of the map is represented Paradise, with rivers and trees; also the eating of the forbidden fruit and the expulsion of the first parents. Above is a remarkable representation of the Day of Judgment, with the Virgin Mary interceding for the faithful, who are seen rising from their graves and being led within the walls of Heaven. The map is chiefly filled with ideas taken from Herodotus, Solinus, Isidore, Pliny, and other ancient historians. There are numerous figures of towns, animals, birds, and fish, with grotesque customs, which mediæval geographers believed to exist in different parts of the world; Babylon, with its famous tower; Rome, the capital of the world, bearing an inscription: '*Roma caput mundi, tenet, orbis fiena rotundi*,' and Troy as '*Civitas bellicosissima*.' In Great Britain most of the cathedrals are mentioned; but of Ireland the author seems to have known very little. Among the points of interest are the columns of Hercules, the Labyrinth of Crete, the Pyramids of Egypt, the House of Bondage, the journeys of the Children of Israel, the Red Sea, Mount Sinai, with figures of Moses and his supposed place of burial, the Phœnician Jews worshipping the molten image, Lot's wife, etc." We must admit that the foregoing does not equal the rapid and racy description of the map as given by the verger when he hurries groups of tourists round the building. His account must be heard to be fully appreciated.

The cathedral library is full of rare and valuable works, the outcome of a monastic collection of books. Many are in chains, and without doubt form the largest and finest collection of books in chains in this country. The oldest volume is a Latin version of the Four Gospels in Anglo-Saxon characters. It is at least a thousand years old, and written on stout vellum. The book-lover will experience some difficulty in tearing himself away from this earthly paradise.

Hard by the cathedral is the Episcopal Palace, with its beautiful grounds near the river. It is formed almost entirely out of an ancient Norman hall, with pillars of timber. Here rich and poor are welcomed to many pleasant functions. The grounds appear to belong to the public as much as to the kindly disposed bishop. His lordship sets an example which others might follow with advantage. On a brass plate on the bishop's garden wall in Gwynne Street, is the following inscription:

Site of the birthplace of
NELL GWYNNE
Founder of Chelsea Hospital, and
Mother of first Duke of St. Albans
Born 1650; died 1691.

In the "Story of Nell Gwyn," by Peter Cunningham (second edition, London, 1903), are a couple of illustrations from photographs taken in 1858, of the humble home in which this celebrated woman was born.

Not far from the cathedral is the Castle Green, tastefully laid out with public walks. The winding Wye and the charming country around may be seen from this elevated position; large trees offer a grateful shelter in hot weather, and the flower beds and green grass delight the eye. In the centre of the ground is a column, sixty feet high, erected in honour of Lord Nelson. Here stood the castle, pronounced one of the strongest and largest of English fortresses. Its historical associations are of national as well as of local importance. As we sit to-day in the pleasant grounds, pictures of the past rise before us. We see issue from the stronghold in 1055, Earl Ranulph, the Norman nephew of Edward the Confessor, to meet on the field of battle Algar, Earl of Chester, and Llewellyn, King of

Wales. The fortunes of war were against Ranulph, and he was defeated and lost 800 men. The Welsh invested the city, and the cry of the dying was heard in a general massacre. In this time of tribulation the glory of the city departed; but not for ever, for it had other dramas to play in history. Soon afterwards Harold the Saxon came on the local scene. He entertained his brother Tostig, who showed his ingratitude by attacking Harold and his followers. Coming down the historical stream of time, we find that in 1139, William Talbot, a partisan of Queen Maud, captured the castle, and held it for three years, when he was driven out of the stronghold by King Stephen. Prince Edward came here a prisoner after the Battle of Lewes (1264), but managed to make his escape the following May. When the Wars of the Roses divided the country in twain, a tragedy was enacted here. After the Battle of Mortimer Cross, Owen Tudor and nine other leading Lancastrian officers were brought here and beheaded. During the not less severe Civil War, between King and Parliament, the castle withstood three sieges. Its end came in 1652, when the Parliamentary Commissioners disposed of the materials for £85. To-day it is a memory of the past. As we recall the scenes and lives of bygone times, we feel thankful that our lot has been cast in happier days.

Let us wend our way through the cathedral close, and leave it to enter Broad Street. Opposite us is the Public Free Library and Museum. It is a building in the Gothic style, and is an ornament to the street in which it stands. It was given to the city by Sir James Rankin, Bart. There is a good circulating library and a carefully selected and valuable reference library, which is extremely rich in Herefordshire books. The museum includes a fine collection of birds and objects of local interest. Some good pictures adorn the walls. It is the head-quarters of the Woolhope Club. It is a most useful and popular institution.

There are several parish churches in the city. All Saints' attracts the most attention, for it has many interesting features which are not usually met with in a parish church. It has undergone a careful and somewhat extensive restoration, which has not destroyed its old-time character. Its tower and graceful spire is 212 feet 4 inches from the ground. We read that in 1871 the spire was repaired, and the weather-cock refixed by Mr. Frith, of Coventry. His fearless and skilful operations were watched with interest and anxiety by the inhabitants. As late as 1892, the whole church was re-roofed, and other work carried out. It is not known when it was built, but Henry III. gave it to the Master and Brethren of St. Anthony of Vienna. There are some finely carved stalls and a remarkable pulpit. The registers include the names of a large number of famous men, including the baptism of the celebrated actor David Garrick. A brass plate on the wall near the vestry door bears the following inscription:

In Memory of
DAVID GARRICK
Who was born in this parish, and baptised in this church,
28th February, 1779,
and was interred at Westminster Abbey.

A house known as "The Raven Inn," situated at the junction of Widemarsh and Manylord Streets, near the Market Place, is pointed out as Garrick's birthplace. Near at hand is the Garrick Theatre. It is asserted at Hereford that Clive, Mrs. Siddons, Kemble, and Garrick started their stage careers here. In the vestry of All Saints' Church is a chained library, perhaps the last formed in this country. It was not until 1725 that William Brewster, M.D., bequeathed the books to the parish. Many of the volumes are good, but by no means rare. No doubt the doctor got his idea of a chained library from the one at the cathedral. After being lost to the church for many years the preacher's hour-glass has been returned. It was formerly placed near the pulpit in sight of the preacher and the people. The example is one of a type common in bygone times, and of which only a few remain. Long discourses were appreciated by the Puritans, and if a clergyman completed his sermon under an hour, he was regarded as a lazy man, and obtained little respect from his critical congregation.

In Wildmarsh Street is the Coningsby Hospital, better known as the Red Coat Hospital, on account of the colour of the inmates' coats. It dates back to the year 1614, when it was founded by Sir Thomas Coningsby, knight, for occupation by eleven poor men and a chaplain. The inmates are old sailors, soldiers, or servants born in the counties of Hereford, Worcester, or Gloucester. Each has a home on the foundation, and a sum of money monthly. The chapel and homes are quaint and well worth seeing. The founder directed that each servitor on his admission is to be supplied with " a fustian suit of ginger colour, of a soldierlike fashion, and seemly laced; a cloak of red cloth lined with red baize, and reaching to the knee, to be worn on walks or journeys, and a gown of red cloth reaching to the ankle, lined also with red baize to be worn within the hospital." The building was a commandery belonging to the Knights of St. John of Jerusalem.

In the rear of the hospital are the remains of the Black Friars' Monastery, founded in 1276. There is also a preaching cross, erected in 1350, and restored by Sir Gilbert Scott. On the White Cross Road was the Lazarus Hospital, said to have been founded for persons afflicted with leprosy and other contagious diseases. Near it is the Lingen's Hospital, instituted in 1609, for the support of poor widows. New buildings have replaced the older structures, but the charities remain; indeed, Hereford is a city of charities. The White Cross Road derives its name from an ancient white stone cross, which is said to mark the site where the market was held in 1660, when the plague raged in the city.

One of the most interesting buildings in Hereford stands in High Town, and is now used as Lloyd's Bank. It is half timbered, and of the style which prevailed in the reign of Queen Elizabeth; it was restored in 1882. The carving within and without is beautifully executed. At one period in its history it was the Butchers' Guild Hall, and over the entrance is the old bull-ring, which was used when animals were baited. A part of the city where the sport took place is known as the Bull Ring. In 1802 a Bill to abolish bull-baiting was thrown out of the Commons. Mr. Windham made a powerful speech in favour of the custom. The brutal pastime continued down to 1835, when it was made illegal by Act of Parliament.

Hereford received its first charter in 1117, and since that period others have been granted which have conduced to the welfare of the inhabitants.

Charles I. recognised the loyalty of the citizens during the siege, and augmented the city arms with the motto: *Invictæ fidelitatis præmium.* The public buildings for conducting the business of the city and county include a Guild Hall, Shire Hall, Town Hall, Corn Exchange, General Hospital, schools, etc.

The rambles and rides round Hereford are delightful. A long and pleasant holiday may be spent in this city on the Wye. The walks along the banks of the river afford much pleasure, and the stream provides a good opportunity for boating. It is an ideal place for a restful holiday.

LUDLOW.

THIS Shropshire town has been extolled in poetry and prose, and its charms entitle it to all the praise it has received. The borough teems with places of interest, and has a long and stirring history. For an extended period it was the home of royalty, and associated with it are some celebrated authors. As one treads its wide but by no means busy streets, breathing its pure air, we are not surprised that its fame is widely known. To have visited Ludlow is to remember its charms.

As we make our way from the station to the castle, we pass "The Feathers," which is among the more famous inns of the country. It is a fine example of the magpie style of architecture. It is described in an old deed in 1656 as an inn, but most probably it was one before that period. Clear proof has been adduced that there was an existing house in 1609, and it has been suggested that as in 1616 there was a celebration at Ludlow of "The Love of Wales to their sovereign Prince," from this circumstance it may have been called "The Feathers." There is some excellent carving without and within this inn, and the finely studded door is of the same antiquity as the building.

The Castle of Ludlow, the chief of thirty-two castles which guarded the Welsh border, was built in its commanding position on a lofty promontory, above the meeting of the Teme and Carve. Its massive

LUDLOW. The Interior of the Castle, 1852.

Norman keep is 110 feet high. It dates back to the eleventh century. We cannot here follow its story at any great length. For an extended period it was a royal residence. It has sunny memories of gladness, and of tragedies which cast a gloom over the pages of history.

When Edward IV. was on the throne he put this stronghold in repair, and here his eldest son was brought up in considerable state. His maternal uncle, Lord Rivers, and his half-brother, Sir Richard Grey, had the chief charge of him, and his tutor was Bishop Alcock of Worcester. Shortly before his death the King drew up a set of rules for his son's daily use at this castle. They embraced orders for his daily attendance at morning mass, his school tasks, his amusements, and for his treatment at table. No man was to sit with him at table without permission of Lord Rivers. During his meals it was directed that there should "be read before him noble stories as behoveth a prince to understand; and that the communication at all times, in his presence, be of virtue, honour, cunning (knowledge), wisdom, and deeds of worship, and of nothing that should move him to vice." The Prince was only twelve when his father died, and at Ludlow Castle he was proclaimed King as Edward V. When a couple of weeks had passed with his guardians he set out for London on the 24th April, 1483, not to sit on the throne, but to perish in the Tower.

Henry VII. had his eldest son Arthur, Prince of Wales, educated here, under the guardianship of a distant relation, Sir Rhys ap Thomas, and the

King frequently visited Ludlow. Before the Prince was sixteen he married Catherine of Arragon, aged eighteen, and he died less than five months afterwards, and in 1502 was buried at Worcester.

In the hall of this castle was first performed, on Midsummer Night, 1634, Milton's masque of "Comus" (the god of mirth). It was written to commemorate the two sons and daughter of the Earl of Bridgwater, President of the Marches of Wales, losing their way at night in Heywood Forest, Herefordshire. They were coming on horseback to Ludlow to witness their father's installation.

Samuel Butler visited the castle at the Restoration, when the President was the poet's friend, the Earl of Carbenny. In a room over the gateway Butler wrote part of his "Hudibras." There are other literary associations linked with this stronghold. The most interesting is the stay of Richard Baxter, as a pupil, with the chaplain, Mr. Richard Wickstead. "During his short residence at Ludlow Castle," it is related in Orme's life of the popular preacher, "Baxter made a narrow escape from acquiring a passion for gaming, of which he gives a curious account. The best gamester in the house undertook to teach him to play. The first or second game was so nearly lost by Baxter that his opponent betted him a hundred to one against him, laying down two pounds ten shillings to his sixpence. He told him there was no possibility of his winning but by getting one cast of the die very often. No sooner was the money down than Baxter had every cast that he wished; so before a person could go three or four times round the room the game was won. This so astonished him that he believed the devil had the command of the dice, and did it to entice him to play; in consequence of which he returned the two pounds ten shillings, and resolved never to play more."

It is not our desire to follow the history of the stronghold in the time of war, for one tale relating to a castle is much like others often told. It was dismantled after its surrender in the Parliamentary Wars in 1646, and allowed to fall into decay; but in its fallen glory it is one of the most picturesque ruins in the country.

An item of folk-lore may be mentioned. It is believed that if a child is suffering from whooping cough, and taken to the castle, to waken the echo with these words, "Echo, please take away my child's cough," a cure will be effected.

There are some remains left of the old town wall, and one of the ancient gates of Ludlow still exists. It nearly blocks the way, but we trust it will long remain as an example of fourteenth century work.

The once Collegiate Church of St. Lawrence is a fine late Perpendicular building. It is ranked among the finest parish churches in England. It replaces a twelfth century church, and the building of the present church lasted into the earlier part of the thirteenth century. Important additions were made, early and late in the fourteenth century. The embattled porch at the south entrance is extremely fine. In the church are many monuments of those connected with the castle, and notable people of the town and district. The collegiate stalls of the College of the Palmers' Guild have spirited and grotesque misereres which attract much attention. Stained glass windows add to the beauty of the sanctuary.

As might be expected the churchyard has a number of curious epitaphs. The following is from the tomb of John Abingdon, "who for forty years drove the Ludlow coach to London, a trusty servant, a careful driver, and an honest man." He died in 1827:

His labour's done, no more to town
  His onward course he bends ;
His team's unshut,* his whip laid up,
  And here his journey ends.
Death locked his wheels and gave him rest,
  And never more to move,
Till Christ shall call him with the blest
  To heavenly realms above

In the churchyard is the Reader's residence, a good half-timbered house bearing the date 1616.

Another place of antiquarian interest is the Grammar School, founded by the Guild of Palmers, and refounded from its property on its dissolution by Edward VI. There is claimed for it the distinction of being the oldest grammar school in England. It has had some famous principals and pupils. Early in the fourteenth century Dondonit, a Breton priest, was the master, and while at Ludlow published several books. He was laid to rest in the churchyard of St. Lawrence, and it is recorded that an epitaph as follows was inscribed to his memory:

* "Unshut" is a Shropshire word for unharnessed.

> In Dunccumb's grave John Dondonit's body lies ;
> His soul, God's grace attend it to the skies ;
> Though absent from his native country here,
> His grave may still be moistened with a tear.

Thomas Wright, M.A., F.S.A., the antiquary and historian, was educated at this school, and wrote a history of the town.

There are, besides a good museum, numerous public buildings, and historic sites, as well as many pleasant walks, which render the little town a desirable place for a holiday sojourn.

LEDBURY.

We see at Ledbury a remnant of Mediæval England. Here we get Jacobean houses in their more attractive style. Not only is it a town to delight the tourist, but it is rich in historical and literary associations. It is situated within easy distance of the Malvern Hills, and may be almost said to be sheltered by them. In the immediate neighbourhood is some charming scenery, and for walks and drives it is a good centre. The origin of the name of the town is a debated matter; some writers say that it is derived from the Welsh "Led," a vale side, while others affirm that it is from the river Leddon, which flows near the town. It was not until the Conquest that its historical importance starts, and in the Domesday Book it figures as Liedeberge.

It was afterwards a borough, and sent two members to Parliament. The stately parish church, dedicated to St. Michael and All Angels, is shown by the numerous ancient remains found during the restoration of the fabric, to stand on the site of a Saxon church. The present building is partly Norman, and has a detached tower and spire. The size and beauty of the church are accounted for by the fact that in the Middle Ages, when Leominster wool reached a high price, Ledbury was the centre of an important clothing industry. Wealth flowed into the town, and the inhabitants devoted much of it to the building of a church which is the pride of the place, and which wins the admiration of those who see it. Here are numerous fine monuments and other famous sculptures. There are within the churchyard and graveyard memorials with quaint epitaphs. There are, it should be noted, in Herefordshire, several places where the towers are built apart from the church, most probably as places of defence.

In the church is the St. Katherine Chapel or Chantry. It has been suggested that it was the Chapter House, and not a chapel or chantry. Here is a very ancient figure resting on a decorated tomb, which is said to be "Sainte Kateryne," the patron saint of the town, of whom a legend is related as follows: "In the reign of Edward II., a certain Catherine Audley, a religious woman, had a revelation that she should only dwell in a town where the bells should ring of themselves. She and her maid, Mabel, coming to Ledbury found the bells ringing without any ringers, and here she built a hermitage and dwelt." Two pieces of land near Ledbury are called St. Catherine's Acre and Mabel's Furlong, and are linked in the popular mind with the legend. Wordsworth put the story into verse:

> When human touch, as monkish books attest,
> Nor was applied, nor could be, Ledbury bells
> Broke forth in concert flung adown the dells
> And upward, high as Malvern's cloudy crest,
> Sweet tones caught by a noble lady blest
> To rapture. Mabel listened at the side
> Of her loved mistress ; soon the music died,

And Catherine said: "Here I set up my rest.
Warned in a dream, I wandered, long had sought
A home that by such miracle of sound
Must be revealed." She heard it now, or felt
The deep, deep joy of a confiding thought;
And there the saintly anchoress she dwelt
Till she exchanged for heaven that happy ground.

One of the most interesting buildings in Ledbury is the Hospital of St. Katherine, founded in 1232 by Bishop Follcott, which happily escaped the general wreckage at the Reformation. It was re-established in the reign of Queen Elizabeth. In modern times it has undergone various alterations. The chapel in Early English style is interesting. During the Civil War it was used as a stable by Cromwell's troopers. In spite of modern additions, which do not harmonise with the past, it is an attractive pile. After passing into the hospital through the central tower, we seem to step into mediæval times.

During the Civil War a battle raged in the streets of the town, when the Cavaliers gained the victory. Much blood was shed, and to-day the marks of the bullets still remain. Ledbury Park, formerly called the New House, the residence of Lord and Lady Biddulph, is a half-timbered mansion, built in 1590, of extreme picturesqueness, at the top of the town, and has charming gardens and a deer park. Here Prince Rupert stayed when he occupied the town.

The Market House in the High Street is a half-timbered building dating back to the time of Charles II., said to have been built by John Abel, and its rent to be used in charity. The design is pleasing, and the upper part of the building stands on sixteen pillars of Spanish chestnut from Malvern Chase. In bygone times it was called the Corn Market House. It was used for storing grain when farmers brought it to the town in bulk. Subsequently it was used for housing wool, hops, etc., and the profits realised were given towards a fund for removing some unsightly houses, known as Butcher's Row, which stood in the centre of High Street. The Market House was restored about 1860, and the upper part is let for meetings, and the butter and poultry market is held in the lower part of the building.

John Abel, the architect of this Market House, was a man of note, who planned some of the finest half-timbered buildings in Herefordshire. Little has been written of his life and work. The following particulars are drawn from Price's "Historical Account of Leominster" (1795). "The most noted architect in this country of his time; he built the Market Houses of Hereford, Brecknock, and Kington, and did the timber work of the new church at Abbey Dore. The said John Abel, being in Hereford city at the time when the Scots besieged it, in the year 1645, made sort of mills to grind corn, which were of great use to the besieged; for which contrivance and service King Charles the First did afterwards honour him with the title of one of His Majesty's carpenters. This architect, after he was ninety years of age, made his own monument, which is in Sarnesfield churchyard, and engraved his own effigy, kneeling with his two wives, and the emblems of his occupation, the rule, compass, and square, and he made the following epitaph:

This craggy stone or covering for an architect's bed,
The lofty buildings raised high, yet now lyes down his head:
His line and rule, so death concludes, are locked up in store,
Build they who list, or they who wist, for he can build no more.
His house of clay could hold no longer;
May Heavens frame him stronger.

JOHN ABEL

Vive ut vivas in vitum æternam."

Abel died in 1674 at the age of ninety seven. He had not only a constructive capacity, but a fine imagination. His outlines are graceful, and his details extremely good. Architecture owes much to his ability, more especially the fine examples of his work in Herefordshire.

The curious custom of sin-eating lingered at Ledbury much later than in other places on the Welsh border. Mrs. F. H. Leather, writing in "Memorials of Old Herefordshire" (1904), deals with the subject in the "Folk-lore of the Shire." She records that on Palm Sunday the day is celebrated in a curious manner in Hentland Church. "The churchwardens," writes Mrs. Leather, "present to the clergyman and each of the congregation, a small cake, which is eaten within the church, as evidence of a desire to cease from all enmities and to prepare for the Easter festival." It would be interesting to know the connection, if any, between this custom and the ancient practice of sin-eating. Formerly a cup of beer accompanied each cake, but this part of the ceremony has now been abandoned. This custom was observed also at Sellack as late as 1867.

The practice of "sin-eating" referred to, peculiar to the Welsh border, was discontinued before the end of the seventeenth century. The following description of it, given in Brand's "Popular Antiquities," is taken from the Lansdowne Manuscripts: "In the County of Hereford it was an old custom at funerals to hire poor people, who were to take upon them the sins of the party deceased. One of them—he was a long, lean, ugly, lamentably poor rascal—I remember that he lived in a cottage on Rosse highway. The manner was that when a corpse was brought out and laid on the bier, a loaf of bread was brought out and delivered to the sin-eater over the corpse, as also a mazard bowl of maple, full of beer, which was also drunk up, and sixpence in money. In consideration whereof, he took upon him *ipso facto* all the sins of the defunct, and freed him or her from walking after death. This custom alludes, methinks, to something of the scapegoat kind in the Levitical law, and though rarely used in our days, yet by some people was observed even in the strictest time of the Presbyterian Government. . . . The like is done in the city of Hereford in those times, where a woman kept, many years before her death, a mazard bowl for the sinne eater."

Another account says the sin-eater "pronounced the ease and rest of the soul departed, for which he would pawn his own soul."

Dr. Schuyler, in his book on Turkestan, describes a corresponding custom: "In Ach Kûrgân . . . he met an old man called an *iskachi*, who made his living by taking upon himself the sins of the dead, and devoting his life to prayer for their souls."

Until quite recent times the ringing of the curfew bell was kept up, and other ancient customs linger in this quaint old town.

In her childhood Mrs. Elizabeth Barrett Browning was taken to Hope End, Ledbury, and there remained until womanhood. It was here that she embarked on a literary career, which placed her in the front rank of women writers. In her works are tender and graceful allusions to her early and favourite haunts. She thus wrote of the scenery about her old home:

> Hills, vales, woods, nestled in silver mist,
> Farms, granges, doubled up among the hills,
> And cattle grazing in the watered vales,
> And cottage chimneys smoking from the woods,
> And cottage gardens smelling everywhere,
> Confused with smell of orchards.

In 1892 was erected in the town the Barrett Browning Memorial, consisting of a Clock Tower, Library, and Reading Room. It is an imposing as well as a useful monument to a good and gifted author.

WEOBLEY.

THE old and picturesque market town of Weobley, Herefordshire, is a favourite haunt of the artist, and, like numerous other places, it has been libelled by a popular " people and steeple " rhyme:

Poor Weobley—proud People ;
Low Church—high Steeple.

It was a pocket borough, and for a long period it returned two representatives to Parliament. We know for certain that as early as 1295 it sent members to the House of Commons, and it may have done so from 1213, but it is to be regretted that the lists relating to Herefordshire down to 1290 are lost. For some cause or other no members were returned after 1306. No reason of a satisfactory nature has been given for the representation being discontinued, but it has been suggested that the trade of the town decreased and its importance declined.

In 1628 it regained its lost dignity. James Tomkins, the then member for Leominster and Lord of the Manor of Weobley, obtained a resolution in the House of Commons ordering a writ to be issued for the borough to return two burgesses, and because " Weobley ought to send burgesses, and the long discontinuance was no loss of its right, for this was no franchise which may be lost, but a service *pro bono publico*." On May 13th, 1628, it once more returned two members, and continued to do so until the passing of the Reform Bill of 1832.

Although it was a pocket borough it nevertheless sent to Parliament some notable men who figure in the pages of national history. William Gregory, a native of the county, was a member in 1678-9. He ably, firmly, and fairly discharged for a short time the position of Speaker in the House of Commons. Next he was made a Baron of the Exchequer and knighted. Colonel John Birch, a celebrated Parliamentarian General, sat from 1679 to 1681, and from 1689 to his death on the 10th May, 1691. In the parish church among other interesting monuments is a life-sized statue of him standing in a recess. At the election which followed the death of Colonel Birch, the nephew of the late member was elected. He did not hold his seat for long, for in the November following, his opponent at the previous contest, Thomas Foley, was declared elected. The result of the polling was:

Thomas Foley, 26 votes.
John Birch, 23 votes.

From the number of votes given it will be seen how few electors in a town had the privilege of sending a member to Parliament.

The famous Lord Eldon, Lord Chancellor, was a member for the borough from 1783 to 1796, and frequently visited the place. In the High Street of Weobley is a large red brick house, in former days known as the Bear Inn; over the principal entrance is a balcony, which was reached by a door from the second story. It was from here the burgesses were addressed by those who sought to represent them, and those who wished to speak generally on matters concerning the county. This and other houses we are informed belonged to the Marquis of Bath, and the tenants only paid a nominal rent on condition that they voted for their landlord's nominee. The rent appears to have been so small that no trouble was taken to collect it. The circumstance appears to have been forgotten; but many years afterwards, when the agent tried to enforce the payment of rent, as no electoral service could be rendered, the householders stoutly refused, and as they had held undisputed possession for twenty years and upwards, claimed the property as their own, and retained it.

Another house still standing is known as Thorne Farm, but in the reign of the Stuarts it was the Unicorn Inn, and here Charles I. slept on September 5th, 1645. The storms of the Great Rebellion had gathered about him. Later the house was called the Crown Inn, in honour of the visit of the King. When in great trouble, on the 18th day of the same month, he again visited Weobley. He was riding about the neighbourhood from six in the morning until midnight.

Nearly opposite the house where the King found shelter, is the old Grammar School, which is small, and has an Elizabethan porch of carved oak well worthy of inspection. Happily, it still remains in a fine state of preservation, although shorn of its ancient glory. The fine old Timber Market and Town Hall, supported by oak pillars, has been swept away. It was in disrepair about half a century ago and was pulled down. The market had passed away, and the power of the burgesses was over, so there was no further use for the building which had been so important in the past in the life of the borough.

The town is very rich in its beautiful houses. One of the most delightful is the Ley, dating back to 1589. It was the old home of the Brydges, a notable county family, which became extinct in 1704. In this house may still be seen a Priest's Hole, or secret chamber. Within living memory it is said that the only entrance to the secret room was through a sliding panel in the wall behind a massive four-post bed. It is some little distance from the town, but it well repays a visit.

Weobley is full of black and white houses, and in one, situated in the High Street, a man named Tomkins became the proud father of thirty-two children, all born in the same room.

In early times Weobley had its castle, and in its palmy days it played a part in historic England; but by the time of the Commonwealth it was useless for defensive purposes, and had no concern in the battles between Roundheads and Cavaliers; to-day its site may be traced, but no ruins are left and the moat has been drained. The stones of its once strong walls made a convenient quarry for the obtaining of materials for humbler dwellings.

The fine parish church is now, and long has been, the crowning glory of Weobley. The spire is very striking and graceful, and is regarded as faultless in proportion. It has a Norman doorway, and many interesting features, including monuments and old stained glass, which delight the student of old churches, and charm the visitor in search of the curious and beautiful in art. Under the monument of Colonel John Birch it is stated: "None who knew him denyed him ye character of asserting and vindicating ye Laws and Liberties of his Country in War, and of promoting its Welfare and Prosperity in Peace." Over the porch is a small sundial with a motto: "One day telleth another, and one night certifieth another."

The place was once famous for its ale, which passed into the proverbial lore of the land. It was not brewed with "the pernicious weed called the hoppe," nor must it be confused with beer. Large quantities were sold in Wales, but towards the latter part of the seventeenth century cider came into favour, and the trade declined; and to use the words of an old writer: "Weobley hath lost the bell for Weobley's ancient ale."

In this peaceful place the busy town toiler finds rest, and many regain health in pleasant rambles along the lovely highways and byways of the district. The Rev. S. Cornish Watkins writes:

Oh! to be in Cider Land
  Far from London's roar and rattle,
Where by gentle breezes fanned,
  All among the orchard stand
Red-cheeked maids, and white-faced cattle;
  Be the weather wet or dry,
April showers, or December snows,
  Flying cloud or sky,
Here's the place where hearts-ease grows.

CHEPSTOW.

THE historically-interesting town of Chepstow is pleasantly situated on the Wye, and for variety of charms few places in England can equal it. There is an old-world look about the town which cannot fail to interest the visitor. In Roman times it appears not to have been a place of any importance. Its name and rise belong to the Saxon era. It is generally agreed that " Ceap," or " Cheap " (as in Cheapside, London), means to buy or bargain, and " Stow " a settlement or town; so we may readily understand that the name indicated a trading-place.

Two of the more important buildings are the castle and the church. The former stands on a bold, rocky eminence. It is an Early English work. On the land side was a deep ditch, and its strong walls were also defended by round towers. During the Civil Wars the stronghold was a place of importance. It was in turn held by King and Parliament. Like other castles, it was long the home of petty tyrants. Castles are not without interest to visit. They show us what the places were like when might and not right prevailed. We may regard them as museums, from which we may learn many old-time lessons.

The Wye flows peacefully past Chepstow Castle. When Shakespeare lived and wrote his undying contributions to English literature, salmon fishing was popular in the Wye. Then, as now, it found employment for many of the townsfolk. We are told by a local poet respecting it that—

> Unlike the flabby flesh in London sold,
> A Chepstow salmon's worth his weight in gold;
> Crimps up, delightful to the taste and sight,
> In flakes alternate of fine red and white.
> Few other rivers such fine salmon feed:
> Not Taff, nor Tay, nor Tyne, nor Thames, nor Trent
> nor Tweed.

St. Mary's Parish Church is the other building of local interest. It stands near the river and is a striking structure, and dates back to early Norman times; it is stated that it was built by a Lord of the Castle at the time of the Domesday Survey, while others believe that it was a priory in the reign of King Stephen, and that it was erected by either Gilbert de Clare or Richard Strongbow. It was attached to the Abbey of Cormeilles in Normandy. The building is Norman in character, and the western door is a fine example of that period. It may be fitly described as a poem in stone. Within the sacred fane are several interesting monuments. None, however, attracts the attention of the visitor more than a plain slab with a quaint inscription placed to the memory of Henry Marten, the regicide.

Marten's curious memorial calls up striking scenes in the history of England when King and Parliament met in that bitter strife for the mastery of the land which ended in Charles I. being beheaded before Whitehall. In that terrible drama Marten played an important part. His life story may be briefly told, although it fills many pages of history, and nearly thirteen columns to tell it in outline in the "Dictionary of National Biography." He was the eldest son of Sir Henry Marten, was born in 1602, at Oxford, and educated in his native city, entering University College as a gentleman commoner, taking his B.A. degree in 1619. At an early age he was admitted to Gray's Inn. He travelled for a time in France, and on his return, much against his inclinations, but pressed by his father, he married a rich widow. It did not prove a happy union, for, as a matter of fact, he was a lover of pretty girls, on whom he spent the greater part of his estate. At one period his reckless living cost his father a thousand a year.

It was in 1639 that Marten started his political career by refusing to contribute to the general loan raised for the Scottish war. This circumstance made him popular, and in April, 1640, and again in the following November, he was returned to Parliament as one of the representatives for Berkshire. He was soon a notable figure in the House of Commons, and advocated the popular cause with zeal.

Possibly he was stimulated by the King publicly calling him "an ugly rascal," and other offensive names, and directing that he should be turned out of Hyde Park. Charles I. displayed great bitterness to Marten, and he figures in the documents issued by his Majesty. Marten was an active member of the Committee of Safety. It is said that he used to snarl at everybody in Parliament. He did not merely confine himself to snarling, for he suspected the fidelity of Percy, the tenth Earl of

Northumberland, and he opened a letter written by Northumberland to his wife. The earl was indignant, and caned Marten. Both Houses complained of a breach of privilege, but the quarrel was privately made up.

When the war broke out Marten subscribed £1,200 to the Parliamentary party, and undertook to raise a regiment of horse. His military career was not successful, and his real power was in Parliament. He was one of the King's judges, and signed his death warrant. Marten's life was not all sunshine during the Commonwealth, but when Charles II. was called to the throne trouble gathered quickly round him. He tried to fly from the country, but gave himself up on June 20th, 1660, in compliance with a proclamation summoning the regicides to surrender "under pain of being excepted from any pardon or indemnity for their respective lives and estates." His trial ended in his life being spared, but the rest of his years were passed in prison. The latter part of his career was spent at Chepstow Castle, and the tower where he was confined is still shown. A good deal of freedom was permitted his wife and family, who took up their quarters with him, and he was allowed to visit the gentlemen of the district. He was twenty years at Chepstow. Southey, when he wrote the following lines, was mistaken in the years of confinement and its conditions:

> For thirty years secluded from mankind,
> Here Marten lingered. Often have these walls
> Echoed his footsteps, as with even tread
> He paced around his prison : not to him
> Did Nature's fair varieties exist ;

He never saw the sun's delightful beams,
Save when through yon high bars it poured a sad
And broken splendour. Dost thou ask his crime?
He had rebelled against the King, and sat
In judgment on him.

Death ended at a good old age Marten's weary captivity. He was buried in the chancel of Chepstow Church, but his body was not allowed to rest there, for it was removed to another part of the building by order of the Rev. Thomas Chest, who was vicar from 1701 to 1740. His nephew wrote on him as follows:

Here lies at rest, I do protest,
One Chest within another;
The Chest of wood is very good,
Who says so of the other?

Over the remains of Marten was placed the following curious inscription:

Here, September the Ninth, in the year of our Lord 1680,
was buried
A True Englishman,
Who in Berkshire was well known,
To love his country's freedom for his own;
Who being immured full twenty years
Had time to write as doth appear.

HIS EPITAPH.

H ere or elsewhere (all's one to you or me)
E arth, air, and water gripes ghostly dust,
N one knows how soon to be by fire set free.
R eader, if you an old tried rule will trust,
Y ou'll gladly do and suffer what you must.

M y time was spent in serving yours and you,
A nd death's my pay (it seems), and welcome too;
R evenge destroying but itself, while I
T o birds of prey leave my old cage to fly.
E xamples preach to the eye. Care then (mine says)
N ot how you end, but how you spend your days.

Aged 78 years.

At the foot of the stone it is stated:

This stone, which formerly marked the grave of Henry Marten was recut during the restoration of the church in 1895.

It is generally asserted that Marten wrote the foregoing lines, but by the better informed the composition is ascribed to his daughter. It seems clear that a scholar like Marten would not have written such doggerel.

The minor antiquities of the town are full of interest, and its walks are pleasant. We regard a ramble from Tintern Abbey to Chepstow as one of the most enjoyable walks in England.

OXFORD.

It is said that this famous educational centre is more noted for teaching manners than for imparting knowledge. There can be little doubt about the university giving a polish to its pupils, and from the high places in Church, State, and other liberal callings which they have taken and are still taking, there cannot be any doubt that the scholastic training is imparted on the right lines. Its colleges are filled with the most promising pupils from the leading public schools of the land. Education and sport here go hand in hand, and the university turns out good all round men.

Situated in the centre of the country, its waterways have been of vast importance, linking the city with the capital of England from early times. The name of Oxford is derived from the Ox-fords which abounded about the place. Some of the local historians have spent much learning to make the statement clear, but to us it seems simplicity itself, indicating the fords where the drovers drove their cattle over the river. We gather from the English Chronicle that in 912 the town was a place of importance, and it must have taken some years to attain that position. During Saxon times it played an important part in the history of the country. Its historic story is a blending of fact and fiction.

OXFORD. South Front of All Souls College, 1837.

It was strongly guarded to keep at bay the Danes and other hostile forces. In Alfred's reign much fighting took place on the Ashdown ridge of Berkshire, opposite to Oxford. We need not linger long among legendary lore, or doubtful history, as the town does not become a place of leading rank until the thirteenth century.

Oxford became a public teaching centre in the twelfth century. As time went on teaching became the profession of the place. The towers and walls of the colleges attract the eye; they appear like a series of stately palaces, the best in architecture and art combine to render them pleasing. Trees, lawns, flowers, with the mellowing touch of time, add to their beauty.

Libraries, the result of ages of careful selection, add to the wealth of these ancient haunts of learning and peace. Traditions of famous teachers and apt scholars linger; men who have added glory to the colleges, and won world-wide reputations as scholars and men of action, while others are remembered for their saintly lives. It is curious to notice how some students seem to carry all before them, while others toil to obtain a pass degree.

In later years learning has been obtained under pleasant circumstances, but it was far different in mediæval times. The colleges were open to educate the poor; he that thirsted for knowledge obtained it here. The boys were frequently brought to Oxford in carriers' carts, and all their expenses, including food and bed, would be at the rate of fivepence a day, and if very poor threepence a day would discharge all expenses. It was a common custom in early times for poor students to go about the country collecting money to pay their university charges. Old account books contain many references to the practice. The disbursements appear to have been small except in cases where the recipients were natives of the parish where the money was given. The largest amount we have noticed occurs in the accounts of the burgesses of Sheffield, and reads as follows:

1573. Gave to William Lee, a poore scholler of Sheffield, towards the settynge him to the universytie of Cambridge, and buyinge him bookes and other furnyture - - - xij . iiij.

The Leverton, Lincolnshire, churchwardens' accounts state:

1562. Gave to a pore scoller of Oxford - - - 2*s.* 0*d.*

Ten years later, in the overseers' accounts of the same parish, is an entry as under:

1572. Relief to Thomas Berry, a pore scholar of Oxford - - - - - - - - 16*d.*

In the parish register of Cawthorne, Yorkshire, under date of August 2nd, 1663, it is recorded:

Cawthorne, for Thomas Carr a poor scholler who was going to Cambridge, and borne in ye parish of Ecclesfield - - - - - 6*s.* 6*d.*

According to the churchwardens' accounts of Kirkby Wharfe, in the year 1697, two poor scholars were presented with sixpence. This begging became such a nuisance, more especially among farmers, that it was found necessary to regulate it by Parliament; it was enacted that no scholar shall beg on the highways until the chancellor has satisfied himself of the merits of the case and granted a certificate. As an example, Bouse, in his "Historic Oxford," cites an instance of Dennis Burnell and John Brown, poor scholars of Aristotle's Hall in 1461, had official testimonials sealed, allowing them to ask alms.

We know from many trustworthy sources how plain was the fare at Oxford in early times, and even to pay for that much consideration and often humiliation was brought into play, but this was not peculiar to Oxford, for the well-known figure of Luther, the monk who shook the world, rises up before us, and in fancy we listen to him singing from door to door to obtain bread.

Early in the history of the colleges, strife between town and students had become a serious matter, and a charter of Henry III., in 1248, was framed to protect scholars from injury by the burgesses. In the event of the regulations not being observed the town authorities were liable to heavy penalties. Among the students a strong feeling prevailed between those from the north and the south. From each part of the country a proctor was chosen down to 1540. The riots between town and gown were frequent and often serious, and the details add largely to the annals of the city. Both parties appear to have been ever ready for a fray.

Many old customs are maintained at the colleges. At Queen's, for example, is the Boar's Head Procession, held in honour of a student who, some five centuries ago, was wandering in the forest of Shotover, conning his "Aristotle," and suddenly a wild boar came springing from its lair at him, with open mouth ready to destroy him, when, with great presence of mind, he thrust the tough tome down his throat, with the annihilating words, "Graecumest!" thus happily saving his own life by causing the death of the monster.

The procession wends it way into the ancient hall headed by a boar's head, and all present join in singing the following version of a fifteenth century carol:

The Boar's Head in hand bear I
Bedeck'd with bays and rosemary,
And I pray you, Masters, be merry,
Qui estis in convivio.

The Boar's Head, as I understand,
Is the bravest dish in all the land,
When thus bedeck'd with a gay garland,
Let us servire cantico.

Our steward hath provided this,
In honour of the King of Bliss,
Which on this to be served is
In Reginensi Atrio.

The Latin line of each verse is sung to a chorus with the concluding words:

Caput apri defero
Reddens laudes Domino.

Not by call of bell but by sound of trumpet are the diners brought together. It seems pretty clear that this is a survival of the old Scandinavian Yule-tide festivities, when a boar was sacrificed to Freya, goddess of Peace and Plenty.

At Queen's another old custom lingers in memory of Robert de Eglesfield, the founder. At dinner, after the loving cup has been passed round, the College Bursar hands to those present a needle and thread with the admonition, "Take this and be thrifty." The threads are of three colours—black, blue, and red—representing the three more important faculties of Divinity (black), Law (blue), and Medicine (red). It may happen that the recipient is not a graduate of either of the faculties, it is then assumed that he belongs to the Divinity, and he receives a black thread.

"This custom," we are told in "Some Oxford Customs," "is supposed to have been introduced as a fanciful play upon the name of the founder, Eglesfeld, aiquille et fil! We are told that when Prince Henry the Fifth, who was a member of Queen's College, was summoned to Court to clear himself of 'certain charges of disaffection,' he appeared in a gown embroidered with eyelet-holes, a needle hanging by a silk thread from every hole!"

The hunting of the Mallard at All Souls College is a well-known Oxford custom. Hearne, in his diary—edited by Bliss—thus refers to the custom of hunting the mallard. "1722-23, January 18. Last Monday, the 14th inst. (the 14th being always the day), was All Souls College Mallard, at which time 'tis usual with the Fellows and their friends to have a supper, and to sit up all night drinking and singing. Their song is the mallard, and formerly they used to wander about the college with sticks and poles, etc., in quest of the mallard, that had been left off many years. They tell you the custom arose from a swing(e)ing old mallard, that had been lost at the foundation of the college (1437), and found many years after in the sink."

We reproduce, as an example of the rest, three verses of "The Merry Old Song of the All Saints' Mallard":

Griffin, Bustard, Turkey Capon,
Let other hungry mortals gape on,
And on the bones their stomachs fall hard
But let All Souls' men have their Mallard.

Chorus—O by the blood of King Edward, O by the blood of King Edward
It was a swapping, swapping Mallard.

The poets feign Jove turned a swan,
But let them prove it if they can:
As for our proof, 'tis not at all hard.
For it was a swapping, swapping Mallard.

Chorus—O by the blood, etc.

Therefore let us sing and dance a galliard
To the remembrance of the Mallard,
And as the Mallard dives in pool,
Let us dabble, dive, and duck in bowl.

Chorus—O by the blood, etc.

The stranger in Oxford usually visits as many of the colleges as time and strength permit, but in such a ramble, where one place gets confused with another, we must decline to bear him company, as we prefer to visit two or three and have them photographed on the brain rather than have blurred and mixed up outlines of the larger number. The Cathedral Church of Christ first claims our attention. It is the chapel of Christ Church College, and the chief church of the diocese of Oxford. Its antiquity is greater than the collegiate establishment which is now associated with it. Its early history goes back to Saxon times. The cathedral, as we see it at the present day, is an example of the transition between the Norman and Early English types. A fine Early English Chapter House is well worth seeing. We cannot designate the college. Previously the pupils had lodged in the college as a "venerable pile." It only dates back to the sixteenth century, and was founded by Wolsey and Henry VIII. We shall not be far wrong if we call it in the words of another, "the most magnificent House of Learning in Europe." Royalty and aristocracy by their wealth and presence, combined with men of mind, from the time of Sir Philip Sidney to John Ruskin and W. E. Gladstone, have rendered it famous for its learning. In all branches of art, science, literature, politics, the Church, and in other callings and studies, Christ Church men have filled the foremost places. The dining hall is the grandest of all mediæval halls in the kingdom, save the one at Westminister. The quadrangle, the most spacious in Oxford, is part of the original plan of Cardinal Wolsey. Other points of interest will detain the visitor and afford enjoyment as the outcome of taste and wealth.

Merton is in some respects one of the most interesting colleges in the city. It is regarded as the Mother of Colleges of Oxford. It was established in 1264, by Walter de Merton, at Malden, in Surrey. Ten years later it was removed to Oxford, and its constitution served as the model of other colleges which followed it. The students were lodged in suitable rooms in the college, and were placed under proper control of the staff of the inns, hostels, etc., of Oxford, and were left to their own devices when not attending classes, etc. Here was fitted up the first common room, and perhaps more important still was established the first College

Library. Mr. J. W. Clark, M.A., F.S.A., our leading authority on the history of libraries in the Rede Lecture, delivered June 13th, 1894, has some important notes on the Merton Library. This library, says Mr. Clark, is attributed by tradition to William Rede, Bishop of Chichester, 1368-85; and it has been so little altered that it may be taken as a type of a mediæval collegiate or monastic library. The room is long and narrow as was customary in early libraries. The books were chained, but the chains have been removed; one or two specimens, however, are left to show the ancient method of securing books to the cases, and that by the provision of desks and seats they might easily be used. The chapel was formerly the Church of St. John the Baptist, and was built in 1264-1310, the high altar dedicated 1277, the transepts date back to 1414, while the tower was built in 1444. It is a striking structure, and the old buildings with modern additions link the past with the present.

We get a good idea of a modern college in Keble, erected by subscription to the memory of the author of the "Christian Year." It was opened by the Marquis of Salisbury, Chancellor of the University, June 23rd, 1870. Butterfield designed a beautiful chapel, which cost the late Mr. W. Gibbs over £60,000, and was solemnly dedicated on St. Mark's Day, 25th April, 1876. The college was founded "for perpetuating academical education definitely based upon the principles of the Church of England, and with the intention of combining sober living and high culture with Christian training."

Having drawn attention to the most important

college, the first and the latest, we must leave the visitor to inspect the numerous colleges which cannot fail to afford pleasure and instruction. Much may be learnt from their history, and from their impressive buildings full of beauty in form and richness in colour.

The museums, picture galleries, and libraries add to the attractions of the city. The Ashmolean Museum claims to be the first public collection of curiosities in this country. It was given to Oxford in 1682 by Elias Ashmole, who had inherited the nucleus from a popular show in London called the Ark, which existed in the days of Charles I. Ashmole greatly added to the collection, and when it came from London it filled twelve carts. It is rich in Anglo-Saxon remains, including King Alfred's jewel, and among the more modern relics Guy Fawkes' lantern. There are interesting and important antiquities from all parts of the world, and it is a great educational force in the city. The picture galleries are rich in works of art, more especially by modern painters. The University Museum was opened in 1860, and is an institution for the teaching and study of Natural Science.

The Bodleian Library was founded by Sir Thomas Bodley, a retired diplomatist, a native of Exeter, born 1544 and died 1612. It is one of the great libraries of the world, and is rich in manuscripts as well as printed books. The Radcliffe Library is one of the sights of the city, as it is housed in a classical building, and of its class the finest in Oxford. Dr. Radcliffe was a native of Wakefield, and a Court Doctor to William III.

and Queen Anne. He left £40,000 for the construction of the library; and smaller sums for a librarian, purchase of books, and other purposes. At each of the colleges are libraries, and in some instances both good and large.

The gardens are an important feature of the city. In 1632 the Earl of Danby founded the Botanic Gardens, with a view of assisting those studying medicine. It has a fine collection of trees and plants, and here one may dream as well as study, for the natural beauties of the place are soothing. The college and other gardens, with their wealth of flowers and greenery, are large and charming.

The city churches are numerous; not only are several of good examples in architecture, but rich in historical and religious associations. The church of St. Mary the Virgin, with its striking spire, was built as a memorial to Eleanor of Castile. Cardinal Newman was incumbent of this church from 1834 to 1843. It was from its pulpit that he preached his "Sermons on Subjects of the Day," and an onslaught on them called forth his "Apologia."

It is recorded that in the chancel the Mayor and Corporation, with halters round their necks, were long accustomed to do penance and pay a fine on St. Scholastica's Day (February 10th), for an outrage committed in 1354 against the university. Some of the other churches are almost as rich in historical associations, and in the past were closely connected with the social as well as the religious life of the city. Those who delight in visiting old churches will find a number here worthy of their study.

In Broad Street is the Martyrs' Memorial, one of earliest and best works of Sir G. G. Scott, R.A. It is modelled on the Queen Eleanor Crosses. On its base it bears the following inscription:

To the Glory of God, and in grateful commemoration of His servants Thomas Cranmer, Nicholas Ridley, Hugh Latimer, Prelates of the Church of England, who, near this spot, yielded their bodies to be burned; bearing witness to the sacred truths which they had affirmed and maintained against the errors of the Church of Rome; and rejoicing that to them it was given not only to believe in Christ, but also to suffer for His sake; this monument was erected by public subscription in the year of our Lord God MDCCCXLI.

Three striking statues of the Martyrs are included in the memorial. The one of Cranmer represents him holding his large Bible with May 1541 marked on the cover. The bailiff's account for burning Cranmer is as follows:

	£	s.	d.
One hundred wood fagots - - - -	£0	6	8
One hundred and fifty furze fagots - -	0	3	4
Carriage of them - - - - - -	0	0	8
Two labourers - - - - - -	0	1	4
	£0	12	0

As we look at this memorial we sigh and reflect on the wrongs done in the name of religion. Some of the darker pages of history come within sight. It is satisfactory to remember that our lot is cast in happier times.

Long the favourite haunt of Royalty, Oxford has been on the side of the monarchs, and shed its best blood for them. When King and Commonwealth drew swords, the town fought for King Charles.

It was protected by walls built in the eleventh century, which may be traced to the present day. Some of the ancient gates were standing in 1771. On a high mound stands a solitary tower, the remains of the castle going back to the reign of William Rufus, and having a long and stirring history. The chief interest of Oxford centres round its colleges. They lift the place from a country town to a city of culture famous in all parts of the world.

CAMBRIDGE.

LIKE Oxford the chief interest of Cambridge centres in its colleges. When we see the stately halls of learning, we almost forget the fact that it is the county town where the business of the shires is transacted. The farmers may discuss crops and the price of beasts, but this seems to be in an undertone, for go where you will the colleges and college-life dominate the town on the Cam.

We need not be told that we are in a town founded in the Middle Ages, there is so much about Cambridge that indicates the fact to those who have made a study of architecture and the planning of places. When railways were constructed the authorities of the university objected very strongly to that link with the outside world being brought near their abode of learning. They feared it would disturb the quietness of those engaged in study, and the result is that the station is some distance from the colleges. The entrance to the town from the station is by no means pleasing, and that from the London Road, down Trumpington Street, is much better, but if first seen from the Backs, it would be difficult to surpass the panoroma presented. Here are avenues of stately trees, standing in well-kept grounds, with charming views of the colleges in the distance. We get from the facile pen of James Payn, in his poem of "The Backs," a pretty picture of the scene. It is far too long to quote, but we venture to give a few of the lines:

Dropping down the river,
Down the glancing river,
Through the fleet of shallops,
Underneath the bridges,
Carven stone and oaken,
Carved with sphere and pillar,
Linking lawn with lawn,
Sloping swards of garden,
Flowering bank to bank;
'Midst the golden noontide
'Neath the stately trees,
Reaching out their laden
Arms to overshade us;
Whilst the winds were heavy
With the blossoms-odours,
Whilst the birds were singing
From their sleepless nests.

The historic tale may soon be told. Some historians attempt to place its origin in the Roman era, while others suggest that it may be traced back to British times, but there is little foundation for their assertions. The castle hill, a curious mound from which an excellent view of the town may be obtained, is supposed to belong to Saxon times.

The name of the place has gone through numerous changes. In 875 it was known as *Grantanbryege*; in the Domesday Book it was called *Grentebrige*. We do not arrive at *Caumbrege* until 1458, and it is not until the sixteenth century that *Cam-bridge* came into use.

Municipal history starts in Saxon times.

CAMBRIDGE. The Market Place, showing the Town Hall and Hobson's Conduit, 1845.

Early in the eleventh century the town was governed by twelve lawmen, and its Thanes had formed themselves into a Guild. Its objects were not unlike the friendly societies of the present time. It afforded mutual help for members in distress, when death took one of the members away the brethren attended his funeral. When a member was sick and away from home, or in the event of his death, he was brought to Cambridge. If a guild-man killed another man by accident his brother members paid compensation to the dead man's friends. If any one killed a guild-brother and refused to compensate the deceased man's kindred, the whole guild would be avenged on him. For more details of this guild and its regulations consult Atkinson's " Cambridge " (1897).

During the Middle Ages were established a number of small religious houses, cells, dependent on the greater abbeys, and at these the young men from Crowland and elsewhere were educated. The origin of the university is lost in the mists of history, but students of the past regard it as an outcome of the ancient religious houses. One circumstance is certain—that it has long been the home of learning. In the earlier times it appears the teaching was conducted in a primitive manner. The scholars started their lessons early in the morning. We have some curious particulars relating to Cambridge in the reign of Henry I. At first, it is said, the students met in a large barn, but in the second year each teacher had a separate room. Very early in the morning one master taught the rules of grammar; at six a second lectured on the logic of

Aristotle; at nine Cicero and Quintilian were construed and expounded, and before twelve a theological class received an explanation of difficult passages of Scripture. Early teaching was not confined to Cambridge, and it was customary in the older grammar schools. At Bewdley, the church bell was rung at 5 a.m., to call the pupils to the grammar school, and this continued till 1801.

The practice gave rise to the following epigram:

> Ye rascally ringers, ye merciless foes,
> Who persecute every friend of repose:
> I wish, for the quiet and peace of the land,
> You had round your necks what you hold in your hands.

However humble may have been the commencement of many of the colleges, they have grown in wealth, and are now buildings of great beauty, and the zeal for learning has been maintained. Men have been students here who have had a foremost part in the shaping of the world in religion, politics, science, literature, and in other directions. One is amazed at the stately piles devoted to education which are to be seen in every direction. There is King's College with its chapel, one of the sights of the world. Henry VI. laid the foundation stone on July 25th, 1446, and it was not completed until about a century had passed. Edward IV. and Henry VII. gave largely to this fabric. The beautiful stained windows belong to the earlier quarter (or a little later) of the sixteenth century. The screen and most of the stalls were placed in the chapel in 1774. It is 316 feet long, 45½ feet wide, and 78 feet high. The service in King's Chapel is not readily to be forgotten. As we write a picture flits before us: we see in fancy Mr. W. E. Gladstone, beside his daughter, Miss Helen Gladstone, principal of Newnham; the affection which was so strong in the family brought father and daughter frequently together, even when he was guiding the ship of state in stormy times.

Trinity is the largest of the colleges, and perhaps not equalled by any other in the world. Henry VIII. founded it by uniting two older foundations. As we wander through the courts and buildings of the college we get some idea of its size. Since the days of the great patron of learning, its royal founder, building after building has been added, designed by the chief architects of the time, from Wren down to Blomfield. There may not be a unity of design in every respect, but on the whole it is most effective. Many of our modern famous men belong to Trinity, we have only to mention such names in literature as Wordsworth, Byron, Macaulay, Tennyson. This latter here enjoyed the friendship of Arthur Hallam. The poet does not seem to have cherished any tender memories of Trinity, and went down without taking his degree. Thackeray was devoted to it, and in his novels introduces it. We must not forget that it was the college of Sir Isaac Newton, but, says a recent writer, the modern history of Trinity for learning begins with the mastership of William Whewell, from 1841 to 1866. He was famous as a scholar, great as an organiser, and generous as a benefactor to the college. He was a power in the realms of learning.

The chapel, completed about 1564, with later additions down to the days of Blomfield, includes much that is worth seeing. The art of our times has increased its charms.

In treasures of literature and art the library built by Wren is to the visitor the chief attraction of Trinity. It is of noble proportions, 200 feet long, 42 feet wide, and 37 feet high, and is well lighted. The carvings of the older book-cases are by Grinling Gibbons, and are much admired. Here are manuscripts in various languages, and brought from distant lands, as well as many relating to this country. The printed books in many instances are rare and all are valuable, including several notable collections. The Capell books relating to Shakespeare merit special mention. Before visiting this library we strongly advise the reading of Dr. Robert Sinker's admirable volume entitled "The Library of Trinity College, Cambridge." It puts one in touch with the treasures of the library. Along each side of the room on the book-cases are marble busts of famous fellows of the college; they include among others Lord Bacon, Isaac Barrow, Sir Isaac Newton, and Lord Tennyson. The bust of Tennyson, by Woolner, was refused admission to the library, because it was held in those days that a bust of a living person might not be placed in the library, and those in authority ordered it to be placed in the vestibule. Tom Taylor, for some time a Fellow of Trinity, made it the subject of some verses, which appeared in *Punch* when he was editor. The following is an extract from the poem:

> the youth
> Who loved the Poet, hoped to see him set
> Within the Library of Trinity,
> One great man more o' the house, among the great
> Who grace that still Valhalla, ranged in a row,
> Two stately ranks—to where the fragrant limes
> Look thro' the far end window, cool and green.
> A band it is, of high companionship—
> Chief, Newton, and the brow-bowed Verulam,
> And others only less than these in arts
> Or science; names that England holds on high.

The bust of the greatest of our modern poets has now been placed within the sacred precincts.

The most striking monument is that of Lord Byron by Thorwaldsen. This beautiful work of art was intended for Westminster Abbey, and was refused by the Dean, Dr. Ireland, on the ground that Byron was not a suitable man to have a monument there. On the Dean's death, in 1842, Dr. Turton, afterwards Bishop of Ely, was approached, and he declined the statue for the abbey. After being in the Custom House vaults for many years it was finally given to Trinity College. In Dr. Sinker's volume will be found a detailed account of the statue which was modelled in Rome in 1831. In the "Life of Thorwaldsen" it is stated: "The poet, in modern costume, is seated upon the ruins of some Greek columns. His head is uncovered. He holds in his hand his poem, 'Childe Harold,' and raises towards his chin his left hand, holding a pen. On one side of the Greek fragment is A O H N H with the owl; on the other, Apollo's lyre and a gryphon. A Death's head is on the broken column. The bas-relief represents the

Genius of Poetry, who tunes his lyre, and rests his foot upon the prow of a skiff." On a table at the back of the statue is exhibited the first letter Byron ever wrote, and as it is always read with interest we give a copy of it:

Dear Madam

My Mamma being unable to write herself desires I will let you know that the potatoes are now ready and you are welcome to them whenever you please.

She begs you will ask Mrs Parkyns if she would wish the poney to go round by Nottingham or go home the nearest way as it is quite well but too small to carry me.

I have sent a young Rabbit which I beg Miss Frances will accept off and which I promised to send before. My Mamma desires her best compliments to you all in which I join.

I am,
Dear Aunt,
Yours sincerely,

Newstead Abbey, Nov. 8, 1798. BYRON.

I hope that you will excuse blunders as it is the first letter I ever wrote.

It was Dean Ireland that refused the interment of Lord Byron in Westminster Abbey. He was laid to rest in a churchyard not far distant from Newstead Abbey. Many pilgrims visit his shrine. The library at Trinity contains many manuscripts. In a book in the writing of Milton is "Lycidas," "Comus," and other poems, and the first draft of "Paradise Lost," showing that the poet first intended to write it in dramatic form. Here is Thackeray's MS. of "Esmond," and the MS. of Tennyson's "In Memoriam," and "Poems by Two Brothers." There are some cases of antiquarian relics and other objects of interest.

At the Backs, after leaving Trinity, one gets perhaps the most charming view in Cambridge. We see in the distance St. John's College, founded by the Lady Margaret Beaufort, Countess of Richmond and Derby, mother of King Henry the Seventh, 1511, on the suppression of a hospital dating back to 1135. It is an imposing building with a striking entrance gateway. Various architects have added and altered the pile, and many are the celebrated scholars who have been educated here. Here came Wordsworth; but he did not take a high degree; he was too much engaged with his poetry, which placed him in the first rank of English poets. Wilberforce and Clarkson were both at this college at the same time, men who freed the slave. Another poet must be named—Henry Kirke White. His poems are not much read at the present time, but his life, so full of promise, is still an inspiration. Born in Nottingham, the son of a butcher, he often carried meat to his father's customers. He passed a year at the stocking loom, then drifted into law; a strong religious feeling induced him to give up the legal profession, and prepare himself for the Church. He had published a volume of his poems, which neither met with praise from the critics nor attained pecuniary success, but gained him the friendship of Robert Southey and William Wilberforce, M.P., who each gave a hundred pounds towards his college expenses.

In October, 1805, White entered St. John's College, Cambridge, and at once made his mark in classics. At the general college examination at the end of the first term, and again in the summer term of 1806, he came out the first of his year. His college was anxious to help a promising student, and in the long vacation of 1806 provided him with a tutor for mathematics. His health was failing, and he was not equal to the strain; consumption had set in, and he was cut down by the hand of death in his rooms on the 19th October, 1806. He was laid to rest in All Saints' Church, a few paces from his college. At the expense of a young American admirer, Francis Booth, the botanist, a tablet was placed above his grave with a medallion by Chantry, and the following lines by Professor William Smyth, one of White's earliest friends:

> Warm with fond hope and learning's sacred flame,
> To Granta's bowers the youthful poet came;
> Unconquer'd powers th' immortal mind display'd
> But, worn with anxious thought, the frame decay'd;
> Pale o'er the lamp, and in his cell retired,
> The martyr student faded and expired.
> Oh! genius and piety sincere,
> Too early lost 'midst studies too severe!
> Foremost to mourn, was gen'rous Southey seen,
> He told the tale, and showed what White had been;
> Nor told in vain: For o'er th' Atlantic wave
> A wanderer came, and sought the Poet's grave;
> On yon lone stone he saw the lonely name,
> And raised this fond memorial to his fame.

When the church was pulled down in which the poet was interred, the monument was removed to St. John's College Chapel, where it attracts much notice. Southey collected his poems and letters and gave to the world "The Remains of Henry Kirke White, of Nottingham, late of St. John's College, Cambridge: with an account of his life." Many editions of this popular work have been published, and it is much valued by lovers of good books. When White passed away many tributes to his life and labours were published. Byron's lines in "English Bards and Scotch Reviewers" are the best known. He says:

> Unhappy White! While life was in its spring
> And thy young muse just shook her joyous wing,
> The spoiler came; and all thy promise fair
> Has sought the grave, to sleep for ever there.
> 'Twas thine own genius gave the fatal blow,
> And helped to plant the wound that laid thee low.

On August 27th, 1811, Lord Byron wrote to Dallas respecting White. "Setting aside his bigotry," said Byron, "he surely ranks next to Chatterton. It is astonishing how little he was known; and at Cambridge no one thought or heard of such a man, till death rendered all notice useless. For my own part I should have been proud of such an acquaintance; his very prejudices were respected."

The beautiful chapel designed by Sir Gilbert Scott, and built in 1864-9, contains much that is interesting, numerous monuments of an ornate character, but none attract the same attention as the monument placed to the memory of the young Nottingham poet and student of promise. The general features of the college are good and well calculated to detain the visitor.

Dr. Hymers, the founder of Hymers College, Hull, was for a long period the tutor of St. John's. Many stories are told respecting him, some are fiction, and handed down from one tutor to another. We have reason to believe the following is true: A Johnian undergraduate, having brought himself under the notice of the police, was sent for by Dr. Hymers, who sternly rebuked him for his misconduct, and stated that the police would shortly come to the college to identify the offender. "You will come here to-morrow morning," said Dr. Hymers. As the culprit was leaving the doctor remarked, "By the way, Mr. ——, if I were you I should shave off that moustache." The use of the razor protected him from identification.

Another college of interest is Magdalen, and was founded by Thomas Lord Audley; it is not one of the larger buildings, and would have little interest were it not for the fact that it contains the library of Samuel Pepys, which he bequeathed to his college. The books are in the cases in which he kept them. Here is his diary in shorthand, which gives such a graphic picture of the manners, customs, and life of the period in which it was written. Pepys was a great lover of forgotten lore, and there is a remarkable collection of ballads and other literary curiosities. The proper pronunciation of Pepys is a puzzle to the general public. Mr. J. Ashby Sterry some years ago attempted to enlighten them as follows:

> There are people, I'm told—some say there are heaps—
> Who speak of the talkative Samuel as Peeps;
> And some, so precise and pedantic their step is,
> Who call the delightful old diarist Pepys;
> But those I think right, and I follow their steps,
> Ever mention the garrulous gossip as Peps.

Matthew Parker was Master of Corpus Christi College from 1544 to 1553. It is one of the smaller colleges, and the students usually prepare for the Church. Two dramatists were educated here, Christopher Marlowe and Giles Fletcher, of Beaumont and Fletcher fame, but its chief scholars have gained renown in the religious world. Parker rose to the proud position of Archbishop of Canterbury. His college holds his name in great esteem, but he was more celebrated as an Archbishop than as a Don. In the library is his great collection of manuscripts. The bequest was made with a curious condition. It was to the effect that if twenty-five of the MSS. are lost, the collection goes to Caius, and if neglected there it is to pass on to Trinity Hall. The counting is conducted with great ceremony. One of the most important MS. in the collection is the original draft of the Thirty-nine Articles.

Milton, on February 12th, 1625, entered Christ's College as a pensioner. His name is associated with a bath, summer-house, and mulberry tree, which are shown with great pride to visitors. King James I. brought into this country in 1609 a large number of mulberry trees with a view of cultivating them in England. It has been suggested that this is a survival of those planted at the instigation of the King.

One cannot pass Peterhouse without looking high up on the outside of the college and thinking of the fire-escape placed there by the poet Gray. He had a horror of fire, and in the event of one he planned a means of quitting the building by means of a rope tied to the ironwork, which remains to the present time. Gray's manners by no means made him popular with the undergraduates. An alarm of fire was raised by them, and straw and paper were ignited at his door. This terrified the poet, and he made his escape by a rope only to land at the bottom in a tub of water. The outrage caused him to leave Peterhouse and settle at Pembroke, where he passed twenty-five years; the last three years he was Regius Professor of Modern History.

Charming courts, beautiful gardens, and a wealth of flowers add much to the attractiveness of the colleges, which, in most instances, are excellent examples of architecture. The rooms in the stately halls are planned with taste, the walls are adorned with portraits of the men who have made the reputation of Cambridge for learning. The skill of the sculptor and the carver has done much to increase its artistic glory. In recent times the master minds of Scott, Blomfield, Pearson, Street, and others have greatly added to the architectural features of the town, more especially that of the colleges.

The educational facilities of Cambridge do not end with the colleges. There are notable museums for the cultivation of art, archæology, and science. The chief is the Fitzwilliam Museum. Richard Viscount Fitzwilliam, of Trinity Hall, who passed away in 1816, left to the university his books, illuminated manuscripts, pictures, and the dividends on £100,000 for the erection of a museum to contain them. The foundation stone was laid November 2nd, 1837, the architect being George Basevi, and he carried on the work until his death in 1845, from a fall in Ely Cathedral. Then followed C. R. Cockerell until operations were suspended for want of funds in 1847. The Entrance Hall was completed in 1875 from designs by E. M. Barry, R.A., at a cost of £23,000; the entire structure cost about £115,000. Some notable collections of pictures have been bequeathed to the institution. There are also fine classical antiquities and objects of interest which cannot fail to instruct and delight the visitor.

The University Library is one of the great libraries of the country, and the ever-increasing additions of books placed on its shelves have at various times outgrown its space, and important enlargements have been made to the building. Lord Acton's library was left to John Morley, and he presented it to Cambridge. The university is rich in the quantity and quality of its books. The college libraries and the one belonging to the university make ample provison for all classes of students and the most bookish of people. Near the university is the Senate House, built in 1722-30 from designs by James Gibbs. Like most of the Cambridge buildings, statuary adds to its attractions.

The Botanical Gardens are extensive, and have a large glass house devoted to various classes of plants, trees, etc., and in the grounds are trees from all quarters of the globe. It is an ideal place for the advanced student of botany and arboriculture. The gardens of the colleges are usually good.

Cambridge churches do not greatly impress the stranger. They yield in interest to the college chapels, which, in many instances, are extremely fine. Great St. Mary's is the parish church, the largest and most important in Cambridge. Here the university sermons are preached. On the site of the present building a church was consecrated in 1351. The present fabric, which is an excellent specimen of Perpendicular Gothic, was started in 1478, but for want of money it made slow progress. Proctors of the university on horseback rode through England with begging letters. The impressive tower was started in 1491, and not finished until 1608.

St. Benedict's Church is pre-Norman, and through the changes of centuries has retained many of its original features. The tower is divided into three well-marked stages, each rather narrower than the one below. The quoins are of long-and-short work, and the whole tower is a good example of Saxon work. The other parts of the building are not so satisfactory on account of the numerous changes.

The Church of the Holy Sepulchre, commonly called the Round Church, is one of the four old circular churches left in this country. Its foundation dates back towards the middle of the twelfth century. It reminds one of the days of the Knight Templars. We need not refer in detail to the other churches, and the many objects of interest in this old English town. Its annals are full of curious and forgotten lore. We may mention that the ducking stool for punishing scolds appears to have been frequently brought into use at Cambridge. Cole, the local antiquary, collected numerous items bearing on this theme. In some extracts made from the proceedings of the Vice-Chancellor's Court in the reign of Queen Elizabeth, it is stated: "Jane Johnson, adjudged to the ducking stool for scolding, and commuted her penance." The next person appears not to have been so fortunate as Jane Johnson, who avoided punishment by paying a fine of about five shillings. It is recorded: "Katherine Saunders, accused by the church-wardens of Saint Andrews for a common scold and slanderer of her neighbours, was adjudged to the ducking stool."

We get several reminders of the olden time in the town. Thomas Hobson, the famous Cambridge carrier, was born about 1544, and died January 1st, 1630-1, and was honoured by two epitaphs written by Milton. Thomas was the son of a carrier, and made much money in the same business. Considerable profits were realised by carrying letters from the university to London. He was the first person to let out horses on hire. The horses were placed in rotation in the stables, and he would not permit one to be taken out of its proper order. This gave rise to the popular saying, "Hobson's Choice." Meaning the only one to select from. In 1830 his visits to London were stopped on account of the plague raging there, and his death followed through lack of his usual occupation. Said Milton, "Death would never have hit him had he continued dodging it backward and forward between Cambridge and the Bell in London."

Much more merits attention in Cambridge, but we must close our account with a few details respecting an old fair. No fair in England was more celebrated than that of Stourbridge. A carefully compiled account of it is given in Walford's "Fairs Past and Present." We are told that the first trace of it is found in a charter granted about 1211, by King John to the Lepers of the Hospital of St. Mary Magdalen, at Stourbridge, by Cambridge, a fair to be held in the close of the hospital on the Vigil and Feast of the Holy Cross. Its history shows how subsequently contentions arose between the town and university of Cambridge, in respect to the profits of the fair. It was held on a large piece of land near the banks of the Cam.

It has been stated that John Bunyan viewed this fair, and it suggested to him the idea of Vanity Fair. We learn from the records of this fair that in 1655 a crimson coat, gaily decorated with taps, was bought for the Lord of Taps, whose duty it was to sample the ale in any or all of the booths of the fair, and see if it was fit for consumption. This office was not formally abolished until 1833.

Down to 1758 a great show was made in proclaiming the fair. A procession as follows proceeded from Cambridge to the fair-ground:

The Crier in scarlet on Horseback
28 Petty Constables on foot
Three Drums
The Grand Marshal
The Town Music (12 in number)
The Bellman in state on Horseback
The Five Serjeants at Mace on Horseback
The Town Clerk on Horseback
The Mayor in his robes on a horse richly caparisoned, led by two footmen in scarlet with wands
The two representatives in Parliament on Horseback
Twelve Aldermen on Horseback (three and three) in their robes, the six seniors each having a Henchman in scarlet
The Four-and-twenty (three and three)
Eight Dispencers in their gowns (two and two)
Four Bailiffs in their habits
The Treasurers in their gowns

The display began to decline after 1758, and was discontinued in 1790, when the Mayor, Bailiffs, and Town Clerk started the practice of proclaiming the fair.

Defoe visited this fair in 1723, and in the following year published an account of it. Referring to the field where it was held, he states that " if the husbandmen who rent the land do not get their corn off before a certain day in August, the fair-keepers may trample it under feet and spoil it, to build their booths. On the other hand, to balance that severity, if the fair-keepers have not done their business of the fair, and removed and cleared the field by another certain day in September, the ploughman may come in again, with plough and cart, and overthrow all, and trample it into the dirt." The waterways to Lynn in bygone times gave rise to its importance. The fair is now shorn of its ancient glory. In the past it lasted several weeks; at the present time it is only held for three days. On one of the days a good trade is done in horses.

BURY ST. EDMUNDS.

CHARLES DICKENS, in his "Uncommercial Traveller," speaks of Bury St. Edmunds as a bright little town. It is a place of considerable antiquity, rich in historical associations and legendary lore. Few, if any, English towns can equal it in its varied charms. It is well planned, clean, and is delightfully situated in West Suffolk. Some attempts have been made by antiquaries to link it with Roman times, but their speculations are of little account. It is a fact that a few Roman coins—and some of them doubtful—have been found within the town. The immediate district has yielded evidence of Roman occupation.

The early importance of the town is derived from its famous abbey, the remains of which are of great interest. Beodricsweorth, or homestead of Beodric, was the name given to the site of the present town. It was here, about 631, that Sigeberht, the King of East Anglia, is said to have founded a church and monastery in honour of the Virgin. From within the walls of this religious house, where he had assumed the *rôle* of a monk, he went forth to battle with the heathen Penda, and was slain. We do not hear any more of Beodricsweorth until the days of King Edmund the Martyr, who was crowned here on Christmas Day, 855. He was a brave and good man, living in stirring times, when might and not right was the order of the day. After defeat in a battle with the Danes, he was taken prisoner. Then his life and kingdom were offered to him if he would renounce Christianity and acknowledge the Danish supremacy. He declined the terms, and in 870 was bound to a tree and shot to death with arrows. He was at last laid to rest at Beodricsweorth, which was named St. Edmundsbury in his honour. His constancy to his faith earned for him canonisation. On the 20th November, the day of his martyrdom, the English Church keeps his name in remembrance. Bury is the Anglo-Saxon Byrig, indicating a town or enclosed place. We need not repeat the idle stories which have gathered round the King's life. The abbey increased in importance, and was ruled by a mitred abbot.

The shrine of St. Edmund became the chief religious centre in Eastern England. It was visited in large numbers by all ranks of the people from the highest to the humblest. Kings and princes came as pilgrims, among them the Confessor, who walked the last mile into the town barefooted. When the first Henry escaped from shipwreck, he came to this shrine to give thanks. Eustace, the son of the Empress Matilda, died at Bury in 1153. He had been plundering the country round, and the convent had refused him supplies. In May, 1157, Henry II. was here wearing the crown of St. Edmund. When the struggle between the King and his sons occurred Henry assembled his army at Bury; the banner of St. Edmund waved before them, and they won the day. Richard I. made several visits to the town. He came hither as a pilgrim in 1189, and was here on St. Edmund's Day before starting for Palestine, and within a few days of his return, in 1194, he came and offered at the shrine a rich banner, taken from the Emperor of Cyprus. Henry III. was visiting Bury in 1273, when seized with an illness which proved fatal. Here, as a guest, Henry VI. spent several months in 1453.

The royal visits are of little account in the annals of the abbey as compared with the gathering which forced King John to observe the conditions of the Magna Charta. On a tablet in the church of St. Edmund it is stated:

Near this spot
On the 20th of November A.D. 1215,
Cardinal Langton & the Barons
Swore at St. Edmund's Altar
That they would obtain from
KING JOHN
The Ratification of
MAGNA CHARTA.

Where the rude buttress totters to its fall
And Ivy mantles o'er the crumbling wall;
Where e'en the skilful eye can scarcely trace
The once High Altar's lowly resting place—
Let patriotic fancy muse awhile
Amid the ruins of this ancient pile—
Six weary centuries have passed away;
Palace and Abbey moulder in decay—
Could Death enshroud the learned and the brave—
Langton—Fitz-Walter—slumber in the grave,
But still we read in deathless records how
The high-soul'd Priest confirmed the Barons' vow
And Freedom, unforgetful still recites
The second birthplace of our Native Rights.

J. W. Donaldson *scripsit.* J. Muskett *posuit,* 1847.

On another tablet are the names of the twenty-five barons appointed to enforce the observance of Magna Charta.

Several parliaments were held here. The most notable was the one in 1446, when Henry VI. decreed the fall of his uncle, the good Duke Humphrey of Gloucester, who was forthwith arrested and imprisoned, and in a few days was found dead, and it is generally believed that he had been strangled.

Down to the days of Queen Elizabeth many monarchs visited Bury, and were notably entertained. Some came here to pass Christmas and other feasts, but in not a few instances they came to perform religious duties. Henry I., after his visit to Pope Innocent the Third in 1132, on his passage to England, was overtaken by a violent storm, and when death seemed near, he made a solemn vow of reformation and amendment of life. No sooner had he arrived safely on land than he proceeded to Bury to discharge his religious duties at the shrine of St. Edmund.

It seems doubtful if James I. visited Bury, but an old ballad says:

King Jamie once in Suffolk went
A-hunting of ye deere
And there he met a Burie blade
All clad in finest gear.

Lamme was the name of the Bury blade, and on learning this, the King observed: "I know not what kind of lamb he is, but I am sure he has a good fleece upon his back."

To understand the life and get the true spirit of

Bury St. Edmunds we must read Carlyle's "Past and Present." From his graphic pen-pictures we can fully realise the important part it played in the olden time. It is not one of the largest, but it is one of the best of the author's books. Anyone visiting the place should not fail to read it.

There is not much left of the ancient abbey. At the dissolution it had a yearly income of £2,366 16*s*., which does not seem a large sum; but the buying power of money was greater in the past than at the present time. In bygone days for a small amount considerable purchases might be made. We find it stated that the manors which then belonged to the abbey are now worth £500,000 per annum. We know from old accounts, pictures and the remains which have come down to us, how large and stately was the ancient pile. The Abbey Gate, the chief entrance to the monastery, is standing, and is a noble monument of the past. It replaced the gateway destroyed by the townspeople in 1327, and was finished in 1377. It is a fine specimen of the Decorated style of pointed architecture. The visitor may enter the monastic grounds by this gate and inspect the remains of the abbey. The churches will also repay careful study; these include St. James's, dating from about 1436. Next to be seen is St. Mary's, Perpendicular in style, and erected at the commencement of the fifteenth century. Both are full of interesting monuments. In St. Mary's is the tomb of Mary Tudor, widow of Louis XII. of France.

Behind the striking Norman Tower (1121-46), forming part of St. James's Church, is the churchyard, known in monastic times as the Cemetery of St. Edmund. It is full of interesting monuments and curious epitaphs. On entering this ancient burial ground the first monument to attract attention is an obelisk to the memory of seventeen Protestant martyrs who were burnt to death during the reign of Queen Mary. On a gravestone is an inscription as follows:

Here lies interred the Body of
MARY HASELTON
A young maiden of this town,
Born of Roman Catholic parents and virtuously brought up,
Who being in the act of prayer
Repeating her vespers,
Was instantaneously killed by a flash of lightning,
August 16th, 1785.
Aged 9 years

Not Siloam's ruinous tower the victims slew,
Because above the many sinn'd the few
Nor here the fatal lightning wrecked its rage
By vengeance sent for crimes matur'd by age.
For whilst the thunder's awful voice was heard,
The little suppliant with her hands uprear'd
Addressed her God in prayers the priest had taught,
His mercy craved, and His protection sought;
Learn, reader, hence that wisdom to adore.
Thou canst not scan and fear His boundless power;
Safe shall thou be if thou perform'd His will,
Blest if He spares, and more blest should He kill.

Another inscription tells the low value human life had at the close of the eighteenth century. Great efforts were made to save the life of the criminal, more especially by Capel Lofft, the poet and friend of poets, and for the part he took in the case on behalf of the poor woman his name was removed from the list of magistrates.

Reader
Pause at this humble stone, it records the fall of unguarded
youth by the allurements of vice and treacherous
snares of seduction
SARAH LLOYD
On the 23rd April 1800 in the 22nd year of her age
Suffered a just and ignominious death,
For admitting her abandoned seducer in the dwelling-house
of her mistress on the 23rd of October, 1799, and
becoming the instrument in his hands of the
crime of robbery and housebreaking.

These were her last words:
"May my example be a warning to thousands."

A number of slight crimes may be cited which brought criminals to the gallows at Bury in the past:

In 1802 John Read, *alias* Oxer, and Thomas Keeley were sentenced to death for burglary at Thrandeston, and were executed.

Robert Clarke, in 1807, was convicted of uttering a forged £1 note to the landlord of the Old Angel Inn, Bury, and was executed.

Two men, in 1802, one for stealing a sheet and the other for stealing a sack of wheat, were sentenced to be whipped one hundred yards in Bury market-place, and were afterwards imprisoned.

In 1804 a man was transported for seven years to Botany Bay for stealing a rabbit. Ten years later a man was imprisoned for six months for perjury, and once within the time had to stand in the pillory at Haverhill on a market day.

A memorial is placed to an author who delighted the reading public in his day, but now his books are little read, and gather dust as they remain unopened on the library shelf. It read as follows:

To the memory of
HENRY COCKTON,
Author of "Valentine Vox," "Sylvester Sound," "The Love Match," and other Works.
His remains were interred in this Churchyard, June 30, 1853.
No stone marks his resting-place. A few admirers of his genius raised this tablet to his memory
A.D. 1884.
His Works are his best Monument.

In early times in this churchyard miracle plays were performed; wrestling and other sports were held, but in 1197 they were forbidden by Abbot Sampson on account of the disturbance which took place between the townspeople and the servants of the abbey. Here a chapel was founded in 1301. It passed through various changes, and in 1637 was a common ale-house and called a common nuisance; later it was used as a blacksmith's shop.

Defoe and others have placed on record particulars of a brutal outrage committed on the pathway running through this churchyard between the churches of St. James and St. Mary. "In the pathway," says Defoe, "between these two churches . . . a tragical and almost unheard-of act of barbarity was committed, which made the place less pleasant for some time than it used to be, when Arundel Coke, Esq., a barrister-at-law, of a very ancient family, attempted, with the assistance of a barbarous assassin, to murder in cold blood, and in the arms of hospitality, Edward Crisp, Esq., his brother-in-law, leading him out from his own house, where he had invited him, his wife and children, to supper; I say, leading him out in the night, on pretence of going to see some friend that was known to them both; but in the church-yard, giving a signal to the assassin he had hired, he attacked him with a hedge-bill, and cut him, as one might say, almost to pieces; and when they did not doubt of his being dead they left him. His head and face were so mangled that it may be said to be next to a miracle that he was not quite killed; yet so Providence directed for the exemplary punishment of the assassins, that the gentleman recovered to detect them, who (though he outlived the assault) were both executed as they deserved, and Mr. Crisp is yet alive. They were condemned on the statute for defacing and dismembering, called the Coventry Act." To-day, as we visit the tombs in this historic burial ground, we can hardly realise some of the tragic stories associated with it.

It was at this town, in 1644, that forty persons were hanged under the ban of Hopkins, the witch-finder. On the Northgate Road is an important historical site. It is called Thing-hou, or "the Hill of the Council or Assembly" of the Anglo-Saxons, and it gave the name to the Hundred of Thingoe. In early times the affairs of the district were discussed in the open air. Down to 1776 it was the place of public executions, and derived its more popular name of Betty Burrough's Hill, from the last person who suffered death there.

A plague of great violence visited the town in 1636, and nearly depopulated the place. At one time no fewer than four hundred families were sick, and were maintained at the public charge. People avoided visiting Bury, and in its streets grass grew. At the bottom of Risbygate Street is the octagonal base of a cross, which was filled with vinegar when the smallpox raged in the town in 1677, so that people attending the market, then held outside the gate of the town, might place in the vinegar their money to disinfect it, while others would dip in their handkerchiefs to save themselves from infection.

The town has many important and interesting buildings, and flowers and trees add much to its beauty. It has charms for the antiquary, and affords delight to the man-of-the-world, and is by no means a sleepy place; indeed, it is not surprising that Dickens selected it for the scene of some of the more diverting events in the career of Mr. Pickwick.

LINCOLN.

It is that poem in architecture, Lincoln Cathedral, which draws strangers to the city, but there is much to interest and instruct those who make a pilgrimage to the place. Lincolnshire is regarded by many as a fenland, lacking in striking scenery. As a matter of fact, few of our English counties are more varied, and have more beauty spots. It has hills and dales, with a wealth of trees, winding streams, dismantled castles, ruined abbeys, and pleasant towns, which make up a delightful holiday haunt. Its history and more especially its rural charms have inspired poets. The Tennysons take the leading place, but others stand high in the realms of literature.

The origin of the name of the city is of considerable historical interest. It takes us back to the days of the dim historic past. It was called by the Britons *Caer-lindcoit*. By the Celts it was known as *Linn-dun*, and when the Romans subdued the land the name was Romanised to Lindum. A name identical with that of London, meaning "the hill fort of the pool." From this we gather that part of the city below the hill was a stagnant mere, of which, at the present time, Brayford Harbour is almost the only remains. The ending of the Roman name Lindum Colonia "proclaims," says Freeman, "the rank which Lincoln held among Roman cities; an ending which it shares with no

LINCOLN. John of Gaunt's Palace, 1834.

other English town or village, and with but one other spot (Cologne) throughout the whole dominion of Rome. Köln and Lincoln are cities kindred in their origin and name, and each proclaims herself simply as the Roman *Colonia*; the city by the Witham keeps her earlier name as well as the title of her Roman rank, and proclaims herself through her long history as the Colony of Lindum."

The British settlement is generally assigned to the enclosed area outside the Newport or Northgate. It was left to the Romans to utilise the steep hill southwards as a means of natural defence, and to move their city in that direction. The first Roman city was small. It measured about 400 yards from north to south and 500 from east to west. There were four gates, of which one still remains, the Newport; this, with the exception of the one at Colchester called Balkerne, is the only Roman gate standing in England. The site of the first Roman city may still be traced. It soon outgrew its narrow boundaries so that it had to be greatly extended, and its extension was southwards, a movement still followed at the present time.

There cannot be any doubt of the importance of the city in Roman times, but its historic story of a colony under Imperial Rome is almost barren of stirring events, and of the shaping of history in this country. It must, however, have been a busy city. The stately tread of the Roman legions must have often echoed in the city. *Ermine Street*, from London to the Humber and into Yorkshire, ran through it, and another road crossed it in the centre of the city, running from east to west. In addition to the roads named the great Foss Way from Bath to Leicester and Newark joined *Ermine Street* at Swine Green, a mile south of the city gate. In 627 Blecca, the prefect of the city, was converted by Paulinus, Bishop of York, the famous Northumbrian Apostle. The site of the first Christian church within the city is known as St. Paul's, which is a corrupted form of the great apostle's name.

A bishopric of Lindsey was founded by Ecgfrith of Northumbria, but Lincoln was not chosen as the bishop's seat. Stow was selected, and its venerable church must be regarded as the mother-church of Lincoln Minster; and until the Norman Conquest, it remained the head of the See.

When the Danes swept the land with the sword in the ninth century, Lincoln was one of their five great boroughs in this country. In no other county in England have they left more abiding traces, more especially in the place-names. Here, as in the other four great towns, Stamford, Leicester, Nottingham, and Derby, a patriciate, and twelve lawmen, whose office was hereditary, ruled the town. It was a sort of commonwealth and independent of the Danish Government. Eadmund, "the doer of good deeds," was the means of winning the people of this country back to Christianity. In 1013 a change took place in the Danish rule in England. The five great boroughs submitted to Swein, the inhabitants were treated with respect, and remained independent communities.

When William of Normandy won the crown at

the battle of Hastings few changes were made at Lincoln. The Domesday Survey shows that the old privileges were retained. The King realised the important position of the place and had the future shaping of it in his own hands. Where the old fortress had stood in 1068 he built a castle, which not only protected the city, but was the key to the eastern counties. At the present time the castle is used as assize courts and as a county prison. It has a stirring history, and is one of the eight known to have been founded by the Conqueror. There are two mounds within the boundary of the stronghold, about 40 feet high. On one stands the Keep, and on the other the Observatory Tower. When the struggle between Stephen and Matilda disturbed the peace of the land, the Queen made Lincoln her headquarters on her retirement from Wallingford. In 1140 Stephen pushed forward his troops and laid siege to the castle. In the battle of Lincoln, which was fought on the slope below the castle, the King was defeated and taken prisoner. Matilda, commonly called the Empress Maud, assumed the throne, but her rule was so unpopular that the barons took up arms for Stephen. The Earl of Gloucester was taken prisoner, and exchanged for the King. Stephen was finally permitted under the Treaty of Wallingford, 1153, to retain the crown during his life, which at his death was to pass to Henry Plantagenet, Matilda's son. Some historians designate her queen regnant. As a matter of fact this is a mistake, for she was never crowned by the Church or the nation.

Six years later, in the piping times of peace, King Stephen spent Christmas at the castle. He wore his crown, disregarding the old superstition:

> The first crowned head that enters Lincoln's walls,
> His reign proves stormy and his kingdom falls.

The castle figures largely in the times when civil strife raged at Lincoln. A notable battle occurred in 1217, the result of King John's breaking faith with the barons and violating the Magna Charta. He was plotting to get Louis, son of Philip, King of France, on the English throne. When John passed away Louis came to England, but those who had promised their support deserted his cause. The Earl of Pembroke, who had been chosen Protector during the minority of Henry, then only nine years old, defeated Louis at Lincoln. This engagement is known as "The Battle of Lincoln Fair." Our first great naval victory was gained at this time, Louis' fleet being nearly destroyed off the coast of Kent.

For a long period little fighting troubled the citizens, until the civil wars rent the country in twain, when father met son on opposite sides and when brothers were fighting under different banners. At the outbreak of the great struggle Charles I. visited Lincoln and was welcomed by 60,000 people. Little did he think then, when the air rang with their hearty cheers, that his career would end at the hands of a common headsman at Whitehall. The castle was held for the King by Sir Francis Fane, who, however, was driven out of it by the Parliamentary troops under the Earl of Manchester in 1644.

In later times the castle became a county prison, and within its walls are not only cells for prisoners, but courts in which to try them and lodgings for the judges. Samuel Bamford, the Lancashire poet and Radical, for a political offence was imprisoned here for a year, and in his "Passages in the Life of a Radical" is the best account of prison life of the period which has come under our notice. Local writers appear to have overlooked the graphic account, which pays a warm tribute to the kindness of justices and jailers. Great liberty was allowed him, which he took care not to abuse, and thus made a great impression on all who came in contact with him. His wife, who inspired his best poetry, was permitted to live with him. Some interesting glimpses of prison life in the past occur in connection with Lincoln Castle. From the top of Cobb Tower, which was roofed over, criminals were executed from 1815 until the "Private Executions Act" in 1868. Prior to 1815, the place of execution was at the corner of the road opposite the north-west corner of the Castle Dykings, and long bore the name of Hangman's Ditch. On March 19th, 1785, some 20,000 people assembled to witness the execution of nine persons, one for highway robbery and the rest for robbery of a slighter character.

Hanging was not the only means of ending life in the eighteenth century; the burning of women was practised long before this period. There is an account of burning at Lincoln in 1722. Eleanor Elsom was condemned to death for the murder of her husband, and was ordered to be burnt at the stake. She was clothed in a cloth "made like a shift," saturated with tar, and her limbs were also smeared with the same inflammable substance, while a tarred bonnet had been placed on her head. She was brought out of the prison barefoot, and, being put on the hurdle, was drawn on a sledge to the place of execution near the gallows. Upon arrival, some time was passed in prayer, after which the executioner placed her on a tar barrel, a height of three feet, against the stake. A rope ran through a pulley in the stake, and was placed round her neck, she herself fixing it with both hands. Three irons also held her body to the stake, and the rope being pulled tight, the tar barrel was taken aside and the fire lighted. The details in the "Lincoln Date Book" state that she was probably quite dead before the fire reached her, as the executioner pulled upon the rope several times whilst the irons were being fixed. The body was seen amid the flames for nearly half an hour, though, through the dryness of the wood and the quantity of the tar, the fire was exceedingly fierce.

Under the shadow of the castle rises the cathedral, a building of great architectural grandeur, and one which dominates the country for many miles round. The See of Lincoln dates back to 1074, when the bishop's seat was transferred from Dorchester-on-Thames by Remigius. The diocese covered much ground, and its bishops played an important part in the making of English history. Remigius built a church, and to-day remains of it may be seen in the central part of the west front. Hugh of Avalon was made bishop towards the close of the twelfth century, and started rebuilding the church in 1192. He commenced his operations at the east end, but died before he had completed his work. The nave was finished by his successors, and in the latter half of the twelfth century the apsidal ending of St. Hugh's choir was taken down, and the presbytery was extended five bays eastwards. The extension forms a striking feature in the cathedral and is the celebrated "Angel Choir," which attracts world-wide attention. It is called the "Angel Choir" from the number of the angelic figures that appear among the carvings. Here are many monuments, including one to Eleanor, wife of Edward I. She died five miles from the city, and her viscera were buried in the cathedral, her heart was taken to the church of the Friars Predicant in London, and her body was laid to rest in Westminster Abbey, not far from the place where her husband's body was laid to rest when death closed his active career.

The towers form a striking feature of the cathedral. The central tower is much admired. "By its dignity in the mass," says Walcot, "and the picturesque combinations with the cathedral which it forms from every point of view, it lends an unequalled majesty to the church. It is the finest central tower in the world." It is only surpassed in height by two cathedral spires in England, those of Salisbury and Norwich. The central tower of Lincoln carried a spire, but this was blown down in 1547. Browne Willis says: "The disaster happened at a time when faith and devotion were at a wretchedly low ebb, and men were rather occupied in unroofing and stripping the temples of God, than raising spires to His honour; and the tower of Lincoln has remained ever since curtailed of its beautiful termination." We might add that the worshippers have remained in safety and without fear from the falling of a steeple. In this tower hangs the famous "Great Tom of Lincoln," a giant among bells. In Macaulay's spirited ballad on the "Spanish Armada," Lincoln figures as spreading the news with the lighted beacon of the approach of the foe. We read:

> . . . twelve fair counties saw the blaze on Malvern's lonely height;
> Till streamed in crimson on the wind the Wrekin's crest of light;
> Till broad and fierce the star came forth on Ely's stately fane,
> And town and hamlet rose to arms o'er all the boundless plain;
> Till Belvoir's lordly terraces the sign to Lincoln sent,
> And Lincoln sped the message on o'er the wide vale of Trent;
> Till Skiddaw saw the fire that burned on Gaunt's embattled pile,
> And the red glare on Skiddaw roused the burghers of Carlisle.

Near the cathedral is a fine statue to Alfred, Lord Tennyson, erected by his admirers in his native county. The Bishop's Palace is a modern building on an ancient site. The historic house of Lincoln is the "House of Aaron the Jew," and it may safely be asserted to be one of the oldest inhabited dwellings in this country. Here resided Belaset de Wallingford, a Jewess, who was hanged for debasing coin in 1290. It was in this year that the Jews were expelled from England. The building has round windows, and the usual features of a Norman house.

Another interesting building is the Stone Bow, situated in High Street. It is a fine example of a fifteenth century town gate. There is a large upper room with a Perpendicular timber roof known as the Guild Hall. Here are kept the interesting and valuable regalia. Here is a bell set up by William Beale, Mayor, 1371, having an involved Latin inscription, which has been translated: "When any good man hears the bell let him open his bag (a brief-bag for the court), and know ye the hall will clear when it rings again."

The Hall of St. Mary's Guild may be pronounced one of the most valuable and extensive ranges of buildings of the twelfth century in England. The guild was the most important in the city. It is called erroneously John o' Gaunt's stables, and keeps alive the tradition that he had a palace nearly opposite St. Mary's Hall, being the home of his third wife, Katherine Swynford, of Ketilthorpe, whom he married in Lincoln Minster, 1386. She was a fair widow with a son, Charles Beaufort, who became Bishop of Lincoln. His mother died during his episcopate, and he had her interred with her daughter near the high altar of the cathedral.

There are numerous churches in the city. Two are especially interesting. St. Peter's at Gowts was built in Norman times. It is to be regretted that recent enlargements have resulted in the demolition of some of the fine Norman work. It has a striking tower. The other is St. Mary-le-Wigford, which has a stately tower similar to that of St. Peter-at-Gowts. In the graveyard of this church is a peculiar epitaph as follows:

> Here lies, believe it if you can,
> Who though an attorney was an honest man.

Many of the old street names are full of historical interest. Mint Street calls to mind the minting of coins, of which examples exist from the age of Alfred the Great to the reign of Edward I. The Bull Ring recalls the days when rich and poor keenly enjoyed the brutal sport. The Corporation bye-laws, like those of other places, contained a rule that no butcher should offer for sale bull beef unless the animal had been baited. "On Guy Fawkes Day, 1802," it is stated in the "Lincoln Date Book," "about eleven o'clock in the morning a bull was dragged into the city amidst the shouts of an applauding multitude; it was taken to the Castle Hill, tied to an iron ring with ropes, and then torn and worried by dogs. The animal appeared to possess great strength, and he soon broke loose, running downhill into the city, to the no small terror of the country people. It being market day, several women with butter, geese, eggs, etc., ran into St. Peter-at-Arches Church during divine service, their livestock making much noise therein. The bull was again secured and baited until four o'clock, when it dropped down dead at the stake." Another cruel sport was cock-fighting. In the "Reindeer," the Corporation had their cock-pit. It was here that King James was made merry by watching two pairs of cocks being placed in the pit at the same time. He attended two services at the minster, and after each touched fifty persons for king's evil.

There are the usual city and county buildings, and an up-to-date Public Free Library, with a good collection of local books, as well as works on the various branches of literature and science. There is a pleasant and well planned Arboretum, and the city has other attractions. There is no missing Lincoln, for " A city that is built on a hill cannot be hid."

COVENTRY.

THE Warwickshire city of Coventry is a place of great antiquarian interest. In spite of modern progress it presents an old-fashioned appearance, and offers a marked contrast to its busy and bustling neighbour, Birmingham. Coventry has a bygone look about it, and in every direction one seems to come into touch with history, while in modern Birmingham everything seems to be given up to trade.

Until the introduction of the cycle, Coventry appeared to have retired from business. Ribbon making had gone, and matters were at a standstill. The new industry put the place once more on its feet, and when the motor-car came along it set the old borough humming. The new industries may have tended to spoil the place in the eyes of the students of the past; but they have increased the wealth and prosperity of the city, and placed it on a line with other centres of trade.

From time to time it is brought into the public eye by its famous Godiva Procession, which ranks among the more important pageants of Merry England. It is to be feared that in the popular story of Lady Godiva there is little that is reliable, but it is quite clear that she was a woman ever ready to relieve those in distress, pious, and a benefactress

COVENTRY. [*From an old print.*

A Performance of a Sacred Play.
Period about the end of the Sixteenth Century.

to religious houses. Her lot was cast in a time when might and not right ruled the land. We have no fewer than seventeen forms of the spelling of her name, but as they all refer to the same person they need not cause any serious consideration. Her brother was Bucknall, Sheriff of Lincolnshire.

Her first husband was taken from her while she was still young, and at an early age she was expected to follow him to the grave. She gave to Ely monastery extensive lands in Suffolk and other parts of the country. We are told that she was a woman of great beauty, and a devoted lover of the Virgin Mary. She recovered from her illness, and before 1040 was married a second time to Leofric, Earl of Chester.

About this time she interested and induced her husband Leofric to help in the erection of a monastery at Stow, Lincolnshire. The couple made considerable benefactions to this religious house.

It is with Coventry that her name is associated in the popular mind. Here her husband had a villa, and here had been a convent, but when the Danes ravaged the district it was destroyed by fire. Godiva induced the earl to found here a Benedictine monastery for an abbot and twenty-four monks. The church was dedicated to St. Mary, St. Peter, St. Osburg (she was the Abbess of the old convent), and All Saints. The Archbishop of Canterbury performed the dedication ceremony. Husband and wife joined in making rich gifts of land to the monastery and church. It is recorded that Godiva made the church resplendent with gold and gems, not equalled in any other sanctuary in England of that time. William of Malmesbury says that the very walls seemed too narrow for the reception of its treasures. Cherished and important relics were deposited here, and we can readily realise that pious pilgrims would visit the shrine. Around this famous religious house would soon grow up a town with a market, and the statement that, when Godiva performed the feat which has given her lasting fame, there was no city, is, we think, a misconception of facts.

According to an ancient tradition, for some reason now lost in the mists of antiquity, Leofric at one period greatly taxed and oppressed the people. His countess was deeply moved to see them suffering, and she determined if possible to deliver them from their oppression. Says Tennyson:

> She sought her lord, and found him, where he strode
> About the hall, among his dogs alone,
> His beard a foot before him, and his hair
> A yard behind. She told him of their tears,
> And pray'd him, "If they pay the tax they starve."

The grim earl heard her words with amazement, and cried in scorn:

> "You would not let your little finger ache for such as these!"
> "But I would die," replied the pleading Godiva.

Tradition tells how her husband laughed, and by St. Peter and St. Paul took an oath exclaiming:

> "O, ay, ay, ay, you talk." She, persisting, said:
> "But prove me what it is I would not do."
> And from a heart as rough as Esau's hand,
> He answered, "Ride you naked thro' the town,
> And I repeal it."

His countess accepted the cruel condition:

> . . . . She sent a herald forth,
> And bade him cry, with sound of trumpet, all
> The hard condition; but that she would loose
> The people: therefore, as they loved her well,
> From then till noon no foot should pace the street,
> No eye look down, she passing; but that all
> Should keep within, door shut, and windows barr'd.

The poet says:

> Then she rode forth, clothed on with chastity.

Her husband's condition complied with,

> . . . . She took the tax away,
> And built herself an everlasting name.

An old story says that a tailor did basely and wilfully bore a hole through his shutters that he might peep at Lady Godiva as she passed. He suffered for the outrage, for, relates the poet:

> . . . . His eyes before they had their will
> Were shrivelled into darkness in his head
> And dropt before him.

The earliest historians do not mention Peeping Tom, and his introduction into the city legend belongs to the reign of Charles II., and was added to the attractions of the Godiva procession in celebration of the freedom of the city. In the past the Mayor and other leading men joined in the popular pageant, but now it is mainly made up of members of friendly and trade societies. The city has two figures of Peeping Tom. One was probably an image of St. George; it was removed from Grey Friars Lane, and placed in its present position, at the north-west corner of Hertford Street, on the formation of that street in 1812. In quite recent times a rival figure was put up at the south-west corner.

On August 31st, 1057, Leofric died. It is generally supposed that Lady Godiva passed away shortly before the Domesday Survey (1085-6).

There is a blending of fact and fiction in the story of Lady Godiva, but little doubt exists that the more important part of the story we have brought before our readers is true, and she will remain a noble example to womankind, although in the altered conditions of life her sex will not be called upon to go through such an ordeal.

After the Norman Conquest the lordship by marriage passed to the Earls of Chester, under whom the place made rapid advancement. Next came the Montalts and the Arundels, and the failure of heirs caused it to pass to the Crown. When Edward III. made his son, the Black Prince, the Duke of Cornwall, he annexed the manor of Coventry to the dukedom for ever. This king gave the place its first charter of incorporation in the year 1344. The great annual fair dates back long before the incorporation of the town, Henry III. having permitted it in 1218.

A singular circumstance stands boldly out in the history of the city. Here, in 1398, Henry Bolingbroke, Duke of Hereford (afterwards Henry IV.), and Thomas de Mowbray, Duke of Norfolk, met to decide a quarrel by Wager of Battle. The scene is immortalised by Shakespeare in his Richard II. The King and many of his nobles were present, and when the Champions were ready for the fray his Majesty stopped the engagement and banished both from England, Norfolk for ten years and Hereford for life.

A parliament was held at Coventry by Edward IV., in 1404, in the great chamber of the Priory, and a second parliament at the same place in 1459. Henry V. was supported by the town in the struggles which ended in his dethronement and death. When Edward IV. assumed the crown the citizens were severely fined for their loyal assistance to the dethroned king. When Richard III. was slain at Bosworth Field and Henry VII. ruled the land, he was welcomed to the city with joy, and a cup and £100 were presented to him. In 1565 Queen Elizabeth visited the city and was warmly welcomed. Mary Queen of Scots spent some of her weary captivity in this city. In 1616 her son, James I., visited the city and was entertained at a great feast. The city was surrounded by walls, which extended to a circuit of three miles, their average thickness being nine feet. Some remains of them may still be seen.

A couple of days after Charles I. had raised his standard at Nottingham, he demanded admission to Coventry, but the Puritans of the city refused to admit the monarch. He then, without success, attempted to take the city by force. Royalist prisoners were sent here, and the strict discipline gave rise to the saying of being "sent to Coventry." Charles II. fined the citizens for closing the gates of their city against his father, and dismantled the walls. For the remains of old religious houses few, if any, towns surpass Coventry.

St. Michael's vies with Holy Trinity, Hull, and St. Nicholas's, Yarmouth, in claiming to be the largest parish church in the United Kingdom. Its graceful spire is a striking object, rising nearly 300 feet. Two brothers, William and Adam Botoner, built the tower between 1373 and 1394. Two sisters, Ann and Mary, added the spire four years later. It was restored in 1888. The church was founded in the reign of Henry I., but little of the original building remains. The present Perpendicular building was erected towards the end of the fourteenth century and the commencement of the fifteenth century. The city was rich in its religious and trade guilds; formerly their chapels were in this church, and screens divided them from the rest of the building, but these have been swept away and the area for the worshippers has been greatly increased. The extreme length of the church is 293 feet, and its greatest width is 127 feet. A curious feature of this church and burial ground is the number of curious epitaphs. On a brass, placed to the memory of a Yorkshireman, in this church is an inscription as follows:

Here lyes the Body of CAPTAIN GERVASE, of the family o Scropes, of Bolton, in the County of York, who departed thi ife the 26th day of August, Anno Domini 1705.

AN EPITAPH WRITTEN BY HIMSELF IN THE AGONY AND DOLOROUS PAINES OF THE GOUT, AND DYED SOON AFTER.

Here lies an Old Toss'd Tennis Ball,
Was Racketted from Spring to Fall
With so much heat and so much hast,
Time's arm (for shame) grew tyr'd at last,
Four Kings in Camps he truly serv'd,
And from loyalty ne'r swerv'd.
Father ruin'd, the Son slighted,
And from the Crown ne'r requited,
Loss of Estate, Relations, Blood,
Was too well Known, but did no good,

With long Campaigns and paines of th' Govt,
He could no longer hold it out:
Always a restless life he led,
Never at quiet till quite dead,
He marry'd in his latter dayes,
One who exceeds the com'on praise,
But wanting breath still to make Known
Her true Affection and his Own,
Death kindly came, all wants supply'd
By giving Rest which life deny'd.

A famous fencing master was laid to rest in the churchyard, and his memorial says:

To the memory of
MR. JOHN PARKES,
A Native of this City.
He was a man of mild disposition, a Gladiator by profession;
Who having fought 350 battles,
In the principal parts of Europe,
With honour and applause,
At length quitted the stage, sheathed his sword,
And with Christian resignation,
Submitted to the Grand Victor
In the 52nd year of his age
Anno Domini 1733.

An old stone, bearing the foregoing inscription, was replaced by a new one some years ago at the expense of the late Mr. S. Carter, formerly Member of Parliament for Coventry. In the *Spectator*, honourable mention is made of John Parkes.

A typographical epitaph is also in the burial ground to the memory of a worthy printer who was engaged over sixty years as a compositor on the *Coventry Mercury*:

Here lies inter'd the mortal remains of
JOHN HULM
Printer,
Who, like an old, worn out type, battered by frequent use
reposes in the grave.
But not without a hope that at some future time he might be
cast in the mould of righteousness,
and safely locked up in the chase of immortality.
He was distributed from the board of life
on the 9th day of Sept., 1827,
Regretted by his employers and respected by
his fellow artists.

The general reader may not grasp the technical terms in the foregoing epitaph, but they will interest the printer and the student of typography.

Another fine Perpendicular church is Holy Trinity. It suffers much on account of being built so near St. Michael's. It is on the cruciform plan; the greatest length is 180 feet, and its greatest width 105 feet. The tower and a graceful spire rise from the intersection of the chancel, nave, and transepts. The interior of the tower is open to the church, and forms a lantern. During a terrible gale on the 24th January, 1665, the spire was blown down, but rebuilt in the two following years. The church stands on the site of one existing in the thirteenth century; only a few fragments of the older building remain. An adjacent Priory appropriated the church. Before the Reformation were a number of chapels and altars within this fabric, and at least two had crypts, St. Thomas's Chapel and the

Mercers' Chapel. Dugdale says that in the time of Richard II. a window was put up to represent Leofric holding in his hand a charter with the following words:

I Luriche for the love of thee
Do make Coventrie Tol free.

At this church a couple were united in marriage who won fame on the theatrical stage. The marriage took place by licence on the 25th November, 1773. The signatures attached to the registers are as follows:

William Siddons.

Sarah Kemble.

The witnesses were Roger Kemble and Mary J. Godfrey. Mr. Siddons is described as of the parish of St. Michael, and Miss Kemble of Trinity parish. The ceremony was performed by the Rev. George Richards, in the absence of the Rev. Joseph Rann, who was vicar of Trinity from 1773 to 1811. In 1776 and the four following years Mr. Rann published an edition of the "Dramatic Works of W. Shakespeare with Notes," in six vols., 8vo. Miss Ellen Terry, the celebrated actress, was born in Market Street, Coventry, 27th February, 1848.

There is much in the church to interest the visitor. In the vestry is a portrait of Dr. Hook, who was the vicar of this church before he was called to a larger sphere of labour as vicar of Leeds, and his zeal for church work, more especially for building new churches, gained for him the title of

"The Apostle of the North." He died Dean of Chichester.

Miracle plays were introduced into this country from the Continent. The earliest pieces were scriptural or, at all events, of a pious character. The earliest record of a performance in England was at Dunstable, about the year 1110, and it was entitled the "Miracle of St. Catherine." They were first performed by the priests as a part of the service of the Church, but later by the members of religious and trade guilds. They retained their popularity until the Reformation.

Coventry was famous for its plays, indeed it has long been famous for its pageants, the chief being the observance of the feast of Corpus Christi. The chief feature of this ceremony was a number of persons in a procession personating scriptural characters. Different guilds performed the mystery or miracle plays at Coventry. A stage was on wheels, and moved from one part to another. The stages on which plays were produced consisted of three floors, the highest representing Heaven, the next Earth, and the bottom one Hell. On one occasion the lower region was accidently set on fire, and, however appropriate the incident, great uneasiness was manifested by the occupants. Such disasters rendered repairs necessary. Here are two or three items from the accounts of the Coventry Mysteries:

Item, payd for mending hell-mowthe - - ij*d.*
Item, payd for makynge of the hell-moth new - xxj*d.*
Item payd for kepyng of the fyre at hell-mothe - iiij*d.*

Hell was generally represented by the imitation of a whale's open jaws, behind which a fire was lighted in such a manner as not to injure the damned who had to pass into the gaping mouth, or the actors personating the demons inside. Among the chief pieces produced by the different guilds were "The Trial and Crucifixion of Christ," by the Smiths', "The Doomsday," by the Drapers', "The Nativity and the Epiphany," by the Shearmen and Tailors'. The play of the Drapers' represented the world in flames. In the Coventry accounts are the following items:

1556 payd to Crowe for makyng of iij worldys - ij*s.*
1558 payd for iij worldys - - - - iij*s.* viij*d.*

A "world" was, of course, destroyed at each exhibition. An entry states:

Payd for settyng the world on fyer - - v*d.*

It would appear that setting one world on fire each day was deemed sufficient. The performers were paid for by the different companies.

Very rarely a new play was put on the stage, but in 1584 the Smiths' Company presented the "Destruction of Jerusalem" (founded on Josephus's account of it). This great effort only took six rehearsals to perfect them for the performance.

In the Middle Ages trade guilds were a great institution in Coventry, and some have come down to the present time. "One of the earliest of these trading guilds," says Mr. W. G. Fretton, F.S.A., "was the Bakers', which dates back to the sixth year of King John, which would be about 150 years before the incorporation of the city by Edward III." Frequently serious disputes and disturbances took place between the Bakers and the citizens, respecting weight and quality of bread. It is stated in the MS. annals of the city that, in 1374, the Commons arose and threw loaves of bread at the Mayor's head as he sat in St. Mary's Hall, and similar proceedings occurred in 1387. This was the method adopted by the inhabitants for showing their disapproval of bread which was light or of poor quality. It was the Mayor's duty to attend to superintend the assize of bread, and see that it was satisfactory in weight and quality.

Among the more important buildings of the city is St. Mary's Hall, which dates back to the end of the fourteenth century. It is the property of the Corporation, and is used for municipal purposes. Here trading companies have had their headquarters. It is a most interesting place, the great hall being especially fine, the oak roof being richly carved. A fine window at the end of the hall is filled with old stained glass, showing full length portraits of the Kings of England and others, above them being their coats-of-arms. John Thornton, a native of Coventry, is said to have executed the work. He was the same man who designed the east window of York Minster. Here is some fine Flemish tapestry, wrought about the beginning of the sixteenth century. The old charters may be seen here in glass cases. In the kitchen is a curious figure on a buttress. A brass plate under it states:

> This Knaves' Post was ormerly affixed to the wall of a house in Much Park street. It was usual to sentence offenders to be whipped at the cart tail from the Mayor's parlour in the Market-place to the Knaves' post and back.
>
> This Post was erected in this place as a relic of the past.
> By order ot the Corporation, May, 1900.

The figure formerly stood in a shallow niche in front of a brick eighteenth century house, about 550 yards from the old magistrates' court, so that the criminal had to walk 1,100 yards when undergoing the punishment of whipping. The last time anyone was whipped at the cart's tail in Coventry was in the early years of the nineteenth century.

There is much in St. Mary's Hall to arrest the attention of the visitor. It has an old-world air about it, which is pleasing and cannot be readily forgotten. Pictures by eminent artists and old furniture add much to its charms. In Grey Friars' Lane is Ford's Hospital for old women. William Ford founded it in 1529; it is a charming specimen of a half-timbered house, and of its class is regarded as one of the finest in the country.

As one wanders about the old city, we are constantly seeing the remains of bygone churches and religious houses as well as places of great historic interest. Here we find a city where the hours may be dreamed away, and in fancy the past recalled. To-day many would be delighted if "sent to Coventry."

LEICESTER.

LEICESTER is a place with a past as well as a present importance. As the visitor leaves the station for the town the fact is realised that it is a growing place, but its progress has not equalled that of Nottingham, Bradford, Sheffield, Hull, and Leeds, and other towns which in recent times have risen to the dignity of cities.

Traditional tales tell us that eight centuries before the birth of Christ the famous King Lear founded the town. The mediæval chronicler, Geoffrey of Monmouth, relates the story; but it is not confirmed by more discriminating historians. Many traces of British remains prove that it was a place of some importance in the days when the ancient Britons ruled the land. Little is reliable that has been written about Leicester as it was before Roman times. About the year A.D. 50, when the Emperor Claudius occupied the throne of Rome, the Proprætor Ostorius Scapula pushed forward into the Midlands at the head of his famed Legions, and sweeping away the British settlement at Leicester, formed his military camp on rising ground above the river, which now forms the older part of the borough. Soon an important town arose, and its site has yielded many examples of urns, pavements, and other Roman remains, displaying artistic taste and refinement. In the town museum may be seen many of these ancient relics.

Some of the roads in the town and district were constructed by the Romans, the greatest of road makers. The Jewry Wall, 20 feet high and 75 feet long, obtained its name from the mediæval *ghetto*; it is composed of Roman bricks and rubble.

About the year 450 the Roman forces were called home to protect their fatherland, and Saxons and Danes came on the scene and dominated the place down to Norman times. The name of the town comes down from the Anglo-Saxon era. It was then known as Leirceastre, or fortress of the Leire, as the river on which it stands was named.

In the year 1068 William the Conqueror advanced towards the Midlands. On his route he took possession of Oxford and Warwick. The town of Leicester made a bold stand against the Norman king. It had then a population of about 3,000 inhabitants, but only sixty-four heads of families were left when the all-conquering invader planted his banner in triumph upon the walls of the town. The Saxon castle, the church of St. Mary, and the homestead and walls of the town were laid in ruins.

A Norman castle was built and stood until 1645, when it was dismantled by Charles I.; and a modernised assize hall, and an artificial earthwork, known as Castle View, are all that remains of the ancient stronghold. All that is left might be called a shadow of the past. There is an old-world appearance about the castle-house and gateway which is very charming, with its wood and plaster walls and greenery refreshing to the eye in this busy hive of industry.

A curious ceremony obtained for many years at

this castle. It was customary for the newly-elected mayor of the town to proceed thither, and in accordance with a charter granted by James I., to take an oath before the steward of the Duchy of Lancaster "to perform faithfully and well all and every ancient custom, and so forth, according to the best of his knowledge." On arrival at a certain place within the precincts of the stronghold, the mayor had the great mace lowered from an upright position as a token of acknowledgment to the ancient feudal earls within their castle. In 1766 Mr. Fisher, a Jacobite, was elected mayor, and like others of his class was ever ready when opportunity offered to show his aversion to the reigning dynasty. He purposely omitted the ceremony of lowering the mace. When the servant of the mayor refused to "slope the mace," the constable of the castle or his deputy refused to admit the mayor. It is not surprising to read that the usage was discontinued after this occurrence, or that, thereafter, the mayor went in private to take the oath.

The old Town Hall is a place full of interest and of historical echoes. It has a quaintness which must be seen to be fully appreciated. It has some fine examples of carving and stained glass, dating back to the days of the seventh Henry. In the large hall prisoners were tried and plays performed. Here Richard Burbage, the creator of Shakespeare's Richard III., acted many times, and the great dramatist, who was a member of the Earl of Leicester's Company, is believed—and with some warrant—to have taken part in plays in this hall.

It was in this old-time hall that the mayor held his

feasts, which were attended by many of the nobility and gentry of the neighbourhood. The late Mr. William Kelly, F.S.A., the well-known local antiquary, gives some curious glimpses of the gatherings which used to take place here. In the "interlude" between the feast and the banquet or the dessert, bears were baited in the room. "In the summer of 1589 (probably at the invitation of the mayor)," says Mr. Kelly, "the high sheriff, Mr. Skeppington, and 'divers other gentlemen with him' were present at 'a great beare-baiting' in the town, and were entertained, at the public expense, with wine and sugar, and a present of ten shillings in gold was also made."

The old town library, after various changes, was housed on the eastern side of the Town Hall. The premises are supposed to have been the Chantry-house of the priests of the Corpus Christi Guild. The old books in the library are both valuable and interesting, and are in excellent condition. The place is well worthy of a visit, and may be seen at certain convenient times without payment. We read that the town-preacher was the means of getting the books removed to the present rooms. The appointment of the town-preacher was held in 1632, when the library was housed here by Mr. John Angel. It has been suggested that the office of town-preacher was instituted as a reaction against the ritual of the day, but most likely the eagerness of the people to hear the expounding of Holy Writ at a time when comparatively few could read, had more to do with its origin. The town-preacher, it should be remembered, addressed the people on politics and social questions, as well as on religious subjects.

The Blue Boar Inn, where Richard III. slept the night before the battle of Bosworth Field, in 1485, and where his corpse was brought back for burial, was pulled down as late as 1829; but a tavern bearing the old name stands on the site.

Of Leicester Abbey, founded in 1143, but little is left to attest its ancient glory. It was here that Cardinal Wolsey, on the 29th of November, 1530, died. He had risen from a humble position to be one of the leaders of his time, one of the greatest of Englishmen. He passed away a prisoner, suffering and disgraced. Shakespeare's picture of the prelate's coming to the abbey in the gathering gloom of a dull November day is one of the finest passages in English literature. Eight years later the religious house was dissolved. There is little to be seen of the ancient fabric, but it is not without interest to visit the site of the abbey and in fancy recall the past, in which it played so great a part.

Trinity Hospital, founded in 1331, is an almshouse for the aged and needy, with a chapel, and numerous olden-time remains. There are many old houses worthy of careful study, which meet the eye as one wanders along the ancient streets. There are five old churches which may interest the stranger, and are a matter of great pride to the inhabitants of the town. St. Martin's Church has a graceful spire 218 feet high. In the churches are monuments of importance. There is a fine statue to the Rev. Robert Hall, a prince of preachers, who was born near the town, and was for some time the eloquent Baptist minister of Leicester. He rose to the highest rank of pulpit orators, with a reputation which was world-wide, and he died in 1831 in the West of England.

Leicester has the usual modern public buildings of a progressive town, including a fine pile of municipal buildings, a free public library, and a museum rich in local antiquities. In the centre of the town is a handsome cross or clock tower (1868), bearing the effigies of Simon de Montfort, Earl of Leicester, Sir Thomas White, Alderman Newton, and William of Wyggeston, notable men in the annals of Leicester. The parks and open spaces of the borough form a pleasing feature.

NOTTINGHAM.

In modern times Nottingham has made great progress, and now takes its place among the leading English industrial cities. It is known as "the Queen of the Midlands," and, situated on the river Trent, is in a picturesque and romantic district. The city as well as the county is linked with ballads and stories of far distant times. Some local historians trace back the foundation of the town to the days of Coelus, King of the Britons, and assert that he was buried here about a thousand years before the Christian era. His place of interment is a debated matter, as Coisfield, Ayrshire, and London lay claim to the honour of being his resting place. He is the "Old King Cole," so familiar to us in song, though it is by no means easy to tell the story of his career. Concerning British and Romans, statements made about the place are of doubtful foundation.

When the course of history reaches Saxon times we are on surer ground. It was then a place of some importance, and known as Nottengaham, meaning a town of caves. During the Heptarchy it was included in the Saxon kingdom of Mercia. When the Danes invaded the country in 787 the town was taken by them, and so strongly was it fortified that the combined forces of Wessex and Mercia failed to drive them from the stronghold.

NOTTINGHAM. The Market Place, 1852.

We gather from the annals of the city that a treaty was made, and the Danes gave up possession of the town and advanced to York. When the Saxons had to submit to the suzerainty of the Danes, and during the period the invaders reigned in Mercia, Nottingham was one of the five great seats of the Danish Government. The inhabitants of Nottingham were much averse to the new rulers. The town was held by the Danes, or Northmen, until 924, when they were dispossessed by Edward the Elder, who did much for Nottingham, including the erection of a bridge over the Trent, which was in use as late as the seventeenth century; he also built a wall round the town.

The battle of Hastings ended the Saxon rule in England. Harold, the last of the Saxon kings, was slain on the eventful 14th day of October, 1066, and the victor assumed the crown of England under the title of William I.

When the Conqueror's forces came into the Midlands a bold stand was made against them at Nottingham, but the inhabitants were quickly subdued, and the population of the place decreased. A castle was reared on the site of the building which is now an art gallery. Much of the tragic history of the town is connected with the ancient stronghold. Lenton Priory, Nottingham, dated back to Norman times. After England had thrown off Papal supremacy in 1534, it survived only five years longer before it was dissolved. To-day it is a distant echo in the historic record of the city.

When the struggle raged between Stephen and the Empress Maud the townsmen supported the

King, and he established a mint here. Henry, the son of Maud, took the town, and it was greatly damaged by him. In 1141 much suffering was caused in the town by fire. Henry II., the next to wear the crown in succession to Stephen, won the affections of the inhabitants of Nottingham by assisting to repair the town, which was in ruins. It speedily rose to be a place of note, and here Parliament sometimes met and transacted important business.

While Richard I. was engaged in the Crusades, John got possession of the castle, and the King had to lay siege to it to drive him out. It is said that in the reign of Richard I. here lived Robin Hood, the famous outlaw. He is sometimes styled the Earl of Huntingdon. When John was on the throne of England, he frequently resided at the castle. It was here that he caused the youthful Welsh hostages to be executed.

Another dark page in the history of the castle relates to the seizing of Mortimer, Earl of March, by Edward III. He was sent to London, and executed "for betraying his country to the Scots for money, and for other mischiefs, out of an extravagant and vast imagination designed by him." An entry was made into the castle by a passage 107 yards in length, which extends from the castle to the river below. It retains the name of Mortimer's Hole, but was made long before his time.

During the struggle between the houses of York and Lancaster, the Yorkists usually held the town. Henry VII. held a Council of War at Nottingham Castle, in 1477, prior to his engagement with

Lambert Simnel at Stoke Field, near Newark. Henry VIII. visited Nottingham in the year 1534, when Papal supremacy was abolished in England,

On a hill to the north of the castle, now called Standard Hill, King Charles I. first unfurled the Royal Standard in 1642, having previously summoned all good subjects able to bear arms to attend. "According to proclamation," says Clarendon, "upon the 29th day of August, the standard was erected about six of the clock on a very stormy and tempestuous day. The King himself, with a small train, rode to the top of the Castle Hill; Verney the Marshal, who was standard-bearer, carrying the standard, which was then erected on that place, with little other ceremony than the sound of trumpets and drums. Melancholy men observed many ill presages about that time. The standard was blown down the same night as it had been set up, by a very strong and unruly wind, and could not be fixed again till, in a day or two, the tempest was allayed. At the start of the Civil War the castle was held for the King, but soon was taken by Parliament, when Colonel Hutchinson was appointed governor, and held it against all attacks. He, in 1651, however, reduced it to ruins to prevent Cromwell from getting possession of it and using it for his own advancement."

At the Restoration the site was granted to the Duke of Buckingham, who soon sold it to the Duke of Newcastle, an old Royalist general. The new owner was eighty years of age, yet full of energy, and in 1674 started building a new castle in a heavy Italian style of architecture, from (it is said) the designs of Sir Christopher Wren. It was finished about 1680. During the riots in October, 1831, over the Reform Bill, the castle was burnt in the daytime by a mob, because the owner had taken an active part in opposing the measure. The Duke of Newcastle received from the Hundred £21,000 compensation, but fearing further mischief, he declined to rebuild the castle. In 1878 it was leased for 500 years by the Corporation, and fitted up as a museum and art gallery.

As one wanders round Nottingham one cannot fail to notice how clean and wide are the streets in the newer parts of the town. In the past it had numerous short and poorly-built houses which have been swept away by the march of progress. Historic sites and not old buildings meet the eye. Churches and chapels are seen in every direction, most of them of recent date. The two older churches are St. Mary's, a fine cruciform Perpendicular building, and St. Peter's, also Perpendicular in style, with a tower and lofty spire. Both contain monuments and other objects of interest which well repay careful study.

Factories are to be seen in many directions. It is here that the lace trade is carried out to perfection. The pride of Nottingham is its extensive Market Place, the largest in the kingdom, and covering five and a half acres. Around it are rows of shops giving indications of wealth and taste.

There are numerous public buildings, including the University College erected in 1880-1, containing lecture halls, classrooms, etc., a natural history museum, and a free library, the latter being one of the best in the country. Not only does it contain books of general interest but a fine collection of local works formed by Mr. J. Potter Briscoe, the learned librarian and author of numerous local historical works. To him we must express our thanks for many facts in this chapter.

Not far from the Free Library is the Arboretum, a beautifully-laid-out pleasure ground, with a wealth of trees and flowers. In the Church Cemetery on the Mansfield Road are some of the old cave dwellings, which have been enlarged and serve for catacombs.

There has long been active literary life in Nottingham, and among the more noted authors, who have made their home in the city at one time or another, may be mentioned Henry Kirke White, Millhouse, the Howitts, and Philip James Bailey.

DERBY.

THE town of Derby is known as "the Gateway of the Peak." It is situated on the Derwent, and although it does not contain much that is very striking, it has some places of interest which repay inspection. As in other busy centres of commerce, many ancient structures have been removed to make room for modern buildings better adapted to the increasing demands of trade. A progressive place seldom has numerous remains of past times, and this, the chief town of one of the most picturesque counties in the kingdom, is not an exception. It is a place of memories and not monuments of bygone times.

Near the town was the Roman station *Derventro*, on the site of Little Chester, through which Ryknield Street ran, and where Roman remains have been found. It was one of the five burghs of the Danes, and before the Norman Conquest it is said to have been held by 243 burgesses. The number declined to 140 at the time of the Domesday Survey. At the battle of Hastings the men of Derby fought for Harold, and from the reduced number we know that many of its strongest men were slain. We know that the town was a place of importance in the kingdom of Mercia in Saxon times. The inhabitants varied their employment by ploughing the land and carrying the sword.

Derby has taken a distinguished place in arms, art, literature, and commerce, and is of ancient origin. Its growth has not been rapid; until the introduction of railways its rise was distinctly slow. When Defoe visited Derby he described it as "a town of gentry rather than trade." To-day, if he could visit the place, he would write differently. Here are factories, foundries, and much work in progress connected with railways. In 1728 the population was 6,000; in 1831 it had reached 22,637; in 1841 it had increased to 37,431. The coming of the railway changed matters; the population has gone up to 122,000, and one out of every eight of the inhabitants finds employment on the line or in connection with it. How different is the Derby of to-day from that of the wet Sunday when Washington Irving was weather-bound at the Bell Inn, and gazed through the coffee-room window, taking a mental note of the dismal commonplace street.

The English kings have frequently visited the old borough, and granted it several charters. Richard I., in the one he gave, stipulated that no Jews were to be allowed to reside in the liberty. Another item of curious history relates to the Society of Friends. At an early period they established a meeting house in the town, and, according to George Fox, were first called Quakers here (1650) by Justice Bennett, "because I bade him quake at the Word of the Lord."

All matters of historical interest wane before the invasion of Charles Edward, the Young Pretender, and his occupation of the town for a few days. He arrived in Derby on December 4th, 1745, with an army of about 5,000 men. The Prince took up his quarters at Exeter House, a fine mansion near the river, which was pulled down in 1854. It was soon clear that he was not receiving the support anticipated, and it was realised that London could not be reached. He did not proceed further south, but his advance-guard occupied Swarkstone Bridge, over the Trent. The day following the arrival of the invaders a stormy council of war was held, which occupied several hours. There were three armies surrounding him, and in the event of an engagement there was little or no prospect of success. Much against his will Charles Edward was induced to make a retreat, and decided next day to march towards Scotland.

During their stay in the town the men composing the army, on the whole conducted themselves well. Some of the common soldiers attended church and took the Sacrament, while others thronged the cutlers' shops to have their swords sharpened. A contribution of £3,000 was levied on the town. We know how failure followed the course of the Prince; how he met with a disastrous defeat at the hands of the Duke of Cumberland at Culloden, and how for five months Charles Edward wandered among the mountains with a price of £30,000 on his head, finally escaping to France.

Some years before the Pretender reached Derby, an important industrial awakening had set in. John Lombe discovered the Italian method of silk-throwing, and introduced it into the town in 1718. The Corporation lent him the Town Hall for his machinery, and granted a long lease of the island swamp in the Derwent at £8 a year, on which to erect a factory. Piles were driven, and a mill was built, 500 feet long and 52 feet wide, containing eight large rooms with 468 windows. The building cost £30,000. Lombe was poisoned by an Italian woman, who had furnished him with the secrets of the trade. His cousin, Sir Thomas Lombe, took up the business and made a fortune of £120,000 out of the industry. In 1736 Jedidiah Strutt invented a machine for making ribbed stockings, and found employment for a large number of people in Derby, but the trade drifted to Leicester. A china factory was established here in 1750, and soon obtained national fame. The ware made there found its way to the table of the King, and was popular in the mansions of the nobility. After a period of prosperity the factory waned, but in modern times there has been a revival under the Derby Crown Porcelain Company (Limited). It is one of the largest and most complete works of its kind in England. On the payment of sixpence a visitor may be taken over the works, and may inspect the choice examples of the potter's art in the extensive show-rooms.

Learning and trade have gone hand in hand. A Philosophical Society was founded here in 1772, and its first meetings were held at the residence of Dr. Erasmus Darwin, a noted physician, a man-of-letters, and a student of science. It formed a library, and collected antiquities from Little Chester and other places, which are now in the Free Library, an institution which is a credit to the borough, and comprises excellent lending and reference libraries, museum, picture gallery, a collection of Derby pottery, local antiquities, and natural history specimens. Inspecting the objects of interest in the museum we noticed a framed set of rules which displays the exclusive spirit of the town in the middle of the eighteenth century.

RULES TO BE OBSERVED IN THE LADIES' ASSEMBLY IN DERBY.

1 No Attorney's Clerk will be admitted.

2 No shopkeeper, or any of his or her family be admitted except Mr Franceys.

3 No lady shall be allowed to dance in a long white apron.

4 All young ladies in Mantuas' shall pay 2*s.* 6*d.*

5 No Miss in a coat shall dance without the leave of the lady of the Assembly Room.

6 Whoever shall transgress any of these rules shall be turned out of the Assembly Room.

Several of the above mentioned rules having been broke through. They are now printed by order and signed by us the present ladies of the Assembly.

ANNE BARNES
DOROTHY EVENS
ELIZABETH EYRE
BRIDGETT BAILY
R. FITZ-HERBERT
HESTER MUNDY

Mr. Franceys, alluded to in rule 2, was an apothecary, carrying on business in the Market Place. He was an Alderman, and displayed great public spirit: he died in 1747, during the year he was Mayor of Derby. In various forms the apron has come down to us from Anglo-Saxon times. Beau Nash, King of Bath, made war against this article of dress. Charles Dickens when in the museum read these rules, which amused him not a little, and he made them the subject of a magazine article. The committee-room of the institution is lined with oak panelling from Exeter House, and it contains a collection of Stuart relics, with a letter written by the young Chevalier to his father from Edinburgh, dated October 22nd, 1745.

There are several old churches in Derby, The chief is All Saints', having a fine Perpendicular tower dating back to the reign of Henry VII. It is 174 feet in height; and has three stages surrounded by battlements and crocketed pinnacles, which are 36 feet more. It is a striking tower, and is the pride of the place. A defaced inscription has given rise to a curious story. The words "young men and maydens" may still be read, and it is said that bachelors and spinsters of the town built the tower. When a maiden born in the parish was married, the young bachelors rang a merry peal. It is more likely that the words formed part of the verse, "Young men and maidens, old men and children, praise the name of the Lord." This large church contains some striking monuments, including one to the famous builder, Bess of Hardwick, who passed away in 1607, and was buried here with the pomp and display that was deemed befitting for one who had played a great part in the age in which her lot was cast. A tradition has come down to us regarding her death, to the effect that it had been prophesied that immediately she ceased building she would die; and her death is reported to have occurred during a severe frost when the workmen were compelled to remain idle, although they tried to mix their mortar with hot ale.

At St. Werburgh's Church Dr. Samuel Johnson married Widow Porter on July 9th, 1735. When the pair were united he was twenty-six years of age, and his "darling Tetty" was forty-nine. Both travelled to church mounted on horseback. The doctor related to Boswell a battle between the couple on their way to church. "Sir," said Johnson, "she had read the old romances and had got into her head the fantastical notion that a woman of spirit should use her lover like a dog. So, sir, at first she told me I rode too fast, and she could not keep up with me; and when I rode a little slower she passed me, and complained that I lagged behind. I was not to be made the slave of caprice; and I resolved to begin as I meant to end. I therefore pushed on briskly, till I was fairly out of sight. The road lay between two hedges, so I was sure she could not miss it; and I contrived that she should soon be up with me. When she did I observed she was in tears." It is given to few to become master before the nuptial knot is tied!

There are numerous old and new churches in the town worth visiting. It is one of those places where church building has made considerable progress. The ancient Bridge Chapel of St. Mary is most interesting, and dates back to early times. The nooks and corners of the town are well worth exploring.

The Arboretum was given to Derby by Mr. Joseph Strutt. It is laid out in an attractive manner, and is rich in trees and flowers. A relic of the plague time may be seen in the Arboretum, and bears on a brass plate the following inscription:

HEADLESS CROSS, OR
MARKET STONE.

THIS STONE formed part of the ancient cross at the upper end of FRIAR GATE and was used by the inhabitants of DERBY as a MARKET STONE during the visitation of the Plague, 1665. It is thus described by Hutton in his History of Derby.

1665, Derby was again visited by the plague at the same time in which London fell under the severe calamity. The town was forsaken; the farmers declined the Market-place; and grass grew upon that spot which had furnished the supports of life. To prevent a famine, the inhabitants erected at the top of Nun-green, one or two hundred yards from the buildings, now Friar-gate, what bore the name of *Headless-cross*, consisting of about four quadrangular steps, covered in the centre with one large stone; the whole near five feet high; I knew it in perfection. Hither the market people, having their mouths primed with tobacco as a preservative, brought their provisions, stood a distance from their property, and at a greater from the townspeople, with whom they were to traffic. The buyer was not suffered to touch any of the articles before purchase; but when the agreement was finished, he took the goods, and deposited the money in a vessel filled with vinegar, set for that purpose.

Derby includes the usual public buildings of a country town. It is not a holiday haunt, but there is much in the place to entertain a thoughtful visitor, those who delight in an unconventional holiday might do far worse than spend a day or two in Derby.

MANCHESTER.

THE cotton and other industries connect Manchester with the trade of the world. It is a place of considerable antiquity, but is more famous for its commerce than its history. Towering warehouses are seen on every hand, and the ruins of ancient strongholds and old religious houses which we usually associate with an old-time city are missing. The place seems wholly to be given up to business, but it is by no means lacking in culture. Here trade and learning go hand in hand. Few, if any, towns display greater public spirit. It has often inspired the policy of the country. Frequently what Manchester thinks to-day England will adopt to-morrow.

Little is known for certain of the early history of this city. It is supposed that the ancient Britons had a fortress here, which passed into the possession of the Romans under Agricola. One fact is certain, that it was the site of an important Roman station. Many traces of their occupation have been unearthed at various periods—not only coins, but examples of walls, etc.

The story of the town for some time after the departure of the Romans is of a legendary character, picturesque, but not reliable enough for the serious student of history. Down to the seventeenth century the tale was told that Tarquin, the enemy of King Arthur, kept the castle of Manchester and met his death at the hands of Launcelot of the Lake. Most likely the place was the scene of missionary labours of Paulinus. Saxon kings and queens are associated with its history, but their lives do not materially add to the importance of the town or district. It was not a growing district, for when the Domesday Survey was made, Manchester, Salford, Rochdale, and Radcliffe were the only places mentioned in South-east Lancashire. The sites to-day of many important towns, the hives of modern industry and progress, were put down as forests and waste land.

Manchester's neighbour, Salford, was granted a charter by Ranulph de Blundevill in the reign of Henry III., which constituted it a free borough. Towards the close of the reign of Edward I., in 1301, a similar charter was granted to Manchester by its baron, Thomas Gresley. The barons exercised great power over the town. It was not until 1845 that the Town Council bought the manorial rights of Manchester from Sir Oswald Mosley for £200,000. The town was granted a municipal charter in 1838, and raised to the dignity of a city in 1847.

The Court Leet, which regulated the life of the town in the olden days, passed many curious orders. Take, for example, the following relating to bread. At a meeting held October 1st, 1561, it was resolved that no person or persons be permitted to make for sale any kind of bread in which butter is mixed, under a fine of ten shillings. Later, the use of suet was forbidden. In 1595 we are told that the Court Leet jury ordered that no person was to be allowed to use butter or suet in cakes or bread, and that offenders were to be fined twenty shillings. If a person sold the cakes, etc., he ran the risk of being fined twenty shillings. We learn from another order, passed on September 30th, 1596, that the inhabitants were not permitted to eat flesh meat on a Friday or Saturday. In the sixteenth century a single woman was not allowed to keep a house or chamber. Even wedding dinners were not to cost more than sixpence a head.

Leland, the antiquary, visited Manchester in 1638, and he describes it as being well built, recognises its trading importance, and speaks of it as being the most populous town in Lancashire. Manchester was made a sanctuary town—a place where transgressors might remain in safety under certain conditions. Henry VIII. was petitioned to take away the rights "because the sanctuary men are prejudicial to the wealth, credit, great occupyings, and good order of the said town, by occasioning idleness, unlawful games, unthriftness and other enormities." The King granted the request.

When the Civil War raged in this country the inhabitants were active in the strife. The place was garrisoned in 1642 by the Parliamentary forces, and withstood a siege of the King's soldiers. At the Rebellion of 1715 the leading clergymen threw in their lot with the Pretender. The inhabitants in the main supported Prince Charles Edward. He proudly entered the town at the head of his army on November 29th, 1745, and took up his residence

MANCHESTER.
Market Street at the beginning of the Nineteenth Century.

in Market Street Lane, until recently called the Palace. He was proclaimed in the town as James III. Many Lancashire people joined his forces, Colonel Francis Townley and Captain James Dawson among the number. These were known as the Manchester regiment. When it was realised that the Stuarts' cause was doomed to failure, the regiment surrendered to the Duke of Cumberland, and the colonel and eight other officers were tried in London, found guilty, and beheaded on Kennington Common. The ruthless conduct of the duke gave rise to a couple of local ballads which are still remembered, called "Jemmy Dawson" and "Townley's Ghost." The former was written by Shenstone, and tells how Dawson's execution was witnessed by his intended bride, and how she died on the spot, broken-hearted.

> The dismal scene was o'er and past,
> The lover's mournful hearse retired;
> The maid drew back her languid head,
> And, sighing forth his name, expired.

Byrom, a Manchester Jacobite and a scholar and poet of more than local repute as the author of "Christians, Awake!" expressed himself in an epigram as follows:

> God bless the King! I mean the faith's defender;
> God bless—no harm in blessing—the Pretender!
> But who Pretender is—or who is King,
> God bless us all—that's quite another thing.

During our troubles with America and France, Manchester supplied men and money on behalf of king and country. In August, 1819, a large gathering of peaceful men met to discuss political reforms, and by a mistaken policy on the part of the local authorities the meeting was broken up and several people killed. It is known as the "Peterloo Massacre."

The Manchester Ship Canal, connecting the city with the sea, and making it an inland port, is a wonderful engineering feat, and was officially opened by Queen Victoria on May 21st, 1894.

The religious life of the city has kept pace with its commercial prosperity. The cathedral, the chief ecclesiastical building, is disappointing, and is unworthy of a wealthy diocese. It was formerly the old parish church, and for that purpose met its requirements, but is not of sufficient dignity for a cathedral. The style is Perpendicular Gothic, mainly dating back to the fifteenth century. It contains some fine monuments; and is by no means devoid of interesting features, which well repay a careful study. The See was founded in 1847. There are many other churches and Nonconformist places of worship, whose pulpits have been filled by some of the greatest preachers of the age.

The Town Hall is said to be the finest municipal building in Europe, was designed by Waterhouse, and covers 8,000 square yards. It was erected at a cost, including interest, of £1,062,565; on the organ was spent £5,269, and the bells and clock cost £6,985. It contains 314 rooms, and round the great hall are twelve mural paintings by Ford Madox Brown. From its tower, which is 260 feet high, may be obtained extensive views of South Lancashire, the charming plains of Cheshire, and the bold hills of Derbyshire. The style of architecture is Gothic. It was opened in 1877. There are numerous other public buildings displaying great taste, and the same may be said of the great warehouses which rise in every direction.

The scholastic establishments, libraries, and parks are the chief glory of Manchester. Foremost is the University, with its colleges, and the Grammar School, founded in 1519 by Hugh Oldham, Bishop of Exeter, and a native of Lancashire. Some celebrated men have been educated there. The most notable scholar is perhaps Thomas De Quincey, a native of Greenheys, Manchester. In later times Harrison Ainsworth, the Lancashire novelist, attended the school. The Free Library was opened in 1852, and owes its origin to Sir John Potter. Not only has it one of the finest reference libraries in the provinces, but it has branches in the various parts of the city. The Chetham library is frequently named as the oldest library in Europe. For more than two centuries the student has entered its doors without let or hindrance. It is rich in Lancashire and Cheshire books and manuscripts. It is a strange experience to leave the busy streets, and retire into the quiet library, which seems to belong more to monastic times in England than to this work-a-day world. It is really the only remains of olden Manchester. Formerly the ancient barons' hall, it was bought by the trustees of Humphrey Chetham, and devoted to a blue coat school and library. The John Rylands library was founded by his widow in memory of her husband, a local worthy. It is a library for students, and contains one of the best collections of books in the country, brought together regardless of cost, and the library is housed in a noble building. There are other excellent libraries in the city to meet the requirements of all classes of readers.

The large and numerous parks, museums, and picture galleries afford endless pleasure and instruction to the residents and visitors. There are many statues, too, of local and national worthies. The city is rich in philanthropic institutions. The Manchester man is more noted for sound common sense than show; as a rule he is a man of culture, with a strong bent for business. The streets are well kept, and in some instances wide. "What art was in the ancient world," says D'Israeli, "science is in the modern—the distinctive faculty. In the minds of men the useful has succeeded the beautiful. Instead of the city of the violet crown, a Lancashire village has expanded into a mighty region of factories and warehouses. Yet, rightly understood, Manchester is as great a human exploit as Athens."

LEEDS.

THIS great Yorkshire city is certainly not an attractive place; it has many fine buildings, but in not a few instances the mean surroundings completely mar their beauty. One of Leeds' most charming singers says, "Great town, your smoke hangs low." No wonder, when we remember the many hives of industry in nearly all directions, which give employment to the sons of toil. It is a city of business and not of pleasure. Here the worker and not the idler spends his days.

Some provision is made for the enjoyment of the toiler by means of parks, picture galleries, public libraries, healthy outdoor sports and pastimes. In the immediate district round Leeds there is some of the finest scenery in Yorkshire.

If the visitor is reaching Leeds by rail, he will be depressed by the outlook, but when he reaches the city, he will be both surprised and pleased at the wide streets, and the many excellent shops. He will at once realise that he is in a city of wealth and taste. The business establishments are among the finest in the provinces. The city may fairly be placed as the best situated industrial centre in this country. The inhabitants have long enjoyed the reputation of being shrewd and honest, and have won a world-wide reputation for fair dealing.

Leeds has a past as well as a modern glory, but its early history is lost in the mists of antiquity. At the time of the Domesday Survey it was a farming village. William the Conqueror gave the manor to Ilbert de Laci, and he sublet it. Maurice Paganel granted a charter, in 1207, to the place. This was the first charter, and proves that in early times Leeds was a growing town. It is said that Paganel built himself a castle; for centuries every trace of it has been swept away, but its site and park to-day figure in the street names of the city. Another street name of historical importance is Swinegate, which is asserted to be derived from Sweyn, the father of Canute the Great. We get an echo to-day of feudal times: the inhabitants were compelled, down to 1839, to have their corn ground at the King's mills. The custom of the "Soke" was only ended by the Leeds Corporation paying the holder of the rights £13,000. The town was first incorporated in the second year of Charles I.

From the Stuarts, Leeds received marks of favour. It was from the first Charles that, in 1626, the earliest Royal Charter was received, and Charles II. granted two, one in 1661 and another in 1684. To this town Charles I. was brought as a prisoner by the Scots, and stayed at the Red Hall, an old mansion situated in Guildford Street, and the rear of the house is known as King Charles's Croft. We are told that John Harrison, a noted local benefactor, repaired to the Red Hall and obtained permission from the guards to present his Majesty with a tankard of prime ale, which he carried in his hand. On Harrison being admitted the King raised the cover of the tankard and found it full of gold and not of ale. Charles quickly hid the money about his person, with feelings of gratitude.

LEEDS. The Central Market, 1831.

Harrison's home was in Briggate, at the top of which stood the Moot Hall, and at the bottom Leeds Bridge, which spanned the river Aire. On this bridge the early cloth-market was held, and largely attended by country cloth-makers. We get a curious sketch of the olden days, written by Norrisson Scatcherd, the historian of Morley. In an account of John Jackson, better known as "Old Trash," poet, schoolmaster, mechanic, stonecutter, land-measurer, etc., who was buried at Woodkirk, on May 19th, 1764, "He constructed a clock," says Scatcherd, "and in order to make it useful to the clothiers who attended Leeds market from Earls and Hanging Heaton, Dewsbury, Chickenley, etc., he kept a lamp suspended near the face of it, and burning through the winter nights; and he would have no shutters nor curtains to his window, so that the clothiers had only to stop and look through it to know the time. Now, in our age of luxury and refinement, the accommodation thus presented by 'Old Trash,' may seem insignificant and foolish, but I assure the reader that it was not. The clothiers in the early part of the eighteenth century were obliged to be on the bridge of Leeds, where the market was held, by about six o'clock in the summer, and seven in the winter; and hither they were convened by a bell anciently pertaining to a Chantry Chapel which was once annexed to Leeds Bridge. They did not all ride, but most went on foot. They did not carry watches, for few of them had ever possessed such valuables." We are told how their wives would wrap up in a little checked handkerchief their dinners, which usually consisted of a small supply of oatcake and cheese. It was men like those we are mentioning who built up the wealth of Leeds, and at the same time made money for themselves.

Such men, we are told, seldom saw a watch, but took much of their intelligence from the note of the cuckoo.

As we pace this famous highway, Briggate, one of the finest streets in the provinces, many celebrated wayfarers are recalled. Leeds took little part in the invasion of Prince Charles in 1745. Many of the victims who were involved in that unfortunate expedition were imprisoned at York for a long period. Some, after being there a year, were forwarded to Liverpool for transportation, and on passing through Leeds, on April 23rd, 1747, sixty-one men and seven women were lodged in the Moot Hall for the night. John Wesley paced this street when he preached in the town. Matters did not run smoothly here. In 1758, writing to his brother, he said, "From time to time I have had more trouble with the town than with all the societies in Yorkshire." The first Wesleyan Methodist Chapel was built in Leeds in 1750. Great has been the work of the Wesleyans since that time. Their churches extend over the city and district, and leading preachers occupy the pulpits. Howard's footsteps were heard in this street in 1788. The philanthropist visited the infirmary, the workhouse, and the prison, and expressed himself pleased with the two former. Leeds has long been famous for its music. In 1714 the parish church had an organ placed in it. Greatly has a love for musical performances increased since that time. The Leeds Musical Festivals are of world-wide interest, and the greatest stars of the day take part in them. Echoes come to us of many notable men and women who have passed along this great highway; they have figured in local and national history, and make up such a large number that it is impossible to find room for even a list of their names.

Kirkgate is another street of note leading to St. Peter's Parish Church, the chief church in the city, whence successive vicars of Leeds have in the past often been promoted to Bishoprics or Deaneries. It was rebuilt in 1839-41 by Dr. Hook, "the Apostle of the West Riding." He is gratefully remembered as one of the great and good vicars of Leeds, and for collecting £30,000 to carry out the work. It is to be regretted that it is not a fine example of church architecture, but still it contains some interesting monuments. St. John's is an interesting church built by John Harrison, a famous local benefactor, and near it is the Harrison Hospital. Several of the modern churches of the city are fine examples of ecclesiastical architecture. The Nonconformist churches are both numerous and, in many instances, an ornament to Leeds.

Among the more important public buildings is the Town Hall; the foundation was laid in 1853, and the building opened by Queen Victoria in 1858. The architect was Cuthbert Brodrick, of Hull; it is an impressive structure with Corinthian columns, and it has a high tower crowned with a dome. The cost of the building was about £140,000. It has served as a model for several of the smaller town halls of the West Riding. Near the Leeds Town Hall are the Municipal Offices. Part of this structure is devoted to an Art Gallery and Free Library. The collection of books brought together is in every respect worthy of the large city, but it merits a better position and a more convenient building. It may fairly be regarded as the best public free library in the country, and has important branches in all parts of the city. The Leeds Institute has done a great work for popular education, and has a useful library. The Leeds Library, founded in 1768, has not only a large number of books, but many which are rare and valuable. There are numerous other good libraries in Leeds. In the Philosophical Hall is a Museum, and here, during the winter months, the leading lecturers of the country appear.

Educational matters have always been kept well to the front. The Grammar School was founded in 1552, and in recent times a University has been established. There is a School of Medicine, and the present Infirmary was erected in 1863, from designs by Sir Gilbert Scott; important additions have been made since that time.

We have only mentioned a few of the public buildings, but we must in conclusion call attention to the new Market Hall, built at a cost of £100,000, and pronounced one of the finest in this country.

Within a short tram ride from the city are the extensive ruins of Kirkstall Abbey. Here one may study the arrangements of an ancient religious house dating back to 1152. The greater part of the remains is Transition Norman, and no one should visit Leeds without seeing this famous abbey.

HULL.

FEW old buildings remain in Hull, for they have been swept away by the march of progress; but the streets in the old town retain their original course, and their arrangement affords a fine example, one of the best in England, of a place founded in the Middle Ages. Edward I. recognised the important position of the port. It then consisted of two places near each other, Wyke-upon-Hull and the Manor of Myton. Wyke was a place of some importance; in 1278 it was granted a weekly market and an annual fair lasting fourteen days. At a much earlier period it had become widely known for its commerce, and in 1198 it ranked as the sixth port in the kingdom, only London, Boston, Southampton, Lincoln, and Lynn having greater imports and exports.

In 1287, Edward I. entered into negotiations with the Abbot of Meaux, the head of a religious house situated near Beverley, for the exchange of lands elsewhere of an equal value to those on which Wyke and Myton stood. In 1293 the negotiations were concluded. The town of Wyke and the Manor of Myton were conveyed to the King by a deed of feoffment, dated from the Feast of Purification in that year, in exchange for lands situated in Lincolnshire.

No sooner had the King become the owner of the place than he gave it the royal title of Kingston-upon-Hull, which remained the legal title down to June 18th, 1897, when it was made the City of Hull. The long title of Kingston-upon-Hull had for many years been shortened to Hull in commercial and other circles. Royal favours were granted to the town. Its government was placed under a Warden (*Custos*) and Bailiffs. Richard Oysel, a Court favourite, was the first Warden, and most probably he induced the King to grant the town its first charter, which may still be seen in the Town Hall. It bears the date of April 1st, 1299, and was granted upon a petition of the inhabitants presented to the King in person, while keeping Christmas in 1288 with Lord Wake at Baynard Castle, Cottingham. The charter made it a free borough with all the privileges of a royal burgh. An improvement was made in the harbour, and the shipping trade advanced rapidly. The place grew in importance until it became one of the chief towns in the kingdom. To meet the increasing demand for money for commercial and other transactions a mint was established. Hull had four furnaces, while Newcastle-on-Tyne, Bristol, and Exeter had only two each.

Edward, when he visited the town in 1300, caused improvements to be made, the chief being the pavement of the streets, and to meet the expense certain tolls were levied on all goods coming into the town for sale. A little later, a couple of burgesses were sent to Parliament. The citizens of Hull are able to regard with pride their long list of members,

HULL. The Market Place, 1831.

which includes many famous townsmen, including Andrew Marvell, the incorruptible patriot, and William Wilberforce, the emancipator.

In the reign of the second Edward, Scotland had, by a splendid victory at Bannockburn, re-established its independence, and we can readily understand that the northern towns of England were anxious about their safety. In 1322 a royal licence was granted for encompassing the town with ditches and castellated walls. In more peaceful times these walls were swept away, their site being utilised for docks.

Edward III., in 1332, on his way to join his army in the north, visited Hull, when the place far exceeded his expectations for its situation and the strength of its fortifications. The King was warmly welcomed by the people, and magnificently entertained by William De la Pole. The King showed his appreciation by knighting his host, and altering the local governorship of the town from warden to mayor. He nominated for the first mayor Sir William De la Pole.

We gather from some ancient bye-laws how the life of the people was regulated in the olden time. The Mayor and Sheriff in and previously to 1452 in the Market Place used to proclaim as follows:—

That all the King's liege people keep his Majesty's peace, and that no burgess or inhabitant draw any knife, sword, or any other offensive weapon in breach of the same under a penalty of 3*s*. 4*d*.

That no man purchase any victuals coming to the market before they be got thither, under a penalty of 3*s*. 4*d*.

That no one offer to sell any corn, nor open his sack before nine o'clock, nor continue it in the market after one, and that no corn be set up out of the market, upon pain of 4*d*. for every bushel.

That no person dwelling within the town buy any fish, flesh, or wild fowl, to sell again to another inhabitant, under the penalty of forfeiting the same, imprisonment of body, and fine to the King.

That no man cast any lastage, straw, or muck, out of ships, keels or boats, into the haven, under the penalty of 6*s.* 8*d.* for every ship, and 1*s.* 8d. for every boat.

That no person cast any ashes, dust, muck, or filth down any staiths under the penalty of 6*s.* 8*d.*

That no tavern keeper, victualler, nor tipler, keep any guest after the bell be rung, on pain of 3*s.* 4*d.*

That no stranger walk out in the night, or be then suffered to wear offensive weapons, on pain of imprisonment.

That no one sell or buy any bread in the town, but what is made or baked therein.

That no one presume to sell a pound of candles for more than a penny, nor a gallon of small ale for more than a penny.

That all butchers cut their flesh in pieces and sell it by half-penny worths, two penny worths, or more as the burgesses have need, according to the quantity and quality.

On the last day of the year 1460 was fought the battle of Wakefield, and among the slain was Richard Hanson, Mayor of Hull, who was on the side of the defeated House of York. The head of Hanson was spiked, with those of other leaders in the fight, on the gates of York.

An entry in the annals of Hull states that in 1549 three of the former sheriffs of the town, named respectively Johnson, Jebson, and Thorp, were fined £6 13*s.* 4*d.* each "for being deficient in the elegance of their entertainments, for neglecting to wear scarlet gowns, and for not providing the same for their wives during their shrievalties." Ten years later a Mr. Gregory was chosen sheriff, and he refused to accept the office. The matter was referred to the Queen in Council, and he was ordered to be fined £100, to be disfranchised and turned out of the town. The order was executed.

The gates of Hull were closed on two critical occasions. On July 4th, 1399, Bolingbroke, Duke of Lancaster, afterwards Henry IV., landed at Ravenspurne, in Holderness, a port long since washed away by the sea. Here gathered round him a number of noblemen who were determined to depose the reigning monarch, Richard II. When the news of warlike movements reached Hull, John Tutbury, the mayor, placed the burgesses under arms, directed the bridges to be drawn up, and the gates closed. The inhabitants were ready for action. Soon the Duke and his followers appeared before the town, and demanded admission. This the mayor refused, saying that "he had sworn to be true to the sovereign, Richard II., and faithfully keep the town for his use, and that he fully intended to do his duty, and never prove false to his oath, and a traitor to his King." On hearing the firm answer to his request, the Duke marched to Doncaster. Happily Henry IV. bore no resentment against Hull, and in the first year of his reign renewed and confirmed the charters of the town.

A still tenser moment occurred in the days of Charles I. Hull at that time had the best magazine of munitions of war in the country. The King hoped to secure them, as they would have given him a great advantage in the struggle. In 1642 he repaired to the royal borough, where he expected a welcome, for it had been greatly favoured by the kings of England, but, to his surprise and disappointment, Sir John Hotham, the governor of the town, closed the gates against him, and the King had to retire to York in discomfiture. Hull successfully withstood two Royalist sieges.

Parliament thanked Hotham for the bold stand made on this critical occasion. His subsequent career was very sad. He felt slighted when Lord Fairfax was entrusted with the generalship of the North, believing that he was entitled to the position. On refusing to obey the orders of Fairfax, he was removed from his generalship. In a jealous pique he decided to transfer his services to the King and deliver the town into his hands. The plot was discovered, and Sir John Hotham had to fly. On reaching Beverley, he was apprehended by his nephew, Captain Boynton, and carried back to Hull, thence to London, where he was tried with his son for "traitorously betraying the trust reposed in them by Parliament," found guilty, and beheaded on Tower Hill.

We find in the "Autobiography of George Pryme," a note showing how closely the town was guarded in past times. Writing of the years from 1781 to 1796, he states: "Hull was formerly enclosed by water, and partly by walls. In my grandfather's times, the gates were closed at ten o'clock at night, and could not be passed without an order, which rule was so rigidly enforced that my great aunt (his sister), who resided a little out of the town, used on evenings of the assemblies to sleep at her brother's house."

In 1745 the gates and walls were put in perfect order in the event of the Pretender's army taking the eastern side of the country, but as we know the west was chosen, and Hull escaped a siege.

Later on docks were built on the site of the old wall and ditches which protected the town in the past. How different are the sights of the city to-day from what they were in bygone times. Sir Robert Constable was gibbeted above the Beverley Gate, in 1537, for high treason. "On Fridaye," wrote the Duke of Norfolk, "beying market daye at Hull, suffered and dothe hange above the highest gate of the toune so trymmed in cheynes that I thinke his boones woll hang there this hundrethe yere."

We may enter the old town over Monument Bridge, getting its name from the Wilberforce Monument, which occupies the site of Beverley Gate. We are soon in Whitefriargate, which obtains its designation from the extensive monastery which occupied the right-hand side of the thoroughfare. At right angles several streets lead out of it, including the Land of Green Ginger, nearly at the end of which stood the Manor House or Palace of the King. In another direction is Trinity House Lane, called after the Trinity House, a place of great historic interest.

Guilds were popular in bygone times, and many exist under altered circumstances in the present day. John Harland, F.S.A., the historian, has outlined one which still survives in Hull, his native town. "In the reign of Edward III., in 1369," says Harland, "some forty-six persons (one-half of whom were wives or unmarried females) assembled in Hull, and founded a guild 'in honour of the Holy Trinity' for the relief of distressed seamen and their widows belonging to that town. Besides burying their dead at the guild cost, and making the usual church-offerings for masses, etc., one of their laws was that: ‘If any brother or sister languish in a perpetual infirmity, so that they had not their own to support them with, such infirm man or woman shall take every week of the goods [money] of the guild eightpence, and at the feast of St. Martin in winter [November 11] one tunic and a little cap.’ Subsequently this association was styled ‘The Guild or Brotherhood of Masters and Pilots, Seamen of the Trinity House of Kingston-upon-Hull.’ In 1457, the guild established almshouses for the relief of poor and impotent seamen, in support of which the masters of ships, and mariners generally belonging to the port, gave what money became due to them in every voyage, ‘as lowage and stowage.’ In 1442 Henry VI., by letters patent, made this guild a body-corporate, and confirmed the grant of lowage and stowage, to be applied to building a hospital (with chapel attached) for the sustentation of the relief of persons who ‘by the misfortune of the sea have fallen into poverty.’ The masters of ships requested the guild to provide them with careful pilots for the river Humber, and this licensing of pilots led to considerable yearly receipts. It has built several hospitals at different times. It is one of the greatest benevolent institutions in the North of England. The house has an old-world appearance, and maintains the customs of former ages. In place of carpets rushes are strewn, and peats take the place of coal."

This guild took the chief part in the production of the Miracle play of "Noah's Flood," which used to be performed on Plough Monday, and which was extremely popular in Hull. A few extracts from a version of this play will serve to show its nature. An actor enters representing God; he deplores the universal wickedness of the world, resolves to destroy it, and all the "folke that are thereon." Noah appears, and is directed by God to build an ark to save himself and family. His sons next enter, and, after some conversation, prepare to build the ark, Noah (the orthography is somewhat modernised) saying—

O Lord, I thank Thee, loud and still,
That to me art in such will,
And spares me and my household to spill,
As I now smoothly find.
Thy bidding, Lord, I shall fulfil,
And never more Thee grieve nor grill (provoke),
That such grace hath sent me till
Amongst all mankind.
Have done, you men and women all,
Go we work, bout din (without noise),
And I am ready bound

Then follow a few words from the wife and sons of Noah about the work before them. Noah commences building the "shippe," and the play proceeds, Noah speaking—

Now, in the name of God, I begin
To make the ship that we shall in,
That we may be ready to swim
At the coming of the flood.
These boards here I pin together,
To bear us safe from the weather;
That we may row hither and thither,
And safe be from the flood.
Of this tree I will make the mast,
Tied with cables that will last,
With a sail yard for each blast.
And each thing in their kind;
With topcastle and bowsprit,
Both cords and ropes I have all mette (measured),
To sail forth at the next wet.
This ship is at an end,
Wife, we shall in this vessel be kept—
My children and thou I would ye in leapt.

Noah's wife replies to him thus:—

In faith, Noah, I would as lief thou slept!
For all thy frynish (nice) fare,
I will not do after thy mede (advice).

Says Noah:—

Good wife, do now as I thee bid.

She replies:—

I' faith I'll not, till I see more need.
Though thou stand all day and stare.

Noah next laments the crabbed nature of womankind. At length the ark is completed, and after receiving from God a list of animals which are to go into it, Noah and his family, except his wife, enter it. Here considerable liberty is taken with the Biblical story, and a strange scene is presented, Noah's wife is a person of whimsical temper. In reply to her husband's appeal to her to enter the ark, she gives vent to a volley of strong language, saying that unless her "gossips" are allowed to go in with her she "will not out of this town." She tells him to "Row where he lists," and get a new wife. Finally, the dutiful Japhet compels his mother to enter by main force, and immediately on her entrance she boxes Noah's ears. He observes:—

Ha, ha, marry, this is hot,
It is good for to be still;
Ha, children, methinks my boat removes.
Our tarrying here grieves me ill.
Over the land the water spreads,
God, do as Thou wilt;
Ah, great God, Thou art so good,
That (who) works not Thy will is wood (mad).
Now all this world is one flood,
As I see well in sight—
This window I will shut anon,
And unto my chamber I will go,
Till the water so great mowe (may)
Be slackened through Thy might.

The window of the ark is now closed for a short time, supposed to be during the period of the flood, after which it is opened, and Noah thanks God for such grace. The Almighty replies, and blesses the patriarch, the play finishing as follows:—

My bow between you and me,
In the firmament shall be;
By every token that you shall see,
That such vengeance shall cease.
Men shall never more
Be wasted with water, as hath been before;
But for sin that grieveth me sore,
Therefore this vengeance.

. . . . .

My blessing, Noah, I give thee here,
To thee, Noah, my servant, dear,
For vengeance shall no more appear;
And now farewell, my darling dear.

This is an example in outline of one of the more serious of the religious plays; but it includes not a few diverting passages for the entertainment of the people. The nautical allusions would be much appreciated in Hull and other seaport towns, and we can readily understand such a piece would be popular in the olden time.

In the books of the Hull Trinity House are many entries bearing on this play. A new "shype" was required in 1421, and it was obtained at a cost of £5 8*s*. 4*d*. In 1447 the wages of Robert Brown, who represented God, were 6*d*., and so continued until 1484, when Thomas Sawyers played the part, and was paid 8*d*., which was increased in 1487 to 10*d*. In 1520 the payment went up to 1*s*., and continued at that rate until 1529. We find in 1469 the wages of Noye and his wyff were 21*d.*; next year they were increased by an additional twopence. In 1485 the payments were separated and also reduced —Noye got 8*d.* and his wyff a shilling. The payment was increased to Noye in 1520 to 2*s.*, and his wyff 18*d.*

The performance used to be given in different parts of the town, and the ark wheeled from one street to another. On it were painted different sorts of animals, and when not in use it was suspended in the Holy Trinity Church. This stately church is one of the largest parish churches in the country. It was founded in 1285, as a sort of chapel-of-ease to Hessle. The dead were taken along the Humber banks for interment at Hessle, and it is recorded that lives were lost and the corpses washed away by the river in tempestuous weather. An appeal to Archbishop Corbridge in 1301 resulted in permission being given for burials to be made in Hull. The transepts are the earliest part of the present building, and date back to the reign of Edward II. It has a fine tower 150 feet high. During the Commonwealth it was used as a house of prayer by the Presbyterians and Independents, and so divided until the Restoration.

News reached Hull on the 3rd July, 1644, of the victory of the Parliamentary forces at the Battle of Marston Moor. The inhabitants were assembled in the church in prayer for the success of their army on the field of battle, when a letter was received by the Mayor, by whom it was hastily perused and handed to the preacher, who read it to the congregation. It was as follows:—

2nd July, 1644. Mr. Mayor. After a dark cloud it hath pleased God to show the sunshine of His glory in victory over his enemies, who are driven into the walls of York, many of their chief officers slain, and all their ordnance and ammunition taken with small loss (I praise God) on our side. This is all I can now write;

Resting Your Assured

FAIRFAX.

At various times from the third decade of the last century some £50,000 has been spent in repairs. It can seat 2,200 worshippers. It contains many beautiful monuments and other objects of interest.

Near the church is the old Grammar School founded by Bishop Alcock in 1486. Here have been educated some famous men; Marvell and Wilberforce are the best remembered. It is now used as a clergy school, and the Grammar School is in another part of the town in a modern building.

We may proceed to the Victoria Pier, named after the late Queen when she visited Hull, and watch the ships on the Humber, which is three miles wide. Matthew Arnold was charmed with the view, as Thomas Carlyle and Alfred Tennyson had been before him. The Humber, when seen from the pier, presents a sight which cannot be forgotten.

We have passed streets which recall to mind the old religious life of Hull, such as Blackfriargate. We may next get into the historic High Street, pass the old site of the home of the De la Poles, see some of the old houses in Hull, and halt at Wilberforce House, a red-brick mansion, and without doubt the most interesting building in Hull. It dates back to Tudor times; it was here that Charles I. was entertained by Sir John Lister in

1639, and here William Wilberforce was born in 1759. It was bought by the town, and is now a museum mainly devoted to local antiquities, including much that relates to the slave trade and objects relating to a local pursuit, the whaling trade, now defunct, but replaced by the trawling industry, which affords support to 30,000 people. No person of taste should visit Wilberforce House without reading a delightful and informing historical story entitled "Andrew Marvell and His Friends," as it throws much light on this house and the Listers who lived in it. We may proceed to the Charter House, founded by Sir Michael De la Pole in 1384. Through the changes of centuries it has provided a home for the needy. It is an institution of great usefulness, and, with its chapel, a place of considerable interest.

St. Mary's Church is well worth visiting. It was founded about 1333, and restored by Sir Gilbert Scott. There are numerous modern churches, including All Saints', from a design by Street. The Nonconformists have some fine places of worship. Albion Church is an impressive building, and its first minister was the Rev. Newman Hall. Fish Street Chapel, which has been removed to another part of the city, has had connected with it several men of more than local reputation. Here the Rev. Joseph Gilbert was pastor, and it was to Hull that he brought his newly-wedded wife, Ann Taylor, one of the authors of "Hymns for Infant Minds." Mrs. Gilbert wrote a charming description of Hull in the first quarter of the nineteenth century. Wycliffe Church is a modern Gothic structure; its pastor for a few years was the Rev. Dr. John Hunter, before he received a call to Glasgow. It was in Hull that the Rev. John Pulsford, the author of "Quiet Hours," laboured for several years.

There are many fine public buildings in the city, some of the more important are the Town Hall, Royal Institution (with its fine library of 70,000 volumes, museum, art gallery, and lecture hall), Hymer's College, Dock Office, Public Free Libraries, Queen's Hall, Royal Infirmary, Children's Hospital, Exchange, School of Art, Victoria Hall, etc.

Thanks to the great ability and energy of Sir Alfred Gelder, five times Mayor of Hull, the town has been transformed, old buildings have been removed, new wide streets made, and attractive shops and public offices erected, which renders Hull one of the finest cities in the country. It has large public parks, but the docks full of ships are of the greatest interest to the visitor. To-day Hull is the same size as London was in the days of Queen Elizabeth. In conclusion, we may describe the transformation of Hull in modern times as a romance in bricks and mortar.

YORK.

THE story of York is a miniature history of England. In the city annals are included events which fully illustrate the shaping of this country. The student of the past may picture the place in prehistoric times from the numerous relics brought to light, which enable him to realise the story not written in words, but plain enough to those versed in the customs of other days. The relics connect the city with the dawn of English history.

We may study the history of York under the Romans without the speculation we are called upon to exercise with regard to the period when it was under early British tribal rule. During the occupation of this country by the Romans, York grew to a place of great importance. The remains of to-day attest its greatness under Roman rule. It is often asserted that it was the birthplace of the Emperor Constantine the Great. He was at York when his father died in 306, and he succeeded to the throne.

York, in the Anglo-Danish period, was a place of stirring events, not less notable in the spread of the Christian faith than the terrible struggles of warlike peoples. The clash of arms often gave way to the song of praise. Here was founded the famous school in which Alcuin was taught, and of which he rose to the mastership before he went in 782 to the Court of Charlemagne. He was the greatest schoolmaster

YORK. The Bridge over the Ouse, 1818.

of his time, and in a dark age kept alight the lamp of learning. York was the home and field of labour of many famous Christian preachers and teachers; it soon became an archbishopric, and its bishop was Primate of the North. The seed planted by those early Christians has grown into a city of churches. A small wooden structure dedicated to St. Peter, where on Easter Day, April 12, 627, King Edwin was baptised by Paulinus, was the commencement of the cathedral. The King began the erection of a stone structure on the site of the rudely-constructed wooden church, but he fell in battle before he had completed it. King Oswald brought the work to a close. Some thirty years later it was restored by Bishop Wilfrid.

Under the more settled Norman kings the cathedral rose in importance, and became one of the most famous fanes in the land. We do not propose to linger over its rise; it is a building of various periods, but displays a unity of design which is seldom equalled and not surpassed. It has withstood the ravages of time, and twice within the last century, viz., February 2, 1829, and May 20, 1840, survived extensive fires. With its lofty towers it is one of the most impressive cathedrals in this country. Within are monuments and windows of beautiful stained glass, which add a glory to the church. Fully to realise its beauty it must be visited. It is a poem in masonry. The curiosities in the fabric are numerous, including a chair in which Saxon kings have sat at their coronation. There is an ivory charter horn, known as the Horn of Ulf, which was given at the High Altar and carried with it his vast estates, an event occurring shortly before the Norman Conquest. The stone screen, which divides the choir from the nave, dates back to the fifteenth century, and is enriched with figures of the kings of England from William I. to Henry VI. One cannot even indicate the interesting features of the cathedral, for they meet the eye in every direction.

In the Chapter House the first three Edwards held their Parliaments. The Courts of Justice were held here from 1298, when they were removed from London, and remained here for seven years. When money has been wanted for the fabric it has freely flowed in, not from Yorkshiremen alone, but from all parts of the world. A world-wide interest is felt in this stately pile.

Under the shadow of the cathedral the churches of the city seem small, but several are of great historic interest and architectural beauty. Days may be pleasantly and profitably passed in visiting the numerous churches. All seem to have a story for the lover of the past, from St. Michael-le-Belfry, near the minster, where Guy Fawkes, the conspirator, was baptised on the 16th April, 1536, to All Saints' on the historic pavement, with its elegant octagonal lantern tower, which used to contain a lamp at night to guide belated wayfarers travelling through the forests near the city.

The remains of religious houses are of unusual interest, and the ruins of St. Mary's Abbey are the most beautiful in the county, some even say in England. Its history is of importance, and linked with Whitby and Lastingham of Saxon times. The Abbots of St. Mary's grew in power, and were mitred and sat with the bishops in the House of Lords. The touch of time has made it a place of rare beauty in its decay.

A ramble along the narrow streets of the city is like walking through a museum. The magic power of Sir Walter Scott and other masters of fact and fiction have given life to not a few of the historic sites in the city. Many of the street names are curious, telling their stories of people, trades, and manners of bygone times. The Guild Hall and the halls of ancient guilds, the remains of monastic homes, the castle, king's manor house, walls and gates of the city are monuments of the past replete with matters of the greatest interest. We do not know a more enjoyable walk than round the walls of York, stopping in our progress to inspect the bars where the chief gates secured the town from the invaders. In the olden time, on the bars were spiked the heads of fallen foes, a custom which may be traced back to early times, and remained until after the battle of Culloden.

In York all classes find something to charm them; the lover of the picturesque may be delighted with its varied beauties, the student may recall the past, and be carried in fancy to distant times; the industrial enthusiast will be pleased with railway enterprise and other rapid strides in this age of peace. Yet even the gigantic modern station occupies the site of an ancient Roman cemetery, from which many strange relics of ancient days have been removed to the museum in the Abbey gardens.

SCARBOROUGH.

If we arrive at Scarborough on a day when crowds are visiting it, and join in the busy throng on pleasure bent, we shall proceed to the sands along fashionable streets, and notice large and modern hotels and many shops which remind the Londoner of Regent Street. It well merits the popular designation, "The Queen of Watering Places." Nature and art have combined in making it a charming seaside resort, but we soon realise that it has a past as well as a present. On the crown of a bold hill stand the picturesque ruins of the castle, and on a lower elevation is the ancient parish church, both having stones of more than passing interest, which find a place in our national annals.

At the present time Scarborough is given up to pleasure, though in distant days it was a thriving port, but as Hull advanced Scarborough declined. To-day, as far as maritime matters are concerned, it is mainly given up to sailing pleasure craft and the fishing industry. In many of the Yorkshire towns a familiar cry in the streets is "Scarborough Herrings," or "White Herrings." The grim fishermen's homes are in the older part of the place, and present a curious contrast with the pretty villas in the modern streets and roads of the borough, where grass, flowers, and shrubs are to be seen in perfection. Poverty and luxury are near each other. Little sunshine seems to enter the dwelling of the toiler, while those that are in easy circumstances live in a round of pleasure.

The story of old Scarborough starts with the castle; it stands on a bold rock some 300 feet above the sea level and commanding the harbour, which in past times it protected. It may have been a stronghold of our earliest inhabitants, though in the ruins no traces of British or Roman work have been found. The Earl of Albemarle and Holderness, in the reign of King Stephen, built a castle, which appears to have been little more than a wall round the plain on the top of the rock and a tower at its entrance.

Henry II. commanded a brave and great castle to be built. It was ably planned, well built, and in such an excellent position as to render it one of the most important fortresses in the north. In 1312 Piers Gaveston, the foreign favourite of Edward II., sought shelter here. The enemies of Gaveston laid siege to the castle, headed by the Earl of Pembroke, and were several times repulsed, but Gaveston had in the end to surrender for want of provisions.

Let us change the scene for a few minutes. Near Guy's Cliff near Warwick, on Blacklow Hill, is a monument bearing an inscription by the celebrated scholar, Dr. Parr, as follows:—

In the Hollow of this Rock,
Was beheaded
By the Barons lawless as himself,
Piers Gaveston, Earl of Cornwall.
This Minion of a hateful King,
In Life and Death
A memorable instance of misrule.

We were alone when we visited the memorial, but the wood was alive with the song of birds, and the flowers growing in rich profusion added a charm to the scene not to be easily forgotten. As we stood reading the inscription the life story of Gaveston unfolded itself in our mind. He was the son of a Gascon knight, who had been a servant to one of the greatest of our kings, the first Edward. The son of the serving knight was chosen by the powerful monarch as the comrade of his weak son, Prince Edward. His influence over the young man was great, and the King realised that it was baneful. In February, 1307, Gaveston was banished, and on the death-bed of the King he commanded his son never to recall him. In spite of this injunction, when Edward II. had commenced his reign, Gaveston speedily returned to this country, and was created Earl of Cornwall.

Gaveston's rise was rapid. He was appointed Custos of the Realm during the King's absence, and other positions of importance were given to him. He was a man able to play many parts well, and was most ambitious, insolent, and avaricious. The honours conferred upon him completely turned his head. He was unpopular with the nobles, mainly perhaps on account of the coarse satire he indulged in at their expense. No doubt he felt secure in the smiles of his King and the lawless men he had gathered round him for protection. Some of his train of retainers, if we are to believe historical notices of his time, were notorious robbers and homicides. The nobles compelled the King to banish him once more, and he was sent to

Ireland in 1308 as an exile. Here the King befriended him, and he was made Viceroy of that country. He was credited with displaying courage and skill in his new position. His Majesty recalled him the following year. Gaveston was again banished in 1311, but in January, 1312, the King welcomed him once more to the shores. It appeared as if this monarch could not do without his favourite.

The barons were so enraged by the King's conduct and Gaveston's overbearing attitude that they resolved to end his life. He had sought protection in Scarborough Castle, and was besieged there by the Earl of Pembroke, to whom he surrendered on condition that his life was spared. The compact was broken. He was conveyed to Deddington Castle, near Banbury. But Guy, Earl of Warwick, whom he had mortally offended by calling him "The Black Hound of Arden," seized him and took him to Warwick Castle, and told him he should feel the hound's teeth. A mock trial was held by torch-light, and the proud Gaveston was taken to Blacklow Hill and beheaded. This story has taken us a long distance from the stronghold of the east coast, but as Gaveston's name is so often recalled in speaking of the castle, we make bold to repeat his history.

When Richard II. came to the English throne in 1377, France was making expeditions against the coasts of England. Andrew Mercer, a Scottish pirate, was taken prisoner and shut up in Scarborough Castle. The pirate's son entered the harbour with some Scottish, French, and Spanish ships, and, out of revenge, carried away vessels. A wealthy London alderman, named Philpot, on his own account organised an armed fleet and chased Mercer, whom he overtook, and after an encounter retook the Scarborough vessels, as well as fifteen Spanish ships, richly laden, and brought them back to the port. The alderman was impeached for raising a navy without the consent of the King, but was honourably acquitted.

During "The Pilgrimage of Grace," when a foolish and fruitless attempt was made by Aske and other fanatics to re-establish the old religion, Scarborough was besieged in 1536. A passage from Speed proves how powerless these fanatics were, although 40,000 met in Yorkshire, ready to take the field and well provided with the implements of warfare. Priests in sacerdotal vestments, bearing crucifixes, preceded the fighting men. Part of the army, under the command of Sir Robert Aske, attempted to take Scarborough Castle. "The garrison," says Speed, "consisted mostly of the servants of the governor, and were without military stores, and in such want of provisions that they were under the necessity of sustaining themselves for twenty days on bread and water only; yet by the great natural strength of the castle, and the skill and intrepidity of the governor, Ralph Evers, or Eures, the assailants were obliged to abandon the enterprise. This insurrection was suppressed without much bloodshed by the Earl of Shrewsbury."

The insurgents cut a sorry figure on the field of battle, and suffered defeat in their engagements.

Most of the leaders were taken prisoners. Sir Robert Aske was executed and hung in chains at York, while Sir Robert Constable, of Flamborough, was beheaded at Hull and also hung in chains.

In 1553 a rebellion was caused by the national discontent at the contemplated marriage of Mary and Philip of Spain. In this insurrection Sir Thomas Wyatt, the son of Sir Thomas Wyatt, the poet, took a leading part. Scarborough Castle was taken by stratagem by Thomas Stafford, second son of Lord Stafford. He disguised his troop as countrymen, and on a market day strolled into the castle with some thirty men, by whom the sentinels were secured, and then the rest of his soldiers were admitted. It was this sudden and successful attack which gave rise to the popular saying, "A word and a blow, but the blow first—like a Scarborough warning." In three days the castle was retaken by the Earl of Westmoreland; and Stafford was tried for high treason, convicted, and beheaded in London.

Sir Hugh Cholmley, during the struggle between King and Parliament, left the side of the Roundheads for the Cavaliers, and held the castle for the King. It was besieged by Sir John Meldrum, who turned the parish church into a battery. Firing had little effect on the castle, but want of food, after withstanding a siege of six months, compelled the garrison to surrender in 1645. Meldrum died of wounds received in his attempts to take the castle, and Sir Matthew Boynton took his place. He was appointed governor of the castle, and three years later declared for the King. From August to December, 1648, it was under siege, and again passed into the power of Parliament. No wonder, with such traitors as Cholmley and Boynton, the Roundheads deemed it the wisest course to dismantle the fortress.

George Fox, the founder of "The Society of Friends," in 1665 was a prisoner here for his faith. At one part of the time he was confined in a room looking over the sea, lying much open, and the wind drove in the rain so forcibly that the water came over his bed and ran about the room, so that he was glad to skim it up with his platter." He seems to have made a profound impression on the officers of the garrison, for they declared "that he was as stiff as a tree and pure as a bell, for they could never move him."

When England was stirred by the coming invasion of the country by Prince Charles Edward, the Young Pretender, the castle underwent some slight repairs, the cost being defrayed by private subscriptions.

The parish church of St. Mary's cannot be truthfully described as an imposing structure, but it is full of interest, and awakens echoes of distant times. The first church built on the site was given by Richard I. to the monks of the Cistercian order. The present church is but a fragment of the original building. Formerly there were three towers, a central one and two at the west end. In the Parliamentary War in 1645 the Roundheads found it a convenient place whence to direct their operations during the siege of the castle. The Cavaliers within the castle stormed the church and destroyed the choir, which was not rebuilt, and the present chancel was formed out of the central tower. Soon after the siege the tower fell and did much damage. It was subsequently rebuilt. At various times the church has undergone extensive restorations and alterations.

Some curious historical and folklore items are connected with this church. In 1694 John Collings, of Scarborough, was executed at Tyburn, without Micklegate Bar, York, for stealing lead and copper from this church.

A pair of stocks used to stand under the church wall, and Sunday was generally the day selected for punishing culprits, so that those attending the house of prayer might see how wisdom was taught.

In the olden time there was a singular custom prevailing in the town of inviting the people to funerals. It was customary for all burials to be announced by the bellman, who concluded his cry thus: "I am to give notice that Mrs. .... of .... will be buried on .... Her husband desires your company at his house at three o'clock, to observe the time of day, and so to church." In the event of the loss of the husband, the wife would issue the invitation.

The vigil of St. Mark's Eve was kept in the past at Scarborough, like many other places. It was a common belief that if a person watched in the church porch, she or he would see those doomed to die during the year pass in procession into the church. About the year 1800 an old Scarborough woman saw figure after figure gliding into the church, turning to her as they glided in, so that she recognised their well-known faces. At last, it is related, a figure turned and gazed at her; she knew it was herself, and, after uttering a bitter cry, she fell to the ground. Next morning, says Henderson, who relates this story in his "Folklore of the Northern Counties," her neighbours found her, and carried her home, but she did not long survive the shock.

Anne Brontë passed away at an early age in Scarborough, where she had come to try and restore her health, alas! in vain. Her grave is out of harmony in this busy town of pleasure, so far from the old home on the quiet moorlands which she loved so well. She had seldom been far from home. Her two novels were "Agnes Grey" and "The Tenant of Wildfell Hall." As a writer of religious poems she displayed greater literary power than as a novelist. A simple tombstone bears the following inscription:—

Here

Lie the Remains of

ANNE BRONTE

Daughter of the

REV. P. BRONTE,

Incumbent of Haworth.

She died aged 28

May 28, 1849.

There is a pathetic interest in the following lines, the last she composed. After they were written the pen was laid aside to rust, and her desk was closed for ever:—

> I hoped, that with the brave and strong,
> My portioned task might be;
> To toil amid the busy throng,
> With purpose pure and high.
>
> But God has fixed another part,
> And He has fixed it well;
> I said so with my bleeding heart,
> When first the anguish fell.
>
> Thou, God, hast taken our delight,
> Our treasured hope away;
> Thou bid'st us now weep through the night,
> And sorrow through the day.
>
> These weary hours will not be lost,
> These days of misery,
> These nights of darkness, anguish-tossed,
> Can I but turn to Thee:
>
> With secret labour to sustain
> In humble patience every blow;
> To gather fortitude from pain,
> And hope and holiness from woe.
>
> Thus let me serve Thee from my heart,
> Whate'er may be my written fate:
> Whether thus early to depart,
> Or yet a while to wait.
>
> If Thou shouldst bring me back to life,
> More humbled I should be;
> More wise—more strengthened for the strife—
> More apt to lean on Thee.
>
> Should death be standing at the gate,
> Thus should I keep my vow:
> But, Lord! whatever be my fate,
> Oh, let me serve Thee now!

The churchyard is full of gravestones bearing quaint inscriptions. Those placed to the memory of sailors are the more interesting. One bearing the date of 1732 bears the following rhyme:—

> Tho' Boreas' blast and Neptune's waves
>   Have tost me to and fro;
> Yet still, by God's divine decree,
>   I harbour here below;
> Where I do now at anchor ride,
>   With many of our fleet;
> But once again I must set sail,
>   Our admiral Christ to meet.

Another epitaph, dated 1730, is as follows:—

> Awake, arise, behold thou hast
> Thy life a leaf, thy breath a blast;
> At night lie down, prepared to have
> Thy sleep, thy death, thy wat'ry grave.

The foundations of the old town wall may still be traced, and one is struck with the smallness of the place in the past.

A fine view of Scarborough is to be obtained from Oliver's Mount, five hundred feet above the sea level. There is a well-known local saying:—

> When Oliver's Mount puts on a hat,
> Scarbro', Fals-grave, and Scalby must pay for that.

Clouds at the top of this hill indicate wet weather. It is a popular error to suppose that Oliver Cromwell battered Scarborough Castle from the top of this knoll.

The Spa is little more than a name. It is the haunt of fashionable visitors, yet it was known as far back as 1698. It has a romantic story; storm and fire have brought about changes. Sir Joseph Paxton planned a saloon and promenade, but the former was consumed by fire in 1876, and the present handsome pavilion was opened in 1880.

Near to the Spa is the Aquarium, an extensive subterranean building in the Moorish style, with a large concert room for entertainments. Refreshments are provided in apartments planned on Eastern models.

The Museum, built in 1828, in the form of a Rotunda, has been enlarged by the addition of two wings. It is close by the Aquarium, and is well worth seeing. There is a fine collection of fossils and specimens of natural history objects found in the district. Local antiquities find a place—including the ancient ducking-stool, used for curing scolding women. It was formerly placed on the old pier, and was last used about the year 1795, when a scold named Mrs. Gamble was ducked, and with this last link with the past we must conclude our historic story of old Scarborough.

WHITBY.

No North-country town has played a more important part in the religious and literary annals of England. In maritime matters it also played a leading part. It is the most picturesque port on the East Coast, and in its especial attractions is not equalled by any other place in Great Britain. The charming river Esk here finds its way into the German Ocean, and at its mouth, built on either side of the stream, stands Whitby, on the right the old town, and on the left the new watering-place, where rank and fashion spend their holidays. To the lover of the past the ancient portion has the greatest charm. The chief glory of the old town is the ruined abbey, which crowns the hill overlooking the red-roofed houses. In the days of our Saxon ancestors, on the then wild spot, stood the monastery of Streoneshalh. It was here that St. Hilda ruled. A member of the Royal Family of Northumbria, she was baptised at York, when only thirteen years of age, with her great uncle, Edwin, by Paulinus, who had come from Kent. For twenty years she led a Christian life in the Court, and then resolved to enter a monastery.

The scene of her probation was in East Anglia, but she only spent twelve months there, for Bishop

Aidan knew her worth, and bringing her back to her native North, presented to her the site of a small monastery near to the banks of the Wear. She was not suffered to remain there long, as she was advanced to be abbess of a larger house at Hartlepool, which had been founded a few years previously by Bega, the first lady in the North of England to take the monastic veil. Here the saintly Hilda toiled for about eight years. Then advancement came, and she was chosen the first abbess of Whitby, and entrusted with building and organising it. Oswin, it is said, gave its site, with that of eleven others, in fulfilment of a vow made that if he won the battle of Winwaed, in 655, he would show his gratitude to God by giving twelve sites for religious houses. The one at Whitby soon grew in importance.

The wisdom of the abbess gained her great fame, and the living sought her advice, while the illustrious dead were interred within her peaceful walls, and among the number Oswin and his queen, Æanfled.

It was here the lamp of learning and piety was kept alight in the Dark Ages. St. John of Beverley was educated here, and from this house no fewer than five monks were raised to the Episcopate, men not less noted for their merit than for their sanctity. Living in a village which arose round the monastery was a poor herdsman called Cædmon, who became the first English poet. He was employed on the monastic estate, and had reached an advanced age before displaying any poetic power. He could not even sing a song. " Wherefore," says Bede, "when all agreed for glee's sake to sing in turn, he no sooner saw the harp come towards him than he rose up from the board and went homewards." Once, when he had done this, and gone from the feast to the stable, where he had the night charge of the cattle, he lay down to rest at the proper time, and a figure appeared to him in his sleep, and, calling him by his name, said, "Cædmon, sing some song to me." "I cannot sing," he replied, and "for that reason I left the feast, and am come hither because I could not sing." He who talked with him answered, "However that may be, you shall sing to me." "What shall I sing?" Cædmon was told to sing the beginning of created things. Soon he praised God the Creator in verse which he had not heard before. When he awoke from his sleep he remembered the poetry he had sung and added more.

On meeting the steward, his superior, he related his experiences and the wonderful gift which he had received. He was conducted to the abbess, by whom he was directed, in the presence of many learned men, to relate his dream, and repeat the verses, so that they might give judgment as to whence his wonderful poetical power was obtained. They all agreed that the Lord had conferred the gift upon him. The following morning more poetry was forthcoming. The abbess realised that he had received a Divine inspiration, and directed him to put aside the attire of a herdsman, assume that of a monk, and enter the monastery. He was taught sacred history, which he put into harmonious verse. He repeated it, and his hearers committed it to memory. His poetry, which dealt with the chief themes in the Old and New Testaments, has come down to us through the changes of centuries. As his knowledge of the Scriptures increased, his poetry greatly improved.

It was once thought that Milton read parts of Cædmon's poetry, and incorporated some of his expressions and sentiments in "Paradise Lost"; but scholars now do not regard the suggestion as well founded.

It is not known how long Cædmon lived after he entered the monastery; but we learn that he there continued composing poetry to the glory of God. His exemplary career won for him the esteem of his brethren. He expressed in the every-day words of the masses the teaching of the Bible, and his life was a light in a dark age. The lofty pile of which the ruins remain was not reared in his day; no doubt the monastery then consisted of a few rude huts covered with thatch. One of the dwellings was used as a hospital for the weak and dying, and when the poet felt the approach of death he repaired to it. His brethren were surprised, for they did not think that his end was near. He cheerfully conversed with them during the evening. Then he asked if they had the Eucharist; but they asked, "What occasion is there for the Eucharist?" They told him that death was not near if he could talk so pleasantly to them. The elements were, however, brought, and, taking them in his hands, he asked if their minds were at peace with him, without any ground of quarrel or enmity. They replied that they were in perfect friendship with him. A similar question was put to him in regard to themselves, and he answered: "My children, I am at charity with all the servants of God." He then prepared for the entrance to another life. Next, he asked when the brethren would be called upon to sing the midnight praises of the Lord. The time, he was told, was near. He said, "Let us wait for that hour"; and signing himself with the sign of the Cross, he sank his head on his pillow and passed away in gentle slumbers.

In the churchyard at Whitby, in 1898, a striking memorial was erected to the saintly poet. It is in the form of a Saxon cross, and the spirit of the seventh-century art is put into nineteenth-century sculpture. The inscription on the monument says it was placed "To the Glory of God, and in memory of His servant Cædmon, fell asleep hard by A.D. 680."

In this abbey was held the great Ecclesiastical Council of 664, when the Northumbrian Church decided to adopt the customs of Rome and Canterbury. Hilda passed away in 680, in the abbey which she had founded and ruled so wisely. Legend and poetry has gathered round her saintly life. She was succeeded by another member of a royal family, the Princess Ælfied, but the glory of the abbey was fading fast. The Danes overran the country, and in *c.* 867-870, the abbey was laid in ruins, and for two hundred years it was a scene of desolation. After the Norman Conquest the ruined abbey of Whitby and others in Northumbria were restored, and the old home of St. Hilda attained an important place among English religious houses. Prayer and praise were heard once more within its walls. The picturesque ruins we see to-day mainly consist of the abbey church, but no part is earlier than the twelfth century.

In the sweeping days of change in the reign of Henry VIII., the house was valued at £347 2s. It belonged to the Benedictines, and was surrendered on December 14th, 1540, by Henry Davall, the last abbot.

On a piece of land known as the Abbey Plain is a tall cross, usually described by the people as a market cross, but more learned authorities regard it as a cross connected with the burial ground. In the district are similar crosses, but the one near the abbey is the tallest.

On the cliffs a little below the ruins of the abbey is the quaint parish church of Whitby. To reach it from below 199 steps have to be climbed. It dates back to the time of Abbot William de Percy, about 1110, and was built for the use of the dwellers in the town and district. Many additions have been made from time to time. It has a three-decker pulpit, old-fashioned pews, and quaint galleries. Words fail to describe the curious aspect of the church. It must be seen to realise its old-world appearance. One writer says that it is suggestive of a ship's cabin.

In the graveyard are many curious epitaphs, many relating to loss of life at sea. On a slab affixed to the east wall is an inscription containing some remarkable coincidences:—

Here lie the bodies of FRANCIS HUNTRODDS and MARY his wife, who were both born on the same day of the week month and year (viz) Sepr ye 19th 1600 marry'd on the day of their birth, and after having had 12 children born to them died aged 80 years on the same day of the year they were born September ye 19th 1680, the one not above five hours before ye other.

Husband and wife that did twelve children bear,
Dy'd the same day; alike both aged were
'Bout eighty years they liv'd, five hours did part
(Ev'n on the marriage day) each tender heart.
So fit a match, surely could never be,
Both in their lives, and in their death agree.

Mary Linskill, the novelist, is not buried in this churchyard, as many suppose, from a misleading inscription on the tomb of her kindred in this graveyard. After giving her name, etc., it is stated, "She wrote for all English readers of the lives and homes of her own country-folk, dwellers 'Between the Heather and the Northern Sea.'" The novelist was buried in the cemetery, where a monument was placed to her memory, the expense being defrayed by public subscription.

The bells of this church call to the house of prayer the many pleasure seekers, those broken down in health and spirits and the weary toilers, too. Mrs. Susan K. Phillips wrote:—

The Whitby bells, so full and free
They ring across the sunny sea,
That the great ocean god, who dwells
'Mid coral groves and silvery shells
Wakes to the summons, joyously.

O'er purpling moors and fernly dells
Sound the sweet chimes, and bird and bee
Pause, hearing o'er land and lea
The Whitby bells.

And as the mellow music swells,
One listener to the Whitby bells
Feels all the days that used to be
Speak in the blended harmony;
They shrine life—death—and their farewells,
The Whitby bells.

The streets and yards of the old town, mainly the home of the humbler members of the community, are narrow, and the houses are small and in marked contrast to the stately buildings of New Whitby. The dwellings of the old town have given shelter to famous men and women. Captain Cook was closely connected with old Whitby. He was a native of Marten, near Middlesbrough, and was born on October 27th, 1728, being the son of a day labourer. His parents removed to Ayton, and there young Cook attended the village school, and during his spare time assisted his father in the fields. At the age of seventeen he was sent to Staithes to learn the business of a general shopkeeper. Here he mixed with the fisherfolk, and became filled with a desire to follow a seafaring life. After being a year and a half at Staithes, he was bound apprentice to Mr. John Walker, of Whitby. He first sailed in the *Freelove*, a vessel of 450 tons, engaged in the coal trade. It was not customary for the ship to sail in winter, and when it was laid up he lived with his master, and the long evenings were devoted to study. Cook made great progress, and in his employer's house in Grapes Lane laid the foundation of his future success. After being five years in the merchant's service, he entered the navy. His first voyage round the world was taken in a vessel built at Whitby. On his third trip round the world he was murdered by the natives of Owlyhee, one of the Sandwich Islands, on February 14, 1777.

There are several novelists associated with Whitby, but none equal in a knowledge of the local folk, the thrilling stories of the town, and the lovely scenery of the neighbourhood to Mary Linskill, a native of the town, who was born here in 1840, and died in 1891. Her birthplace was a humble house in Blackburn's Yard. She was the daughter of the parish constable. At an early age she was a milliner, later a teacher, and lastly a famous author, the friend and companion of the great and gifted, and, above all, the gentlest and kindest of women. The magic of her pen has given a world-wide interest to Whitby.

The trade of the town has nearly all gone. The whaling industry, for which it was once famous, is now dead, the jet trade has decayed, and shipbuilding is carried on only to a limited extent. The fisherfolk exercise their calling on the mighty deep, and their joys and sorrows have inspired many authors to tell in poetry and prose the stories of this hardy Northern race.

DURHAM.

THE cathedral and castle at Durham crown a hill which takes the form of a peninsula surrounded on three sides by the river Wear, and in bygone times on its fourth side by a moat. The well-wooded hill-sides add much to the beauty of the scene. It is one of the most pleasing pictures in old England; even a hurried view of it from the railway carriage as the train passes the city leaves a charming impression on the memory.

Legendary lore adds a romantic interest to the history of the city, but unlike many ancient towns its origin is not lost in the mists of antiquity. It arose about the year 995, when the bones of St. Cuthbert were brought hither by Bishop Aldhuin, from Ripon, and a church was built to enshrine them. We need not linger over the stories told of the wanderings of the monks for many weary miles.

> O'er northern mountain, marsh and moor,
> From sea to sea, from shore to shore,

they bore for seven years the corpse of St. Cuthbert, before a final resting place was found for it. The Dun Cow guided them to the site of the future shrine of the saint. On the cathedral of modern times the circumstance is rudely illustrated in sculpture. The monks, assisted by Uthred, the Northumbrian king, cleared the ground of trees and tangled thickets, and a shelter was constructed of boughs and wattles for the remains of the saint. A church was completed about six years later, and most probably this was the beginning of the city of Durham. Here were brought the bones of the Venerable Bede, and his last resting-place is the Galilee Chapel in the west end of the cathedral. It is more in harmony with his life than the busy haunts of men engaged in industrial and commercial pursuits such as his old monastic homes of Jarrow and Wearmouth have become.

Shortly after the Norman Conquest the bold sons of the North suffered much at the hands of the invaders. The northern parts of the country were laid waste, and for a time the monks of Durham had to flee for their lives. The church was plundered and profaned. As soon as the Normans had retired and the monks had returned to Durham from Lindisfarne, Malcolm, King of Scotland, invaded England, and desolation blighted the district.

The first Norman king realised that the men of the North must be kept in check. Durham was raised to a Palatinate, and on Walcher, the Norman Bishop of Durham, were conferred all the powers of an independent prince. After his officers had assassinated his friend, the great Saxon Liulph, the populace rose and murdered the bishop. This infuriated the King, who with fire and sword spread misery once more over the North country. A castle was built at Durham to keep the people in submission.

DURHAM. From the North-East, 1834.

The first church was swept away, and on its site William de Carileph began, about 1092, the erection of the present cathedral. It is a fine example of Norman work, massive, yet not lacking beauty of design, and was built for the ages. It has been happily described as "half church of God, half castle 'gainst the Scot." Under great bishops and builders for four hundred years the stately pile rose in boldness and beauty. Since 1500 the fabric has undergone extensive renovation. The bold central tower is 214 feet high, and the two western towers 138 feet. It remains to-day the noblest example of Norman architecture in England. In the past, pilgrims crowded to the shrines of St. Cuthbert and the Venerable Bede, and their offerings greatly added to the wealth of the church. The See of Durham increased its riches from various sources, but still the guiding animal which determined the site of the cathedral enters largely into its history. A local proverb still current says: "The Dun Cow's milk makes the prebends' wives go in silk."

On first coming into his See the Bishop of Durham used to take part in the observance of a singular tenure. Far back, in the days when the first Richard occupied the throne, it is recorded that Hugh Pudsey, "the jollye Bishop of Durham," bought from the King the title of Earl of Sadberge for himself and his successors. On the arrival of a newly-appointed bishop it was the duty of the Lord of the Manor of Sockburn or his representative to meet his grace at the middle of Sockburn Ford, or on the Croft Bridge, which spans the river Tees. After hailing him Count Palatine and Earl of

Sadberge, he presented him with a falchion, saying as follows:—

> My Lord Bishop, I here present you with the falchion wherewith the champion Conyers slew the worm, dragon, or fiery flying serpent which destroyed man, woman and child; in memory of which, the king then reigning gave him the manor of Sockburn, to hold by this tenure, that upon the first entrance of every bishop into the county this falchion should be presented.

The bishop, after receiving the weapon in his hand, promptly and politely returned it, and at the same time wished the lord of Sockburn health and long enjoyment of the manor. The last time the ceremony was performed was in April, 1826, when the steward of Sir Edward Blackett, the lord of Sockburn Manor, met on Croft Bridge, Dr. Van Mildert, last Prince-Bishop of Durham.

A similar service used to take place when the bishop took up his residence at Auckland Castle. He was presented here with a falchion, and addressed as follows:—

> My Lord, I, on behalf of myself, as well as several others, possessors of the Pollard's Lands, do humbly present your lordship with this falchion at your first coming here, wherewith, as the tradition goeth, he slew of old a mighty boar which did harm to man and beast. And by performing this service we hold our lands.

The cathedral is not rich in monuments, but its ancient associations are of the greatest interest. On the north door is the grotesque old sanctuary knocker. A ring is held between a monster's teeth. The person claiming sanctuary raised the ring of the knocker, and sounded it to obtain admission to the church, where, for a time, he was out of reach of the avengers. In the sacred building were men on duty night and day, ever ready to quickly open the door. A bell was next tolled to make known the fact that a man had taken sanctuary. When the refugee sought protection an early intimation was made to the prior, who gave injunctions that he was to keep within the limits of the churchyard, which formed the boundaries of this sanctuary. In the presence of a witness, a detailed account had to be given of the crime committed—dates, names of persons, places, etc., were carefully noted. In cases of murder and manslaughter, the weapon employed had to be mentioned. A gown of black cloth, having on its left shoulder a cross, known as the Cross of St. Cuthbert, was given him to wear. The badge was, we are told, "to the intent that everyone might see that there was such a freelige granted by God unto St. Cuthbert's shrine, for every such offender to flee for succour and safeguard of their lives."

The refugee at Durham was allowed protection for thirty-seven days, and provided with food and drink and bedding by the convent. If within that time he failed to make peace with his adversaries, he had to abjure the realm. He lost his property by the proceeding, but saved his life, or evaded some barbarous form of punishment which often resulted in mutilation of a most painful character.

Connected with the ringing of the curfew bell is a curious item of old-world lore. Every night of the week except Saturday it is rung at nine o'clock. On Saturday evening long ago a ringer went up the tower, according to custom, but disappeared in a mysterious manner and was not seen any more. Popular belief says the Evil One carried him off.

Since that time the curfew bell has been silent on Saturday night.

In bygone times acrobatic performances were by no means uncommon on churches. It is related by Raine that in 1237, Prior Melsonby was elected Bishop of Durham, and that the mitre was taken from him for encouraging a rope dancer to perform his feats on a cord stretched between the towers of the cathedral. The man fell and broke his neck.

One might linger longer over the annals and legends of the cathedral, but other places remain to be briefly noticed. The castle occupies the site of the palace of the Saxon bishops, and was burnt down in 1069, and rebuilt as a fortress by William the Conqueror in 1072. It suffered from fire, and in 1174 was rebuilt by Bishop Pudsey. Since then many additions have been made, and for a long period it was the residence of the bishops, but is now used as a residence of students at the Durham University. A college was founded here by Cromwell, but it was suppressed at the Restoration. It was in 1833 that the present university was opened for students. There are many points of interest in the castle. The libraries connected with the cathedral and the university are of considerable importance.

CARLISLE.

THE Border city of Carlisle is richer in historical memories than in ancient buildings. To-day it has a modern appearance, and one looks in vain for the picturesque remains of the olden time. It is pleasantly situated on a gentle eminence in a far-reaching plain, where the Calden and Petteril mingle with the Eden. The strong walls which surrounded the city, with its three gates known as the English, Irish, and Scots gates, have been swept away.

A cannon was formerly fired at night to warn those who desired to enter the city that they must do so without delay, and those who wished to leave must promptly depart. The gates, once closed, remained shut until sunrise next morning. In the past few, if any, gates in this country were more carefully guarded than those of Carlisle.

The heads of the rebels were displayed over the gates, and often struck terror into the hearts of Scotsmen when they were invading England. An old lady from Dumfriesshire related to Allan Cunningham the terror felt in the hearts of the Scotch at seeing the heads of their countrymen thus exposed to view. Relating to one of the heads—that of a comely youth, with long yellow hair—a pathetic story is told, and it adds romance to the history of

Carlisle. "A young and beautiful lady," so runs the tale, "came every morning at sunrise and every evening at sunset to look at the head of the yellow-haired laddie, till at length both the lady and the head disappeared. The incident is commemorated in a song, in which the sick-hearted damsel bewails the fate of her lover." A couple of verses are as follows:—

White was the rose in my lover's hat
  As he rowled me in his Lowland plaiddie;
His heart was true as death in love,
  His hand was aye in the battle ready.

His long, long hair, in yellow hanks,
  Wav'd o'er his cheeks sae sweet and rud-dy;
But now it waves o'e Carlisle yetts,
  In dripping ringlets soiled and blod-dy.

At the rebellion of 1745, when the Highland soldiers were passing southward, they did not enter the city by the Scotch-gate, on which "the grim and ghastly heads of their brethren were exhibited."

A stranger in Carlisle will first direct his steps to the castle, and as he winds his way along, historic ground will recall the past to his memory. In Roman times it was a place of some importance, but beyond the relics which have been found at different periods, little is left to remind us of the days when the proud Romans were located here. The great wall in the immediate district is a lasting monument of their military skill and industry. There can be little doubt that in Roman times the city was one of wealth, and that its leading inhabitants lived in luxury. The remains which have come to light attest the truth of the assertion. When the Romans had been withdrawn from England in the fifth

CARLISLE. The News Room and Library, 1838.

century, to protect their crumbling empire at home, Carlisle was for centuries the scene of strife, and among those who fought for it were the Pict, Caledonian, Angle, and Celt. During the Roman occupation the two former had been kept at bay, but when the Romans had departed they swept southwards, and their battle-cry rent the air, and cast a terror over the land. Poetry, in its old ballad form, connects the city with King Arthur and his knights, a connection which gave rise to the title of "Merrie Carlisle." The designation seems out of harmony with its quiet business life at the present day.

The site of the castle, or castles (for here have been reared strongholds at different periods in the annals of Carlisle) stood on a hill overlooking the Eden. Here the site was moated by the Roman vallum, which cut across the neck of the headland on which the stronghold stands. In 876 the Danes ruined the town, and for over two centuries it did not regain its power, until the reign of William Rufus. At the point of the sword he drove them away, and in 1092 built a castle for the protection of the people who colonised the town afresh. In later Norman and Edwardian times important additions were made. Richard III. was constable while Duke of Gloucester, and he is credited with the erection of the Tile Tower in the wall which runs from the castle to join the west wall of the city. It was left for Henry VIII. to adapt the interior of the building for cannon. At this castle Mary Queen of Scots spent some time at the commencement of her long and weary imprisonment. The apartments she occupied here commanded a delightful view of the Eden Valley. From the battlements she could obtain a distant view of her own land, and dream of the days when she might recross its border line to assume the rule of Scotland—dreams never to be realised. Her captivity ended in death at the hands of the headsman on a dull February morning, in 1587, in the Banqueting Hall of the Castle of Fotheringay.

Bonnie Prince Charlie took up his quarters at the castle, a circumstance which entailed terrible punishment on the leading citizens. The ravages of time, and more especially the hand of man, altered and reduced the old fortress, and at the present time little of its ancient grandeur is left. One of the most heroic deeds of the olden days is still recalled. In 1596, under cover of night, Buccleuch rescued Kinmont Willie from imprisonment in this stronghold.

The next place of interest to be visited is the cathedral, which is replete with historic memories, but by no means impressive in appearance. It owes its origin to William Rufus. After he had re-established the town, he left as governor when he returned southwards a rich Norman priest called Walter, who started building a church, to be dedicated to the Virgin Mary. He did not live to see it finished, and the first Henry had the work completed. In 1133 the King founded the See of Carlisle, and the church commenced by Walter the priest became the cathedral of the newly-formed diocese. It has suffered on four occasions from fire, the greatest damage being done in 1292. All was destroyed except the outer walls of the aisles, including the belfry and bells. Here one may study every variety of style, from Norman to Perpendicular. The nave, long used as a parish church, is Norman, and it is cut off from the choir, which is mainly in the Decorated style, and one of the finest in the country. The central tower is by no means imposing, being only 127 feet high, and formerly supported a spire of timber, but this was removed in the eighteenth century. Many of the details of the cathedral are extremely fine, but the chief glory is its east window, which is one of the finest in the kingdom, perhaps unsurpassed in the world.

Some officers inspected the English cathedrals in 1634, and said that Carlisle Cathedral was "more like a great wide country church than a fair and stately cathedral." Eleven years later, when the Parliamentary troops had captured the city, they pulled down the nave to repair the fortifications. It has been pointed out that most probably the Norman church was partly built of stones from the Roman wall, and it is curious to find six centuries later the western part of the same church being destroyed in order to repair the city walls.

In the Journal of George Fox, founder of the Society of Friends, is an account of his preaching in the cathedral in 1653. He relates how some "heard him gladly"; but we are further told "rude people of the city found their way into the building, and the governor was obliged to quell the tumult with musketeers."

The cathedral played an important part in the time of war, for its bells and beacons gave alarm when the enemy was coming to the city. When the young Pretender was defeated, Jacobite prisoners were confined in the cathedral, and much damage was done by them. Many of the monuments, especially those of modern times, are full of interest, and repay careful inspection.

The usual buildings of a county town are to be seen. The more important are the Redness Hall, which dates back to Edwardian times, and overlooks the green market. It was there animals were baited. The hall has a room for each of the old guilds of the city. Another house belonging to the same period is in King's Arms Lane. A good specimen of a seventeenth century domestic building is Tullie House, situated between the cathedral and castle. It includes a public free library, a subscription library, and a reference library extremely rich in local books. There is also a picture gallery and an excellent museum with antiquities belonging to the city and district, ranging from Roman remains to the stocks and pillory belonging to the not far distant past. In all respects the institution is worthy of the city.

MONMOUTH.

In Monmouth there is a feeling that we are in Wales. It is perhaps an echo of the past which haunts us. Before the Principality was divided into twelve counties by Henry VIII., Monmouthshire was a part of Wales, but the King decided to include it among the English counties. He assigned for Parliament two knights for the shire, and a burgess for the borough. A change was made in May, 1895, when the House of Commons decided that the county for civil purposes should belong to England, and so far as religious matters and laws were concerned Monmouth was to belong to Wales.

The town is delightfully situated, with hills in every direction; and the river Wye, which is here augmented by two streams, the Monnow and the Trothy, adds a charm to the scenery. Monmouth is built mainly on the old red sandstone, is clean, and has many points of interest, and the usual offices of a county town. There is a pleasant blending of the past and present in the place. The streets and shops are lighted with electricity.

In the olden time the town was protected by a wall and moat, and could be entered by four gates. To-day only one remains, venerable with age, for it dates back to the year 1270, and is known as Welsh Gate on Monnow Bridge. It may be regarded as a curiosity rather than a place suitable for defensive purposes, but within living memory warlike preparations were made within its walls. The western side of the gateway contains several rough holes. These, says the late Mr. R. Waugh, were for musketry in anticipation of the advance of the Chartists on Monmouth County Gaol, after their attack on Newport in 1839; the gateway would then have been an effective military post, for the river was not fordable in consequence of the heavy rains which had delayed until daylight the entry of the Chartists into Newport, otherwise intended to have been effected at night. Could the old walls speak, strange would be the story we should hear from 1270 to 1839; how the foe had been kept at bay, and the town saved; tales would be told how gallant knights had left their sighing lady loves, as they bravely rode under its archway to war, never to return, meeting death on the field of battle, while others would come back covered with glory. As one gazes at this monument of other days, many pictures flit across the mind, more or less pleasing, but all connected with the heroic conduct of the men of Monmouth.

Castles along the Marches of Wales were numerous, and to-day one may visit the ruins of not a few fine examples of the strongholds of bygone ages. Little is left of Monmouth Castle; it remains more a place of memories than a specimen of a fortress. It is stated that the castle was reared on a British fort. Here was a Saxon fortress to restrain the inroads of the Welsh. We are told in the Domesday Survey that the castle was held for the King by

MONMOUTH. The Church of St. Thomas and part of the Monnow Bridge, 1801.

William Fitz-Baron. Camden asserts that it was built by John of Monmouth in the days of Henry III. Here lived in splendour John of Gaunt, and his son Henry Bolingbroke, afterwards Henry IV. On August 9th, 1387, here was born Henry V., that same Harry of Monmouth who, at the battle of Agincourt, gained a glorious victory against great odds, and established his fame as a great soldier. He was a devout and just King, and led a pure life, yet he did not display mercy to a conquered army.

Monmouth stands in two parishes, one called St. Mary's and the other St. Thomas's, situated in Overmonnow. The graceful spire of St. Mary's Church is a notable landmark, being 200 feet in height. The present church was erected in 1736, on the site of an old building, described by Speed as a beautiful church, which statement is confirmed by other writers. It was called the Monk's Church, and here was written the fabulous history of Great Britain, by Geoffrey, surnamed Monmouth and Ap-Arthur. A curious story is related of the bells of this church. When Henry V. had left the harbour of Calais after the wars with France, thus runs the tale, the inhabitants of the town were so delighted that they started ringing the bells of their church. The King was so much annoyed by their action that he put back into the harbour, and brought the bells to England, and presented them to his native town. The church of St. Thomas is small, but interesting, and some parts of it seem to indicate that it was built before the Conquest, as it contains examples of Saxon work. Near it in the street was an ancient cross, which in recent times has been restored.

The sports and pastimes of the place were varied and popular. Bull-baiting was an appreciated form of sport, and even to-day echoes of this form of cruel amusement come down in tales told by sire to son. Badger-baiting was popular. Archery, quoits, fives, tennis, and bowls were favourite forms of diversion for spending the evening. The leading bowling-green was on the site of the garden of the Gloucestershire Banking Company, Monnow Street, in which is a summer house, where Lord Nelson and a party of friends on August 19th, 1802, "took their coffee, and passed the evening in high glee."

Prior to the formation of turnpike roads in 1755, and for some time afterwards, Mr. Waugh says wagons were not in use in Monmouthshire. Grain and all other merchandise were brought to the town on the backs of packhorses. The grain was sold in bulk and not by samples as at present. On a market day some 500 horses would come into Monmouth by the Welsh gate, each animal carrying five imperial bushels of corn. The horses were permitted in front of the houses, and wide sheds were erected for them. It was customary for pent-houses to be erected before nearly all the residences in the town, and for farmers to place their grain in them till sold. The persons providing the pent-houses took out of each sack a small measure of its contents as payment for accommodation.

After the roads were made, stage coaches were employed, and partly used for passengers. Before a person ventured to undertake a journey to London and back he made his will; the road was difficult to travel along, and it was beset by highwaymen. The start was made at two o'clock on Monday morning, and the traveller was timed to reach London on the following Saturday night.

The annals of peace are far more entertaining reading than those relating to war. The historic story of Monmouth is full of interest, more especially of the times which are so near to us, but in this high-pressure age appear so distant. Monmouth is a place in which we get into touch with the olden time.

CHESTER.

FEW cities at home or abroad are more picturesque and historically interesting than Chester, situated on the Dee. It is well known as the haunt of the antiquary, artist, and searcher for the beautiful, and all must find something to please them. The origin of the place is lost in the far distant past, and round its earlier ages have gathered legends which later writers have linked with its history.

When we deal with the city in Roman times we are on surer ground than when legendary lore comes under consideration. The many Roman remains which come to light from time to time help us to realise its importance at that period, and remind us that the name Chester is derived from Castra, a fortified camp. The walls which surround the city and form such a delightful promenade follow the old lines of the Roman fortifications. They are kept in an excellent state of repair, and enable us to understand fully what an old English town was like before cannon and powder played their part in bygone warfare.

A number of towers are erected on the walls from which distant views of the country may be obtained. The county, which is called the "seed-spot of English gentility," has some stately halls and other historic piles. One of the towers is of red sandstone, and is called "King Charles's Tower." The unfortunate Stuart King watched from this site the defeat of his troops on Rowton Moor in 1645. The

CHESTER. The East Gate.

Parliamentary forces completely put the King's soldiers to rout, and when the King saw the battle was lost he made his escape from the city. He left word that if assistance did not arrive within eight days the city was to surrender, but stubborn courage enabled the defenders to hold out for twenty weeks. No assistance came, and at last hunger compelled the loyal citizens to open their gates. The Water Tower is one of the most picturesque bits of ancient Chester. It is supposed to have derived its name from the fact that, in the olden times, the Dee came up to its walls, and the water was deep enough to enable vessels of a considerable size to be moored to it. When day is drawing to its close, and sunset comes, the "Sands of Dee" present a remarkable sight, which inspired Canon Kingsley to write his imperishable song. We can picture Mary calling the cattle home, and how she met death when

> The creeping tide came up along the sand,
> And o'er and o'er the sand,
> And round and round the sand,
> As far as eye could see;
> The blinding mist came down and hid the land;
> And never home came she.

What a marked contrast to the escape of Charles was the triumphal arrival of the Saxon Edgar. He was rowed over the Dee to St. John's by six kings, and he proudly sat at the stern. The annals of the city deal largely with Saxon times, and are replete with interest, but our object is more to make a survey than relate the history of Chester.

A visitor should first walk round the walls, noting the objects of general interest in the city and the scenery of the country around. Many objects of minor interest will arrest his attention as he strolls along the path at the top of the walls.

The cathedral should next be visited, and we doubt not that some disappointment will be felt. It has a plain and modern appearance; it has little rich ornament and appears more like a parish church than a cathedral. It is a massive structure of crumbling red sandstone, irregular in style, from Norman to Late Perpendicular. It has a massive tower of 127 feet, and this helps to redeem the plainness of the structure. The interior contains numerous features of interest which will detain the visitor. If he be a man of literary taste he will be struck by the composition of some of the monumental inscriptions. Here is a fine example copied from a tablet near the door:—

To the Memory of
JOHN MOORE NAPIER,
Captain of Her Majesty's 62nd Regiment,
Who died of Asiatic Cholera
in Scinde
on the 7th of July, 1846,
Aged 29 years.

The tomb is no record of high lineage;
His may be traced by his name;
His race was one of soldiers.
Among soldiers he lived; among them he died;
A soldier falling, where numbers fell with him,
In a barbarous land.
Yet there was none died more generous,
More daring, more gifted, or more religious,
On his early grave
Fell the tears of stern and hardy men,
As his had fallen on the graves of others.

"Surely," says Mr. Francis Bond, "one hears the trumpet on the dusty field of Meeanee, and the word of command of the stern old general. The inscription can be by none other than Sir Charles Napier." There is not much in verse that rings like these few lines of prose.

The cathedral was formerly the church of the abbey of St. Werburgh, which was for 650 years one of the richest in England. After the dissolution of the religious houses it became the cathedral church. It has undergone restorations under the directions of Sir Gilbert Scott and others. Some of the details are full of interest, but it lacks the dignity which one associates with the larger, and even the smaller, cathedrals of this country. The best of music and a skilfully-trained choir add a charm to the services which cannot easily be forgotten.

Playing at ball in the olden time used to be extremely popular at Chester on Easter Monday. It is said that the ball was forced into the cathedral. "Strange as it may seem," says the Rev. G. S. Tyack, in "Bygone Cheshire," "it is nevertheless asserted that the Bishop and Dean took the ball into the church, and it was bandied about between them and the choristers during the singing of the antiphon, a practice which, to say nothing of its reverence, can scarcely have assisted much in the rendering of the said antiphon." Chester was also one of the most famous places in England for mysteries, or miracle plays—pageants which formed such a curious feature in bygone religious life.

There are several interesting churches in the city; for example, St. John's Church. A part of this ruined Roman fabric has been restored. It was a cathedral church for some years during the eleventh century, when the See was removed from Lichfield to Chester. The present bishopric of Chester was constituted in the reign of Henry VIII.

The Irish poet, the Rev. Thomas Parnell, D.D., author of "The Hermit," one of the most beautiful poems in the English language, died at Chester when on his way from London to Ireland. His mortal remains found a resting-place in Trinity Church. His ancestors were natives of Cheshire, and of long standing, at Congleton. It does not seem out of place for the poet to be buried in the land of his forefathers.

Near to this church is the Yacht Inn. It is a fine gabled house, and was at one time the leading hostelry of the city. Dean Swift invited the cathedral dignitaries to supper, but they took no notice of his invitation, and he revenged himself by scratching on the window the contemptuous lines:

> Rotten without, and mouldering within,
> The place and its clergy are all near akin.

There is little left of the ancient castle, some part of which may have had its origin in Roman times. Here stood the fortress erected by the Saxon Princess Elfleda in 907. William the Conqueror, in 1069, added largely to the building, and it is not surprising that he is credited with its erection. All has been swept away with the exception of Cæsar's Tower. On its site are barracks and county buildings. In 1867 there was a Fenian plot to seize Chester Castle. Some fifteen hundred Fenians arrived in the city on February 11, but towards night it became known that they had been betrayed by some of their own brotherhood, and they beat a hasty and undignified retreat.

The Rows are perhaps the chief charm of Chester, and strike the stranger with surprise and pleasure. One has to see them fully to realise this curious feature of Chester architecture. It is not easy to trace their origin, nor yet to describe them. Quaint Thomas Fuller spoke of them as "galleries wherein passengers do go dry without coming into the street, having shops on both sides and underneath, the fashion whereof is somewhat hard to conceive. It is worth their pains who have money and leisure to make their own eyes the expounder of the manner thereof, the like being said not to be seen in all England; no, nor in all Europe again." Camden and other writers notice the peculiar style of building of these Rows at Chester, and some suggest that they are of Roman origin. They consist of shops at the lower storey facing the road, with larger shops set well back on the second storey, having rooms over the broad walks. Steps from the road lead to the Rows. In these later times much rebuilding has taken place in Chester, and the old style has been retained. Timber and plaster, largely used, give a most picturesque appearance to the houses.

Many of the old houses should be carefully inspected, but we can only linger over a few examples. The chief historic house of bygone Chester is Derby House, or Stanley Palace; it is known by both these titles. The date of the erection is 1591, according to a carving in front of the palace. It is a fine specimen of the architecture of its period in this country, with slight indications in the details of the transititon to the Italian style. Within its walls the seventh earl spent the last night before he was beheaded in the Market Place at Bolton on October 15, 1651. At the outbreak of the Civil War he was appointed by the King lord-lieutenant of the counties of Chester and Derby, where it was supposed he had great influence. He is said to have shed the first blood in the Civil War in a skirmish at Manchester on July 15, 1642. His influence and ability were over-estimated. By the King he was mistrusted, and he was not supported by the people.

In Westergate Street is "God's Providence House," originally built in 1652, and rebuilt on the old design in 1862. On the main beam under the gable is the inscription :—

GOD'S PROVIDENCE IS MINE INHERITANCE,
1652.

From this pious legend the house obtains its name. It has long puzzled visitors, and even residents. The generally-accepted theory, and, we think, the correct one, is that when the plague in the seventeenth century desolated the city, this was the only house in the street that escaped the fearful scourge.

Another remarkable dwelling is Bishop Lloyd's House. It has been questioned if this just bishop had any connection with the house that bears his name. He was Bishop of Chester from 1604 to 1615, where he died at the early age of fifty-five. It is recorded of him that he treated the nonconforming clergy with much leniency, protecting them from persecution as much as he could. There are numerous other houses which merit consideration, but we have not space to linger over their history.

The Dee Mills must be seen, and will recall the Jolly Miller of the Dee. He and his mills are linked with story, proverb, and song. His well-known song seems to be destined for all time:—

> I care for nobody, no not I,
> And nobody cares for me.

Old-world Chester favourably impressed Washington Irving. He introduces it into his "Sketch Book." "I shall never forget," wrote the American author, "the delight I felt on first seeing a May-pole. It was on the banks of the Dee, close by the picturesque old bridge that stretches across the river from the quaint little city of Chester. I had already been carried back into former days by the antiquities of the venerable place, the examination of which is equal to the turning over the pages of a black-letter volume, or gazing on the pictures of Froissart. The May-pole on the margin of that poetic stream completed the illusion. My fancy adorned it with wreaths of flowers, and peopled the green banks with all the dancing revelry of May Day."

The echo of another old custom comes down to us which was once common in the city and country, and under slightly different forms still lingers in the more remote parts of the county. On All Souls' eve it was customary for both men and children to go from door to door a-souling—i.e., begging for soul cakes, or anything else good-natured folk were disposed to give. Sometimes a play was performed, but in all instances the following or a similar song was sung:

You gentlemen of England, pray you now draw near
To these few lines, and you shall hear
Sweet melody of music all on this evening clear.
For we are come a-souling, for apples and strong beer.

Step down into your cellar, and see what you can find,
If your barrels are not empty, we hope you will prove kind;
We hope you will prove kind with your apples and strong beer.
We'll come no more a-souling until another year.

Cold winter it is coming on, dark, dirty, wet, and cold,
To try your good nature, this night we do make bold;
This night we do make bold with your apples and strong beer,
And we'll come no more a-souling until another year.

All the houses that we've been at we've had both meat and drink,
So now we're dry with travelling, we hope you'll on us think;
We hope you'll on us think with your apples and strong beer,
For we'll come no more a-souling until another year.

God bless the master of this house and the mistress also,
And all the little children that round the table go;
Likewise your men and maidens, your cattle and your store
And all that lies within your gates we wish you ten times more:
We wish you ten times more with your apples and strong beer,
And we'll come no more a-souling until another year.

Many public modern buildings are most artistic, and are in keeping with the ancient city. Among them may be mentioned the Grosvenor Museum. It merits a visit, for it is rich in local antiquities, and is a credit to the taste and public spirit of Chester.

OLD ENGLISH TOWNS

ELSIE M. LANG

(PART II.)

DOVER

To many of the hundreds of travellers who daily pass through Dover, it is merely a bustling modern port from which they can cross to France in the shortest possible space of time. Perhaps they may catch a glimpse of the castle, or the cliffs on either hand recall to their minds allusions to the "white cliffs of old England," but that is all. Yet it is a place of unique interest, and modern though its present aspect is, dates back to the days of the ancient Britons; in fact, when our first chronicles begin, it was already an important and strongly fortified port, and universally recognised as the key to England. Julius Cæsar sailed for Dover when he set out upon his great invasion, and although prevented from landing by the sight of "armed forces . . . stationed on all the hills," he returned immediately after his victorious attempt at Deal and took the town by storm. A hundred years later, when the Romans renewed their conquest, their first care was to erect at Dover as a beacon tower to guide their ships across the Straits, the pharos which still stands upon the castle heights, and is undoubtedly the oldest building in the kingdom. Dover can boast yet another building, dating from the first century, the church of St. Mary-in-the-Castle, the tower and nave of which, in the opinion of archæologists, were erected by the Romans as a fortification and joined to the pharos by an arched passage, concrete foundations and part of the arch being still in evidence. The chancel, transepts, south doorway, and some of the windows appear to date from the fourth century, and probably the Romans transformed it into a church shortly before they quitted the country. It bears traces of a Saxon restoration, and possesses a coffin-lid belonging to the same period.

William the Conqueror, who came straight to Dover from his victory at Hastings, found it an important and prosperous town with a guild-hall, a strongly fortified castle, and a great Benedictine monastery, and boasting special municipal privileges which had been granted by Alfred the Great for a successful repulse of the Danes :—his soldiers left it a heap of blackened ruins. For this lawless act, however, they received severe punishment, and the astute William, who fully recognised the value of the portsmen's friendship, compensated the latter in such royal fashion that the town speedily rose like a phœnix from its ashes. The Benedictine monastery dated from Saxon times, and was known as St. Martin's-le-Grand; its first home had been in the castle, its second in the market-place, but the monks grew so lax and indifferent that in the reign of Henry I. Archbishop Corbeuil turned most of them adrift and built a new priory and church called St. Mary and St. Martin Newark (new work) outside the town. Various parts of these buildings

DOVER. The Castle.

are still to be seen, some in ruins, but others in a state of perfect preservation, for the site is now occupied by Dover College, and the beautiful refectory, one of the finest specimens of a Norman refectory in the kingdom, is used as the college hall.

Dover's wealth has from time immemorial been drawn from two sources: traffic with the Continent and the Norfolk herring fisheries; the former, of course, increased considerably under the Norman kings, and as for the latter, when their ships were no longer needed to keep the French at bay, the townsmen were able to send a larger fleet to the fishing. Thus Dover grew and prospered and was made head of the corporation known as the Cinque Ports, which is still in existence, although the other ports, Romney, Sandwich, Hastings and Hythe, have long since sunk into decay, owing to the perpetual silting up of their harbours by the wash of the sea. The installation of the Lord Warden of the Cinque Ports, an office combined with that of Constable of Dover Castle, and at present held by Lord Brassey, is still conducted with the old-time pomp and ceremony. The freemen of the Cinque Ports were advanced by the Conqueror to the dignity of barons, and were privileged to send four of their number to hold a silken canopy aloft upon four spears over the King's head at his coronation, and to sit upon his right hand at the banquet afterwards.

It is naturally in the castle that the history of the town centres. Of the earliest fortifications, the work of Britons, Romans and Saxons, little now remains except the earthworks of the middle ward and Earl Godwin's Tower in the outer wall, and it is to the Normans that we owe most of the present buildings, with additions and restorations made by succeeding generations. The ancient place of entrance is still in use, and British, Roman, Saxon and Norman feet have wended their way up the path that leads to the Colton Gate. The castle covers about thirty-five acres, and consists of three wards; the wall surrounding the outer ward contained twenty-seven towers, one of which, the Constable's Tower, with Norman drawbridge, portcullis and gates, is now used as the main entrance and considered "one of the grandest gateways in England." It was formerly known as Fiennes Tower after Sir John de Fiennes, who, with a band of eight other knights, was set to guard the castle by the Conqueror, each receiving in return for his service certain manors or "knights' fees." Eight other towers in the outer wall perpetuate their memory, Fulbert de Dover's, Arsick, Crevequer, Mamignot, Fitzwilliam, Averanche, Porthes and Peverell, the last-named, containing a gateway, ditch and drawbridge, being the entrance to the middle ward. The inner ward stands on much higher ground and is surrounded by a polygonal wall called the Curtain, which is strengthened by fourteen towers and entered by two gates, the King's Gate, on the north, leading from the outer ward, and the Palace, or Duke of Suffolk's Gate, on the south, from the middle ward. In the centre of the inner ward rises the keep, a splendid square pile with some of its walls more than twenty feet thick; it was built with the curtain and towers in the reign of Henry II.

First of the many names connected with Dover

Castle is that of Godwin, Earl of Kent, father of King Harold, to whom is attributed the existing Saxon work, together with much of which no trace remains. He was a sturdy champion of the townsfolks' rights, taking their part against the King. The first constable was Odo, Bishop of Bayeux, half-brother to the Conqueror, whose rule was one of oppression and exaction; he cared nothing for the interests of the town, as an entry in the Domesday Book bears witness; viz., "In the entrance of the port of Dover there is a mill" (belonging to the bishop), "which shatters almost every ship by the great swell of the sea, and does great damage to the King and his men." The townsfolk were goaded so far as to appeal to their ancient enemy, Eustace of Boulogne, for help in a vain attempt to take the castle from him; however, not long after he fell into disgrace with the Conqueror and had to leave the town. Greatest of all the early constables was Hubert de Burgh, the most famous Englishman of his day, but perhaps best remembered now as the kindly custodian of the luckless Prince Arthur. He held the castle during the Barons' War, when the Dauphin of France, at their invitation, came over to seize the throne of England, and began by attacking Dover Castle. It was the most terrible siege the castle has ever sustained; the French erected machines round the walls for the ceaseless discharge of huge blocks of stone, and wooden towers on the edge of the ditch from which invisible soldiers kept up an incessant shower of darts, but the besieged, encouraged by De Burgh, met the attack with a dashing gallantry which compelled the enemy to fall back for awhile, though the Dauphin vowed he would never leave the place until he had taken the castle and hanged every man in it. Then came the news of King John's death, but still De Burgh held out, and neither bribes nor a threat to hang his brother, who had been captured by the French, before his eyes, could move him; his sole answer being: "Let not Louis conceive at all a hope that I will surrender the castle. As long as I draw breath never will I resign to French aliens the castle which is the very key and gate of England." The attack was therefore renewed with greater fury than ever, but without result, and eventually the arrival of reinforcements forced the French to beat an ignominious retreat. The Dauphin collected a fleet for a second attempt, but De Burgh, with a few of the Cinque Port ships, drove him back before he reached the coast. Directly peace was restored De Burgh proceeded to strengthen the castle and built the outer ward with its wall and towers, several of which are connected by subterranean passages with other parts of the castle. Part of this wall and the cliff on which it stood fell down in an earthquake in Queen Elizabeth's reign. Dover also owes to De Burgh its old Town Hall, formerly known as the Maison Dieu, which he founded as a hospital for the rest and refreshment of the many pilgrims who were continually journeying backwards and forwards to France. Henry VIII. suppressed the hospital, and the building, fallen into decay, was used as a brew-house or victualling yard until 1852, when it was restored to all its former beauty and converted into a town hall. Its windows are filled with stained glass after designs by Sir E. J. Poynter, P.R.A., and represent famous personages and events in the history of the town. In 1868 a council chamber was added to it, and in 1882 the Duke and Duchess of Connaught opened the adjoining or new town hall, the windows of which contain pictures of some of the constables. Up to the days of the Tudors the castle was used as a royal residence, and many a king has been here on one of the most important occasions in his career :—Richard I. stayed in Dover Castle before setting out full of gallant enthusiasm for the Crusades ; Henry III. after his disastrous French campaign, and again when the Barons had risen against him ; Edward I. was confined in the castle as Prince of Wales during the same Civil War, and later on met with a very different reception when he landed at Dover on his way back from the Crusades to receive the crown of England. Edward II. brought his beautiful bride Isabella straight to Dover Castle from her French home, current gossip proclaiming them the " handsomest pair in the world." Henry V. landed at Dover after his famous victory at Agincourt, and was carried up to the castle on the shoulders of the enthusiastic crowds, who rushed into the water to meet him.

As for Dover harbour, that unceasing anxiety and expense to the good burgesses of Dover, its history, properly speaking, begins in the reign of Henry VII. In early days the river ran out into the sea under the castle cliff, and the ships, which were then quite small, could sail up to Buckland, where the harbour apparently was. At the beginning of the fourteenth century a great fall of the cliff turned the course of the river westward, and the wash of the sea having built up a pebble beach on the western side of the bay, the drift of the current changed, and the waves, of enormous strength during the frequent south-easterly gales, began to beat upon the town, causing endless damage and choking the mouth of the river and harbour with beach. To prevent this a strong wyke or sea wall had been built across the sea-front, but it could not long withstand the force of the waves, and as ships were now being built on a much larger scale a stone pier was erected running from the western beach into the sea, to protect the town and form a harbour for the shipping, and so great a boon did this at first prove that the seamen gave it the name of Paradise Pent. Before forty years had gone by, however, it was partially destroyed, and the entry into the harbour so choked up that " horses and drags " were required to clear a passage before any ship could enter or leave the port, and the mayor and burgesses in despair sent a petition to Henry VIII. stating that " unless some remedy be provided the inhabitants, ship-owners as well as others will be forced to forsake the town." Luckily for Dover Henry fully recognised the great national importance of its harbour, and he came down and inspected the town himself, with the result that a great restoration and fortifying of both castle and harbour was put in hand, and a new pier built on a plan that seemed to promise well. But Dover harbour has been the grave of many engineering reputations, and a source of much quarrelling, bad feeling and disappointment. The new works very soon proved to be a failure, and as no more money was forthcoming, matters were soon as bad as ever, and so continued until Sir Walter Raleigh drew the attention of Queen Elizabeth to the town. Once more money was granted, all sorts of schemes were suggested, and another pier built; but a violent storm spoilt most of the new work, and for the next two centuries the pier was constantly in need of repair and the harbour entrance choked up. To meet the heavy expense a harbour tax was imposed and the ancient custom revived of a drum being beaten by the mayor to summon every householder on pain of the fine of one shilling to repair to the harbour with a shovel and clear away the shingle; and once after a great storm had done incalculable damage every able-bodied person had to assist in making a mud wall to keep out the sea. A letter is still extant, superscribed "in haste, post haste, or all's lost; port, town and people" in which the writer describes "a fearful inundation" and begs that a Commissioner be immediately sent down from Trinity House "to see the danger of desolation." At last, after various other schemes had been tried, the harbour was in 1791 put into a fairly satisfactory condition, and ships drawing twenty feet of water could enter it without damage. But it was the nineteenth century which assured the future importance and usefulness of Dover Harbour. The great Duke of Wellington strongly advocated its extension into a National Harbour of Refuge, and although more than sixty years went by before money was actually voted by Parliament for this great undertaking, the Admiralty Pier, which is to form its western boundary, was built in 1847-71, and various other works carried out for the improvement and enlargement of the existing harbour. The memorial stone of the outer harbour was laid by the late King Edward when Prince of Wales in 1893, amidst the greatest possible rejoicing, and the work is now far advanced; when it is completed Dover will be the proud possessor of a magnificent national harbour covering an area of 685 acres of water, in which twenty of the largest battleships and any number of cruisers and smaller boats can ride in safety.

Meantime, among many other improvements effected in the town, enormous care and expense have been lavished upon strengthening and arming its defences. It was at the time of the scare of an invasion by Napoleon, when William Pitt was Warden, that the first earthworks were thrown up on the Western Heights and armed with cannon, and forts erected along the sea front in which a strict watch was kept night and day. Since then more than a century has elapsed, and now upon the Western Heights may be seen the Citadel, Grand Redoubt, and Deep Redoubt, splendid specimens of modern fortification, while in the castle 4,000 soldiers can be assembled, and, at the end of the Admiralty Pier, in a turret which no stranger is ever allowed to enter, some heavy guns lie hid ready for immediate action.

Truly Dover may be reckoned chief among our fortified towns.

NORWICH

THE fair city of Norwich has been variously called the " City in an Orchard," the " City of Churches," and to those who gaze down upon it from the lofty battlements of the castle in its centre, or the green heights of Mousehold Heath rising up beyond its great cathedral, the reason for both titles is clearly apparent. Picturesque it is still in many an odd corner, and although the march of modern progress has swept away much that is old, we cannot but rejoice in widened streets and well-kept thoroughfares when we recall the Black Death ever lurking in the dim depths of the narrow mediæval streets with their picturesque signs and house-fronts, to break out now and again in an epidemic that robbed the good city of half its population, and the terrible skin diseases that necessitated the building of innumerable leper hospitals.

The origins of Norwich are so ancient that they are lost in the mists of time, but the earliest historians inform us that the invading Romans found a settlement here surrounding a fort which they named Venta Icenorum, held by a tribe called the Iceni, who, led by the heroic Boadicea, made so stubborn a resistance that even when they were subdued the Romans had to erect a strong camp at Caistor, and maintain a military force there to keep them under; it served, moreover, to help keep out the fierce vikings, Danes and Angles, who were continually swooping down upon the coast of Norfolk, and endeavouring to effect a landing. When the Romans at length, recalled by the needs of their own empire, left England defenceless, the Northmen overran the county in such numbers that it came to be known as Norfolk, the land of the North folk. The Angles were the first; under their cyning or king, Offa, they settled at Cyning's ford, now Conisford, the oldest part of Norwich, down by the river at the foot of the Castle Hill. Some antiquaries think they raised the artificial mound on which the castle stands, and erected a stockade; at any rate, the burgh in their days grew into a place of considerable importance; it was the seat of a royal mint, and we have coins that were minted here by King Athelstan in the tenth century. Then, says the Saxon Chronicle in 1002, "Swegen came with his fleet to Northwic and wasted and burned the burh," and the Danes took possession of the land; antiquaries assure us that 256 out of the 740 Norfolk parishes were settled by them, and Christianity, which the Saxons had introduced, had to make way for the worship of Woden until the time of the converted Canute. Tombland (the Danish tomland meaning vacant land), was the centre of Norwich in those days. Here the market was held, and the citizens met to discuss the events of the day; all the main streets led up to it, and here were the church of St. Michael, the principal church in the burgh, and the earl's palace. By the

NORWICH. Bishop Hall's Palace.

time of the Conquest Norwich had grown into a town containing 1,238 burgesses, and was considered one of the most important cities in England. One of the townsmen, Ralph de Guader, whose mother was a Breton, had fallen into disgrace shortly before, and fleeing the country, had sought refuge in William's Norman Court. He managed to worm his way into the Conqueror's favour, and following in his train when he went to invade England, managed to secure the earldom of East Anglia, and to become lord of the town out of which he had been cast. For a time all went well, and Guader was very busy ; he built a timber keep on the top of the castle mound, and surrounded it with a deep ditch. He also followed the example of the Norman nobles, and established a new burgh in which some of the Normans, Bretons and Flemings who had come over with the Conqueror took up their abode, also a number of Jews under the special protection of the King, who found their treasure chests very useful. But the restless treachery of Guader's ambition was not satisfied, and at the magnificent bride-ale which celebrated his union with FitzOsbern's daughter, he hatched a plot against his new King, which led to his undoing ; he was not strong enough to carry it through, and forced for the second time to flee from Norwich, he left his brave bride to hold the castle a little longer. Great was William's wrath, and it fell not only upon Guader and his followers, but also upon the innocent townsfolk, particularly those who lived in the old burgh, and so many of them were killed or exiled that they could no longer hold their own against the newcomers, and the centre of the town was removed to Mancroft, where the new burgh was.

William now bestowed the earldom of Norfolk upon Roger Bigod, one of the many bold, arrogant, turbulent barons who thronged the Court, always seeking to extend their power, always on the eve of rebellion, and entrenching themselves in the massive castles they built all over the kingdom. Bigod and his sons erected the great stone keep that dominates Norwich, but before it had risen upon the castle mound a yet greater edifice had grown up below.

Herbert de Losinga, a brilliant and courtly young priest, high in the favour of William Rufus, bought from him the bishopric of East Anglia, and afterwards realising and repenting this act of simony, determined to build in expiation a great cathedral. He purchased the Cowholm, a wide meadow east of Tombland, and effected an exchange with Bigod by which he obtained possession of St. Michael's church and the earl's palace, both of which he removed, and then proceeded to lay the foundation stone of what is still "the most perfect of Anglo-Norman cathedrals," and "has come down to our own day with nearly the entire shell of the original fabric intact." The presbytery choir, the north and south transepts, and the three beautiful chapels, St. Mary's, St. Luke's and the Jesus, are all the work of Losinga, and his effigy stands over the outer door of the north transept. The nave and cloisters, which are the second largest in England, were not completed until the twelfth century, and in consequence of their slow construction we can study in them the whole development of Gothic architecture. The nave is of unusual length. The best views of the cathedral, which is unfortunately situated on some of the lowest ground in the city, are to be obtained from the south-west angle of the cloisters, and from the Ethelbert and Erpingham gates. Alongside the church Losinga also founded a Benedictine convent for sixty monks, between whom and the townsfolk there soon came to be perpetual feuds; these usually came to a head on Fair Day, a fair having been granted to the town on the foundation of the priory. The monks were frequently the aggressors, and used to shoot arrows and throw stones at inoffensive citizens strolling across Tombland. On one occasion the monks sallied forth from the priory, drank and caroused, fought and plundered, and did so much damage that the townsfolk in revenge burnt the close, the gates and adjoining buildings, and carried off everything they could lay hands on. Several monks were killed and the prior escaped to Yarmouth, where he appealed to the King. Rough justice was dealt out all round: the ringleaders were executed, or dragged about the city by horses until they died; the prior was imprisoned, and the townsfolk had to pay a heavy fine towards the restoration of the cathedral.

The Jews, too, were seldom left in peace. They were the physicians, pawnbrokers, and usurers of the community, and occasionally became very rich, but scandals were frequently got up about them, and every one conspired to defraud them. They were robbed and imprisoned, banished and killed. The King would remit debts to them and extorted money from them whenever he wanted it. King John ordered the teeth of Isaac of Norwich to be drawn out one by one until he consented to yield up 10,000 marks; this famous Jew's house, once known as Isaac's Hall, is still standing in King Street, and in later days passed through the hands of the Yelvertons, the Pastons, and Chief Justice Coke. The worst persecution of the Jews was in 1144, when they were accused of crucifying a little Christian boy and burying him in Thorpe Wood; the body was exhumed and the child canonized as St. William, Boy and Martyr. A history of the affair was written by a monk and a shrine set up in Norwich Cathedral, to which numberless pilgrims travelled. Henry V. left his coronet in pawn with the Jews of Norwich when he went to the French Wars, taking with him amongst others the gallant Sir Thomas Erpingham, builder of Erpingham Gate.

In 1252 the city was enclosed with walls and a ditch. The woollen and weaving trades, upon which the prosperity of Norwich has been chiefly based, were by this time beginning to grow; even in the twelfth century an old chronicler tells us the Norwich men were "for the most part weavers, they knew not how to bear arms in knightly wise." Weaving had been introduced into Flanders by the grandfather of Queen Matilda, wife of the Conqueror, and was brought into this country by the Flemings, many of whom had come over to England at the Conquest, while others were included among Losinga's army of foreign workmen and Stephen's foreign mercenaries; thus for more than a century there was a constant influx of Flemings into England. By the

NORWICH.

The Cathedral.

end of the thirteenth century eight Cistercian convents were established in or near Norwich, and as this order derived the greater part of its income from sheep-breeding and wool, the woollen trade of Norwich increased by leaps and bounds. About 1330 John Kempe came from Flanders with his family and servants and settled in Norwich, where he taught his system of weaving. In 1338 a further number of foreigners settled in Norwich, and the town began to be very crowded. Again and again the Black Death appeared, and in the fourteenth century it carried off so many of the working-class that the labourers felt themselves in a position to insist on higher wages and better conditions. All over the country there was great discontent and rioting, and at Norwich 40,000 malcontents gathered round John Littester, a dyer, known as the "Idol of Norwich." Their first step was to send for the Governor of Norwich, who was one of the handsomest and bravest men of his time, and having by sheer force of numbers compelled him to appear before them, their leader thus addressed him:— "Robert, you are a knight and a man of great weight in this county, renowned for your valour; yet, notwithstanding all this we know who you are; you are not a gentleman, but the son of a poor mason, just as ourselves. Do you come with us as our commander, and we will make so great a lord of you that one-quarter of England shall be under your command." But Sir Robert was faithful to the trust reposed in him by his king, and indignantly rejecting their proposals he set about him with his sword, and killed twelve of the rebels, besides wounding many others, before he was overpowered and cut into bits. Having wrung a large amount of money from the frightened townsfolk, the rebels entrenched themselves at North Walsham, making their camp secure by piling up around it gates and tables, and anything on which they could lay hands, and enclosing it with a deep ditch. Meantime the townsfolk waited in fear and trepidation. When news of the rising reached the ears of Spencer, Bishop of Norwich, who had been away travelling, he clapped on a helmet and coat of mail, and taking a sword in his hand, called on every man able to bear arms to follow him ; hundreds joined him and they set off hot-foot for the rebel camp. Led by the fiery bishop, they bore down upon the unsuspecting insurgents with such extraordinary fury that in a very short space of time the ringleaders were captured and the camp was completely at their mercy. The conflict over, the bishop resumed his episcopal robes, heard the confessions of the captives and accompanied them to the gallows.

By the fifteenth century civic life in Norwich was a gaily-coloured, flourishing affair; the trades had grouped themselves into guilds, of which the first and foremost was " The Gild of St. Mary, called the Great Gild of Norwich," and on high days and holidays they had brilliant pageants or gave performances of quaint miracle plays. All the great families of Norfolk had town houses in Norwich, the Fastolfs, the Erpinghams, the Pastons, the Yelvertons, and many others. The Duke of Norfolk had his palace here, and his son, the Earl of Surrey, a mansion both on Mousehold Heath and in Surrey Street. Every monastic establishment in the county also had its town house or inn. But though the town grew wealthy and the trades flourished, there was much misery among the poor, who were oppressed by the wealthy landlords, and in 1549, unable to bear it any longer, a band of peasants armed themselves with pikes and scythes, and swore that their wrongs should be redressed. Robert Kett, a tanner, was their leader, and they encamped upon Mousehold Heath in huts of turf, roofed with boughs. In a few days their numbers had reached 20,000, and Kett felt emboldened to take possession of the Earl of Surrey's mansion, which he turned into a prison, shutting up in it all the gentlemen he could capture, one of whom was the mayor. Every day he held a court under a tree known as the Oak of Reformation. There he drew up a petition containing a list of grievances which he sent to the King. In it the peasants begged that the lords of the manor should no longer be allowed to enclose the common lands; that "prests or vicars that be not able to preche and sett forth the woords of God to hys parisheners may be thereby putt from hys benyfice; that all bonde men may be ffre, for God made all ffre by His precious blode sheddynge; that all the rivers be ffre and comon to all men for fyshyng and passage, and that pore men's chyldren of ther paryshe should be taught the boke called the Cathakysme and the prymer." This petition, simple and pathetic though it was, left the King indifferent; he merely sent a herald to proclaim pardon to all that "wolde humbly submit themselves and depart quietly every man to his house." Kett replied: "Kings are wont to pardon wicked persons—not innocent and just men. We have done nothing to deserve such pardon, and have been guilty of no crime. We therefore despise such speeches as unprofitable to our purpose." For a time they kept the King's troops at bay, aided by the secretly sympathizing townsfolk, fighting being confined to skirmishes in the streets and alleys, but at length the Earl of Warwick, with a large army of Italian and German mercenaries, drove them forth to Mousehold Heath and forced them to open battle at Dussyn's Dale. The inexperienced peasants had no chance against the highly-trained mercenaries in the open, and they went down like grass before them, dying where they stood, but holding on undauntedly until Warwick, struck by admiration and pity, promised the survivors pardon if they would surrender, Kett and the ringleaders alone being hung on the Oak of Reformation.

In 1564 the trade in woollens and worsteds declined to such an extent that the workers were sore put to it, and Elizabeth, in the hope of reviving it, permitted a number of Dutch and Walloons, fleeing from the Duke of Alva's persecutions in the Netherlands, to settle in the town, into which they introduced the making of "bayes, sayes, arras, mockades and such like," to the great advantage of the city. On the whole they lived peaceably with the inhabitants, and it was said of them, "They live wholly of themselves without our charge, and do beg of no man, and do sustain all their own people." In 1582 their numbers had increased to

4,679. When Elizabeth paid a visit to the city one of the many pageants arranged in her honour was called the "Artizan Strangers' Pageant," which included representatives of all the various manufactures of the city, and had eight little girls spinning worsted on one side of the platform and eight knitting on the other. To them was due the introduction of printing into the city, the first Norwich book being printed by Anthony Solen in 1570. Doubtless it was the memory of former persecutions of the many foreign citizens that made Norwich so zealous in the raising of forces and money to repel the Spanish Armada.

The Howards, who were now the Dukes of Norfolk, attained great eminence, the Duke of Norfolk in Elizabeth's reign even aspiring to the hand of Mary Queen of Scots. In 1602 he began to build a wonderful palace in Norwich, which took fifty years in the making, and was esteemed one of the most magnificent buildings in England; it had splendid gardens stretching along by the river, with a tennis court and walks twenty feet wide, and in it the reigning duke feasted and entertained right royally; here Charles II. was once a guest, on which occasion he knighted Thomas Browne, the famous author of the "Religio Medici," who lived for many years in a house near St. Peter Mancroft, and was buried in that church. Sir Thomas was one of the most learned men who ever lived in Norwich, the most renowned antiquary of the day, interested specially in Roman remains. It was the discovery of some Roman urns at Norwich that was the occasion of his writing "Urn Burial."

Another most famous citizen of Norwich was George Borrow, who was clerk in a lawyer's office in this city. It was in the cattle mart that he first met the gipsies, whose wild free life and strange haunting dialect appealed to him so strongly; in the long summer evenings he used to sit with them by their camp fires on Mousehold Heath, listening to the curious tales which stood him in such good stead when he wrote "Lavengro" and "Romany Rye." His younger brother was a pupil of the famous artist, of whom Norwich is justly proud, "Old Crome," whose father had been an innkeeper in the worst part of Norwich. As a boy he was apprenticed to a sign painter, and on his rare holidays used to wander over Mousehold Heath and drink in the loveliness which he afterwards immortalised in his pictures. He was the founder of the Norwich School of artists, one of whom was Cotman, the son of a Norwich silk mercer. Crome lies buried in St. George, Colegate, where there is a tablet to his memory.

For five hundred years the great castle was used as a gaol, but it is now the property of the Corporation, who have converted it into one of the finest museums in the country.

BRISTOL

Bristol is a city of merchants, and the churches and charities they have founded. It was the Saxons who first discovered what an excellent harbour was afforded by the river Avon near its junction with the Frome, and they speedily turned the little town that already stood on the river banks into a port which in after years was rivalled in importance only by London itself. The first known date connected with its history is furnished by two silver pennies of the reign of Ethelred the Unready (978-1016), which have an inscription signifying that they were struck at Bristol. The earliest merchants dealt in slaves, young men and girls, whom they obtained by force and sold in the market-place or shipped to Ireland. This traffic in human beings was strictly forbidden after the introduction of Christianity, but the Bristol merchants contrived to evade all laws even after the Conquest. At last Wulfstan, bishop of Worcester, came to plead, and so wrought upon them that with one exception they promised to give up their wicked trade, and turning upon the merchant who remained stubborn they put out his eyes and drove him from the town. This, however, was by no means the last of the slave trade in Bristol; centuries afterwards it again became a source of great profit to the town.

In early days the Frome and the Avon entirely surrounded Bristol except for a narrow neck of land on the Gloucestershire side, on which in 1088 the castle was built, and, being on an eminence, the highest point of the present Castle Street, it commanded the harbour as well as the one approach by land. A bridge spanned the Avon just where it does now, and beyond it the town centred round the carfax formed by Wine and Corn Streets, and High and Broad Streets. To render it even more secure it was enclosed by walls; no wonder that in Norman days Bristol, besides being one of the richest, was considered the most impregnable city in England. Nothing of the castle now remains except the entrance to the banqueting hall in Tower Street, the sub-structure of the chapel and a large room in Castle Street, while the site of the old drawbridge is occupied by the tramway centre, one of the busiest parts of the town.

After the Conquest all sorts of religious communities settled near Bristol, and among them the Knights Templars, who lived for a century or more in the present parish of Temple and built the Temple Church. The hospital of the Bons Hommes was also instituted about this time, the beautiful chapel of which, recently restored, is now known as the Mayor's. At the beginning of the twelfth century the Abbey of St. Augustine was founded, and when four hundred years later Henry VIII. suppressed the monasteries and raised Bristol to the dignity of a bishopric, the abbey chapel, partly restored and rebuilt, became the cathedral, although it did not attain its present size and beauty until a

BRISTOL. The Temple Church.

generation or two ago. Nothing of the original building now remains except the Norman gateway and the chapter house.

In the thirteenth century the channel was cut through which the Frome now flows, and the old one filled up, and a second bridge was built over the Avon to connect Redcliff and Temple with the town of which they soon became part. Bristol by this time was doing a thriving trade in wool, cloth of home manufacture, soap also made in the town, fish caught along the coast and in great request for fast-days, leather from the tanneries already springing up along the banks of the Avon, and wines from the south of France, a branch of trade introduced by Henry II. when he married Eleanor of Aquitaine. By degrees the various trades formed themselves into guilds, each having its own district: the weavers occupied Temple, and numbered among them some of the wealthiest citizens in Bristol, one of whom, Thomas Blanket, gave his name to that useful article which he manufactured in great quantities; their guild chapel, dedicated to St. Katherine, still stands near the Temple Church. The fullers or tuckers lived in Tucker Street, the corn-dealers in Corn Street, and so on. The chief guild was, of course, the merchants', which in the fifteenth century developed into the famous corporation known as the Merchant Venturers. Many of the members of this guild lived magnificently in great houses luxuriously furnished, but in spite of their wealth and splendour and the beautiful buildings already in existence, Bristol in mediæval days was a dirty and squalid town. The streets, unsafe for vehicles on account of the many cellars for the storage of merchandise which ran underneath them, were very narrow and dark, with great bulkheads over the shops, stalls encroaching upon the roadway and a drain running down the centre into which the refuse from all the houses streamed. It is not surprising that three leper hospitals were considered necessary, and that when the Black Death came in the fourteenth century it wrought so great a destruction that "the whole strength of the town perished," and grass grew in the principal streets. But when the visitation was over, those who survived and upon whom the whole wealth and trade of the town devolved, set to work with the energy for which the men of Bristol have always been renowned and, hiring a large number of the rural population to come in and work for them, they gradually built up the prosperity of the town anew and by the beginning of the fifteenth century it was more thriving than ever. The trials through which they had passed, however, were not without effect upon the burgesses of Bristol: religion began to occupy a far more important place in their lives, and they devoted great sums of money to restoring and building churches and the relief of the sick and poor; pilgrimages were frequent, the festivals of the Church were observed with ceremony and rejoicing, and no new enterprise was undertaken without a priest's blessing.

The exquisite upper stage which has caused the Temple Church to incline slightly to one side dates from this period, and so does the restored fabric of St. Mary, Redcliff, that thirteenth century church which was afterwards praised by Queen Elizabeth as "the fairest, the goodliest and most famous parish church in England." Its restoration was due to the liberality of William Canynges, chief of the merchant princes of that age, whose trade with northern Europe far exceeded that of any of his contemporaries. He was five times mayor and twice represented Bristol in Parliament; his good deeds were endless, and towards the close of his life he retired from the world and, taking Holy Orders, spent his last few years at Westbury-on-Trym.

During the fifteenth century there was a great revival of learning, and the eager desire for knowledge which was felt all over England, took the form in Bristol port of attempts to discover the unknown lands which it was confidently believed existed on the other side of the Atlantic. These attempts were directed by John Cabot, a Genoese merchant, who, after sundry visits to Bristol, had settled in the town in 1491. For six successive years Bristol men sailed with him in search of the "Island of Brazil and the seven cities," and returned disappointed. In 1498 they set out for the seventh time, in five ships, and accompanied by Cabot's son Sebastian, and after a voyage of nearly two months, their perseverance was rewarded by the first sight of the new world, and, landing, they planted the flag of England on the coast of North America a year before Columbus discovered the southern continent. After sailing round the Gulf of St. Lawrence, John Cabot returned to Bristol, where he met with an enthusiastic reception and was hailed as the "Great Admiral," but Sebastian went on further along the coast of Labrador "until seyng suche heapes of Ise before hym, he was enforced to tourne his sayles." He brought back to England as a present to the King three savages who "were clothed in beasts' skins and ate raw flesh, and were in their demeanour like brute beasts." England, however, had few charms for him, despite the fact that Bristol was his birthplace, and he soon left it to enter the service of the King of Spain. These discoveries were followed by others described by Richard Hakluyt, then a canon of Bristol, in his famous book, "Navigations, Voyages and Discoveries," and enthusiasm for foreign trade grew until every one who could scrape together a little money invested in some such enterprise. This private trading, however, proved a great hindrance to the Bristol merchants, and they complained to the King, who gave them a charter, which conferred upon them the title of the Merchant Venturers of Bristol, and forbade any one else to trade beyond seas. Another great hindrance to the merchants was the Spaniards, who continually attacked their ships, and great were the rejoicings in Bristol when the Spanish Armada was defeated, as the Neptune Fountain in Victoria Street bears witness.

By the end of the seventeenth century trade with the southern States of America and the West Indies was thoroughly established, and the golden age of Bristol commerce had set in, sugar and tobacco were at first the chief imports, but the great plantations in which they were grown being worked by negroes, the Bristol merchants soon discovered that slaves were more profitable still, and traffic in human life became for the second time the chief source of the town's wealth. For bars of iron and other manufactured goods they purchased negroes on the coast of Africa, packed them tightly together in the holds of their vessels, and sailed for the West Indies, or the southern States. Many of the poor wretches did not survive the horrors of the voyage, but they had cost little, and their loss did not affect the merchants who, their human freight disposed of, reloaded their ships with sugar and tobacco for the journey home. For more than a century and a half the infamous trade went on, and it only came to an end when the noble efforts of Wilberforce brought about the abolition of slavery. Meanwhile, Bristol flourished exceedingly, the docks were crowded with West Indiamen, the yards with vessels in course of construction, the great sugar refineries, one of the sights of the city, were in full swing, and the whole town was pervaded with the pleasant hum of bustling prosperity. The merchants' wealth caused the King himself to pay them court, and the voices of visitors to the town, among whom were the famous Evelyn and still more famous Pepys, were loud in its praise. Defoe stayed in Bristol when he was collecting material for his "Tour Through the Whole Island," but unfortunately it was when he had just been made bankrupt and he had in consequence to spend most of his time in hiding from the bailiffs, a circumstance which earned him the title of the "Sunday Gentleman." It was at Bristol that Defoe saw Alexander Selkirk, brought thither by the sea captain who had rescued him from his uninhabited island, and learnt the story of his adventures upon which he afterwards founded "Robinson Crusoe."

Best and greatest of all Bristol's many merchant princes, the man whom the town will never grow weary of honouring, and whose birthday is regarded as the most important day in the year, and celebrated with prayer and feasting, speechmaking and collections for the poor, was Edward Colston, whose chief pleasure lay in spending his great wealth for the benefit of his native city. On all sides there are memorials of him: the splendid school at Stapleton was his gift, so were the almshouses on St. Michael's Hill, the charity school in Temple Street, and the merchants' almshouses in King Street. His statue stands in the centre of the gardens near the tramway centre and a hall in memory of him was opened in 1900 on the site once occupied by a Carmelite monastery. He died in 1721, in the days when the Hotwells was a fashionable resort that rivalled Bath in elegance and popularity.

Another man, or rather youth, whose fame is now world-wide, did much, although unconsciously, for Bristol, the ill-fated Thomas Chatterton, for it was his daring forgeries which first aroused in the town an interest in literature. He was born at Bristol in 1753, his family having been connected with the town for centuries, and was educated at Colston School, leaving at an early age to be apprenticed to a small solicitor. He relieved the tedious drudgery of the office by writing verse and dreaming of fame, but, fearing he would never obtain a hearing for his poems, he pretended they were the work of one Rowley, an imaginary chaplain of Canynges, and that his father had found them in the muniment-room of St. Mary, Redcliff, when he was sexton there. His statements were believed, and the successful publication of the poems tempting him to continue he produced the "Rise of Peynctynge in England," and had the audacity to send it to Horace Walpole. That astute authority was deceived for the time being, although he afterwards discovered his mistake, and Chatterton, full of hope, came to London. Three months' starvation, however, in an obscure lodging completely disillusioned him, and utterly despairing, he put an end to himself at the age of seventeen. His work shows traces of great genius, and but for his unnecessary and most unfortunate imposture, he might have lived to enjoy an honoured position in the world of letters. It was soon after his death that Hannah More, the poetess, began her literary career. Her work, unlike his, was greatly appreciated in her lifetime, but is seldom read in the present day. She helped her sisters to keep a select boarding-school in the town, and a public hall bearing her name now stands on the site of the house and garden in which they lived for many years. Robert Southey's is another and greater literary name connected with Bristol. He was the son of a linendraper in Wine Street, and went to school at the Fort on St. Michael's Hill. One of his greatest friends was Robert Lovell, the Quaker poet, son of a pin-maker on Castle Green, and the other was Coleridge, whom he first met in Bristol in 1794; all three were ardent Revolutionists, and their dream was to found a settlement in the New World where all should labour for the common good and live in peace and harmony. Fired with youthful enthusiasm they gave a series of lectures in the town, which were very popular, and brought them a publisher, a young man named Joseph Cottle, who issued from his shop the early poems of the three, which included Coleridge's "Ancient Mariner." They married the three daughters of a Bristol tradesman, and often returned to the town in later life.

The trade of Bristol began to decline a hundred years ago, largely owing to the keen competition of Liverpool, but Bristol men have set to work with a will, and there is every reason to believe that she has a future before her not unworthy of her past.

GUILDFORD

RISING from the banks of the gently gliding Wey in the heart of the North Downs, which, in sweeps of moorland, green pasturage, and wooded upland lie upstretched around, Guildford is one of the most picturesque of our county towns. Cobbett, writing of it in his "Rural Rides," in October, 1825, says: ". . . the town of Guildford, which (taken with its environs) I, who have seen so many many towns, think the prettiest, and taken all together, the most agreeable and happy-looking that I ever saw in my life." The most plausible explanation of its name is that an ancient trade guild ruled the place, and that there was a ford over the river at the foot of the High Street, and certainly the story of its guild, or Gild-merchant as it was called, is very closely interwoven with the history of the town.

The first mention of Guildford is in the will of Alfred the Great in A.D. 900, wherein he bequeathed it to his nephew Ethelwald; when Ethelwald died it reverted to the Crown, and continued to be Crown property and a place of royal residence until the time of the Tudors. From the reign of Ethelred II. to the reign of Henry I. it was the seat of a royal mint, the earliest coins bearing the name of Dunstan, evidently the famous Archbishop, who is known to have been a skilled worker in metals. In the Domesday Survey is the entry :—" In Guildeford King William possesses 75 tenements in which reside 175 men." These " tenements " were mostly down on the west side of the river, and there the wool and cloth trade began, later to become so important, but when the castle was built at the beginning of Henry II.'s reign, another part of the community grew up under the shelter of its walls on the east side. By the twelfth century the wool and cloth trades were in full swing. The reason Guildford was chosen to be a seat of these manufactures was, not only that the water of the river was particularly good for the fulling, but because in the neighbourhood were to be found three plants which were constantly used by the dyers : the fullers' teasle, the buckthorn and the woad, all of which still flourish here. The great day of the year was the Feast of St. Blaise, the patron of the town and of all woolcombers. On this day no work was done, High Mass was observed in St. Mary's, alms were given to the poor, the Gild-merchant met for the election of officers and for a banquet, bonfires blazed on all the hills, and early next morning the new officers made their communion together " at the Mass at the church nigh unto the river, where the fulling took place." The church referred to was the first of the four churches which have stood on the site of the present St. Nicholas. St. Mary's, which, though added to and restored, dates back to the eleventh century, is the oldest building in Guildford. By the time of Richard II. the cloth trade of Guildford had become so important that an Act of Parliament was passed concerning it, and the ancient Company known as the Merchants of the Staple, whose officers examined the various cloths of the country and made reports thereon, granted a certificate to the town in 1482, stating that they had no fault to find with the Guildford cloth-workers and that their cloth was " honest," and accordingly allowed their arms, a woolsack tied at the four corners, to be included in the arms of the town. Queen Elizabeth issued an order that every inn in Guildford was to have a sign with a woolsack painted upon it hung over the door on penalty of a fine of six and eightpence. She also bestowed upon the mayor as his staff of office a rod of the rare Campeachy wood, which was used to dye objects of special value and importance. In the seventeenth century the trade had begun to decline. This, according to Aubrey, was because of the clothiers' " fraudulent practice " and " avaricious method of stretching their cloth from 18 yds. to 22 or 23, which being discovered abroad they returned their commodity on their hands and it would sell in no market." Archbishop Abbot, the town's chief benefactor, whose father had been a Guildford clothier, took great interest in the trade and did his best to revive it. He gave £100 to be distributed in £5 portions to every man who would set up a loom in the town, and later he allotted certain rents, amounting to £100 a year, for the employment of young persons in some manufacture to be carried on in the town. He also required the brethren of his hospital to wear gowns of Guildford blue cloth when they attended Divine service. His efforts, however were of only temporary avail, and by 1755 the trade had entirely died out. Many of Guildford's chief benefactors had been clothiers or cloth manufacturers, and various memorials of the trade remain; the mill at the foot of the town is still called the Fulling Mill, there is a building in a passage in the High Street which has always gone by the name of the Manufactory, while the approach to the caverns near the castle is known as Rack Close because the large wooden racks were set up there on which the dyed cloths were placed out in the sun to dry.

The story of the birth of Archbishop Abbot, most distinguished of Guildford's sons, is an interesting one, as told by Aubrey:—" His father was a Cloathworker and he was born at the first house over the bridge in St. Nicholas parish (now, 1692, a public house known by the sign of the Three Mariners) and his mother when she was with child of him dreamt, that if she should eat a jack or pike the son in her womb would be a great man; upon this she was indefatigable to satisfy her longing as well as her dream; she first enquired out for the fish; but accidentally taking up some of the river water (that runs close by the house) in a pail she took up the much-desired banquet, dress'd it and devour'd it almost all. This odd affair made no small noise in the neighbourhood, and the curiosity of it made several people of quality offer themselves to be sponsors at the baptismal font when she was delivered; and three were chosen who maintained him at school, and at the university afterwards. This dream, etc., was attested to me by the Minister and several of the most sober inhabitants of the place." Abbot was educated at the

Free Grammar School, and at Balliol College, Oxford; in 1597 he was elected Master of University College; in 1609 he was created Bishop of Coventry and Lichfield, in 1610 Bishop of London, and in 1611 Archbishop of Canterbury. "He did first creep, then run, they fly into preferment, or rather, preferment did fly upon him without his expectation," wrote Fuller. His last years were saddened by an unfortunate accident: when deer-shooting at Bramshill he unwittingly killed a keeper who had twice been warned to keep out of the way; he was horribly distressed, pensioned the unfortunate man's widow and imposed upon himself several severe penances, but this was not the end of the matter. Certain bishops-elect who were jealous of him, among them Laud, who was afterwards to take his place, refused to receive consecration at his hands. A commission was therefore appointed to sit in judgment upon the matter and foreign Universities were invited to give their opinion; meantime he retired to Guildford and stayed in the hospital he had founded in the High Street, busying himself with its affairs. Eventually it was decided to go through the formality of giving him a free pardon, and as three of the bishops-elect still held back, they were consecrated by the Bishop of London. As to the fine hospital which is still the most important building in the High Street, he wrote in his preface to the statutes:—"My affection leading me to the town of Guildford where I was born, and where my aged parents lived many years with good report I thought upon the erection of an hospital there which I have dedicated to the blessed Trinity." The inmates were to be unmarried persons not less than sixty years of age, inhabitants of Guildford or resident there twenty years. It is nearly three hundred years since the foundation-stone was laid, but the institution still flourishes, the buildings are unchanged, the old furniture and fittings may be seen in all the rooms, and the inmates number twenty-two. The Archbishop's coat-of-arms—three golden pears—most beautifully painted, appear in many of the windows, frequently with the motto: "Clamamus Abba Pater,"—"We call Abbot our Father." In the chapel which faces the entrance in the extreme left corner of the quadrangle are two very beautiful stained glass windows, part of which—containing the stories of Isaac and his two sons—is believed to have been bought by the Archbishop from the chapel of the old friary, a very important Dominican establishment in the Middle Ages, now entirely vanished except for a memory in the names of Friary Street and Walnut Street Close, where the monks planted their walnut trees. In the room over the great entrance of Abbot's Hospital, the window of which looks into the quadrangle, the Duke of Monmouth was confined after the battle of Sedgemoor, on his way to London. A portrait of the Archbishop hangs in the board-room. On the same side of the High Street, a little farther down, is the town hall, first mentioned in the thirtieth year of Elizabeth's reign, when it was enlarged and the "Queen's armes and the armes of this towne sett in the windows at the north end." In 1683 the front was rebuilt. The fine clock has a history: John Aylward, a clockmaker, came to Guildford with the intention of setting up in business, but was forbidden by the Gild-merchant on the ground that he was a "foreigner," *i.e.*, not a native of Guildford. Not to be beaten he set up a workshop just outside the town, and made this clock, which he presented to the borough, to the admiration and delight of the townsfolk, who immediately granted him the freedom of the town. He settled in the High Street, in the premises now occupied by Mr. Perkins, and worked there at his trade for many years.

There are quite an unusual number of old houses in the High Street, some of which were probably built with stones from the castle as parts of it were removed. No. 25 has been called one of the most remarkable houses in England; it has a wonderful old staircase, elaborate plaster ceilings and marble mantelpieces, and can generally be seen on application by the courtesy of the owner. The Angel Inn has a fine old hall, surrounded by a gallery, and a clock dated 1658; underneath the Angel and the Savings Bank opposite are two thirteenth century crypts or vaults, which with the castle and St. Mary's are the only really mediæval buildings left in the town. They still contain traces of ancient frescoes and probably formed part of a monastery of White Friars which once stood here, the Angel Inn occupying the site of the ancient guest-house. In Spital Street is the Royal Free Grammar School, founded in 1507 by Robert Beckingham, a wealthy London grocer :—

"And benefactor principall
Or more was Beckingham :
For first in Guildford by his gift
The name of free-school came."

The original building was soon found to be too cramped, Edward VI. made a grant towards the expenses of a larger site, and the present schoolhouse was erected in 1557. Many distinguished men have been students in this school, including an Archbishop, six Bishops, a Speaker, two Lord Mayors of London, a great Greek scholar and a Colonial Premier. A treasured possession of the school is the chained library, containing eighty-nine books; there are only eight of these libraries in the kingdom. It is also notable as being the first place in connection with which cricket is mentioned—in Elizabeth's reign.

As for Guildford's churches, Holy Trinity contains the tomb of Archbishop Abbot, removed from an earlier building; St. Nicholas has the beautiful Losely chapel, which was for more than three centuries the burial-place of the More family; each time that the church was rebuilt it was carefully preserved and connected with the new building; it contains the finest collection of monuments in Guildford; St. Mary's has an Anglo-Saxon tower and a Norman nave and chancel, the latter used to be twelve feet longer; but in the days of George IV., when the Prince Regent used to drive down to Brighton through Guildford, the lane outside the church was so narrow that his carriage had great difficulty in passing, and in a fit of irritation one day he promised the townsfolk a handsome sum if they would widen the roadway; this they accordingly did, not by curtailing the county gaol opposite as they could easily have done, but by sacrificing a portion of St. Mary's chancel; in spite of their zeal no money was ever forthcoming from the Regent.

The castle has not had an eventful history; it was mostly used as a gaol, the royal residence being a palace in a park at the north of Guildford, built by Henry II., and long since vanished. It was taken by the Dauphin of France in John's reign when he invaded England at the request of the Barons. James I. granted it to Francis Carter, and passing from hand to hand it was eventually bought by the Corporation, and in 1886 laid out as a town pleasure ground. Near it are some chalk caverns, once evidently used as quarries; Henry II. converted them into a storehouse for wines from his vineyards in Gascony and Poitou, which he used to sell to the people, forbidding the consumption of any other wines until his stock was disposed of. The only occasion on which these caverns are mentioned in history is in 1688, when the women and children of Guildford hid in them, fearing a civil war when William of Orange landed in England.

Guildford has a daughter town in the U.S.A., Guilford in Connecticut; it came about as follows: in 1639 some forty traders left England for America, they were "Congregationalists and Puritans, driven from their native land because of their religion." Henry Whitfield was their leader, and when they settled in Connecticut they "called the place Guilford in remembrance of Guildford, a borough town, the capital of Surrey, where many of them had lived." Guilford contains the oldest house in U.S.A., built of stone as a fortification against the Indians, and in it Mr. Whitfield's family lived. It now belongs to the town, and is used as a museum in which the townsfolk place every object connected with their early history they can gather together. Whitfield was a great friend of the Rev. John Wilson, at that time Rector of St. Nicholas, to whom Dr. Cotton Mather alludes in one of his works as the great Guildford preacher from whose teachings he derived his religious beliefs.

LIVERPOOL

THIS great seaport, which is one of the largest in the world, and apparently a mere growth of modern times and centre of twentieth century commercial activity and progress, has its mediæval memories, although its antiquities may have been swept away by a practical and ruthless corporation. It is true it cannot boast, like Dover, of Roman remains, as vast forests covered its site in those ancient days, but as far back as the reign of Richard Cœur-de-Lion, when Chester harbour became too silted up for the approach of heavily laden vessels, men recognised the natural advantages of the small inlet in the estuary of the Mersey that went by the name of Lithepool, or Liverpool (Pool of the sea). Protection of course in those troubled times was essential, and it was not until they had built a castle at the top of what is now Lord Street that they began upon the town. It consisted at first of the four streets, Castle Street, Dale Street, Water Street and High Street, with a great cross, called the High Cross, to mark their meeting-place. To this budding township King John granted a charter which, written in a neat, clear hand on a small parchment, is still preserved among the muniments of the city, inviting such of his subjects as were able to settle therein, and promising them special privileges. The new port was useful for shipping troops and stores to and from the recently conquered Ireland, but beyond that the trade was small, as it was long before the days of manufactures or of commerce with distant lands, and after the three streets now known as Chapel Street, Tithebarn Street, and Old Hall Street had been added, the whole containing about a hundred and sixty-eight houses, the town remained just as it was for at least four centuries. But towns were small in the Middle Ages, and it was regarded as an important place even in the thirteenth century, as when the first Parliament was held in 1296 Liverpool furnished two members, paying their travelling expenses and wages for their services. Two places of worship sufficed until the beginning of the eighteenth century; indeed, one of these, St. Mary of the Quay, built in 1464, was turned into a Free Grammar School in Elizabeth's reign; the other, St. Nicholas, was built in 1356 on the same site as the present church.

The Wars of the Roses left their mark upon the little town, its trade fell off, its population decreased, and though the burgesses made every effort to stay the decline, it continued until Elizabeth came to the throne; then, in desperation, they sent their M.P. to her with a petition, describing their troubles and begging for aid, ending with the words: " Liverpool is your own town. Your Majesty hath a castle and two chauntries clear, the fee farms of the town, the ferry boat, two windmills, the custom of the duchy, the new custom of the tonnage and poundage which was never paid in Liverpool before your time, and the commodity thereof is your

Majesty's. For your own sake suffer us not utterly to be cast away in your Grace's time, but relieve us like a mother." The Queen straightway sent down Lord Derby, attended by numerous lords and gentlemen, to enquire into the matter, and the town regaled them "with a banquet of delicious delicates of two courses of service." The result was so satisfactory that on the anniversary of the Queen's accession the mayor caused "a great bonfire to be made in the market-place, and another anenst his own door, giving warning that every householder should do the like throughout the town, which was done accordingly. And immediately after caused to call together his brethren the aldermen and divers others of the burgesses, and so went all together to the house of Mr. Ralph Burscough, alderman, where they banqueted a certain time, which done Mr. Mayor departed to his own house accompanied of the said aldermen and others, a great number, upon whom he did bestow sack and other white wine and sugar liberally, standing all without the door, lauding and praising God for the most prosperous reign of our said most gracious sovereign lady the Queen's most excellent Majesty." Among her other bounties the Queen made a grant towards a Free School. Emboldened by her interest, the town made a final effort to throw off the yoke of Chester, which city had always been jealous of the Port of Liverpool, claiming it "as a mere creek within its jurisdiction," and of late had been particularly arrogant because it was backed by a powerful company of merchant adventurers to whom the Queen had recently granted a monopoly. The Mayor of Liverpool went up to London to declare that " Liverpoole hath ever heretofore been reputed and taken for the best port and harbour from Mylforthe to Scotland and so hath always been proved, with all manner of ships and barks, owners, masters and mariners." A long course of litigation followed, but the good burgesses of Liverpool stuck to their guns with indomitable perseverance and, eventually triumphing, shewed their appreciation of the decision in their favour by sending a hogshead of wine to " the right Worshipful the Master of the Rolls."

Grateful though they were to the Queen, the burgesses rebelled when her troops were quartered upon them for what they considered too long a period during the Irish wars. They were wont to stand upon their rights, but they did not disdain honest labour, for we are told that when an effort was made to mend the streets which were sadly in need of repair, the mayor " in his own proper person laboured himself." In Elizabeth's reign Liverpool was represented in Parliament by the most illustrious of her M.P.s, Lord Bacon. The largest of the ships which went out of the port at this time was forty tons, worked by twelve men, and the port only possessed twelve vessels; sometimes they went as far afield as Spain and Portugal, taking with them herrings and salmon, and bringing back iron and wine, and there is one mention of a cargo of Manchester small cottons, showing that the Lancashire manufactures were beginning.

With the dawn of the seventeenth century were visible the first stirrings of the new life that was to make Liverpool one of the first ports in the world.

Woollen manufacture started in the West Riding, and the Manchester merchants began to buy yarn from Ireland, and to return thither the manufactured article, all the trade, of course, passing through Liverpool. In 1628 Charles I. sold the Crown rights in the town and lordship of Liverpool to Lord Molyneux, in whose family the constableship of the castle had been hereditary for many generations; he laid out Lord Street, originally Lord Molyneux Street, built a bridge over the Pool brook, for which he paid a rent of 2d. a year, and made a road (now Church Street), across the Common; he then handed the lordship with all dues and customs over to the Corporation on a lease of one thousand years for the rent of £30; an agreement his descendants must have bitterly regretted, as the dues and customs thus valued in 1672 produced in 1886 a revenue of £260,698, and of course in the present day are worth far more.

Richard Mather, a minister at the old chapel, Toxteth Park, was one of the early upholders of the Protestant faith, and being in consequence silenced by the Bishop, escaped in disguise to Liverpool, and from thence took ship to New England, where he became very popular and distinguished; Cotton Mather, the famous historian of New England, was his grandson. In those days the Corporation of Liverpool took the greatest interest in all matters connected with the church; they appointed the minister, paid his "wages," and kept a careful eye on all his doings. He had to "weare the srplus ev'y Sabothe, and ev'y holiday at the tyme of Dyvine Service," and "cause his haier to be cut of a comly and seemely length in such decent manner as best befitteth a man in his place." Besides his wages and his house he was allowed "a reasonable milk cowe whilst he remaineth a preaching minister here and shall have allowed yerely for her keepinge ov' his twenty pounds wages the sum of 46s. 6d., but if the said Mr. Lappage shall hereafter publicly murmer or sue for more allowance, then this order to be void." When in 1622 the first public clock was placed in the "Chappel of Liv'poole, to the great benefitte and pleasure of the inhabitants" . . . the minister promised that he would "well and duly dureinge the tyme of his ministrie at Liv'poole keep and sett the said clock. And if he shall neglect the doeinge of the same, that then he is willinge that forth of his wayges from the towne of Liv'poole soe much money shall be abated and defalked as the tendinge and keepinge of the said clocke shall lye in." When the Commonwealth was instituted and Cromwell issued an order requiring all ministers in the presence of their congregations to subscribe to an engagement, to be "true and faithful to the government established without king or House of Peers," the Liverpool minister was one of the many who refused, and was in consequence ejected from his position. However, he afterwards repented, and on promising to "subscrybe to the Ingudgment," was reinstated.

The town suffered several sieges during the Civil War, and being "in a great p't destroyed and burnt downe by the Enemie," Parliament issued an order that "500 tons of Tymber be allowed unto the Towne of Liverpoole," for its rebuilding, and

" that the said 500 tons be felled in the grounds and woods" of certain Royalist lords. A decree also went forth that the Castle was to be dismantled, the Corporation becoming tenants under the Crown. The streets were now lighted for the first time, it being ordered that " Two Lanthorns with twoe candles, burneing ev'ie night in ye dark moone be sett out at the High Crosse, and at Whyte Crosse, and places p'pared to sett them in ev'ie night till past eight of the clock by ye Srjant and Water Ballive. This to be obs'ved from All Saints to Candlemas." The Civil War, of course, had checked the progress of the town, but at the Restoration, when the affairs of the kingdom had settled down into their normal course, a steady tide of progress set in which has gone on increasing right up to the present day; the discovery of new lands extended the commerce of the port all over the world; the names of its merchants became famous, and the town itself began to expand in all directions. Hitherto its limits had been marked by the Pool Stream, which ran along what are now Byrom, Whitechapel, and Paradise Streets, and was crossed by three bridges; the streets were only seven or eight yards wide, without footpaths, and having a gutter running down the centre; the roads leading out of Liverpool, even the highway to London, had simply a strip of paving in the middle for packhorses, but were impassable for carriages up to the middle of the eighteenth century. The houses were small and mean, of wood or brick, and with thatched roofs. The water of the town was obtained from the old Fall Well, which stood on the Great Heath, near the corner of what are now St. John's Lane and Roe Street, and it had to be ordered that " Noe Manner of p'son shall wash either yarne or woole there upon paine of three shillings and four pence for ev'y offence." The Great Heath extended from what is now Whitechapel to the present Crown Street, and was used for public meetings, demonstrations, and the practice of archery. The two hills now occupied by St. James's Cemetery and University College were used as stone quarries. In 1660 the common lands which extended between what are now Hanover Street, Park Lane, and Wapping were " taken inn, and inclosed, at the town's charge, and mannaged for ye best use and benefitt of ye towne." In 1673 the High Cross was pulled down to make way for the first Town-hall and Exchange, " a handsome building . . . the same sett upon pillars and forthwith sett out as Mr. Maior shall think meete." This site is now occupied by the Liverpool and London Insurance Offices. As the commerce of Liverpool went on increasing, the harbourage in the Pool was found insufficient, and an act of Parliament was obtained authorising the Town Council to borrow £6,000, construct a dock and levy dock dues on all ships entering the harbour, and thus came into being what was afterwards known as the Old Dock, the beginning of the largest system of floating docks in the world. The architect whose idea it was, settled in Liverpool and had a long and prosperous career; he was appointed Harbour Master, chosen architect for St. George's Church, and finally elected Mayor, when he built himself a handsome mansion in Hanover Street. This dock was soon found to be too small, and extended. At the beginning of the eighteenth century Union Street and Fazakerley Street were made; the stream which fed the old Pool was arched over and Paradise Street and Whitechapel formed; forty-five lamps were ordered for the lighting of the town; the ruins of the castle were removed, and fine mansions began to appear in various parts of the town, particularly in Hanover and Paradise Streets. The most imposing building of the time was the Exchange, now the Town-hall, which was completed about 1760. By the middle of the century five large churches had been built. In 1796 the title of Earl of Liverpool was conferred upon Lord Hawkesbury, subsequently Prime Minister, and very proud the good burgesses were to see the name of Liverpool in the peerage.

There were two blots on the fair name of Liverpool in the nineteenth century, privateering and the slave trade; for the former there was excuse, as the trade of the city suffered so severely during the seven years' war between France and Spain, the War of American Independence, and again when war with France broke out, that little legitimate business could be done, and other countries having set the example Liverpool did but follow suit. Indeed, when in 1793 war was declared with France the commerce of Liverpool was so seriously affected that a general panic set in, numerous mercantile houses of the highest standing were ruined, and a run on the banks took place. After considerable discussion among the merchants, chief of whom were John Gladstone and William Rathbone, it was resolved to apply to the Bank of England for a loan and to Parliament for permission to issue certain notes to the value of £300,000 for three years, a wise and public-spirited measure that saved the commerce of the city. As for the slave trade, by the middle of the century the majority of the Council were engaged in it, and in 1771 105 slave ships sailed from Liverpool to the West Indies, carrying 28,200 slaves. William Roscoe, attorney, of Liverpool, published a pamphlet, demonstrating its inhumanity and bad policy and urging its abolition, but the Council strenuously opposed him and paid the Rev. Raymond Harris £100 to write a reply; they also despatched various petitions and delegates to London; in fact, so deeply were they involved that when slavery was actually abolished it was three years before the town made good its losses. Despite these commercial crises, however, many canals were constructed towards the end of the eighteenth century; the opening of trade with India, and the application of steam power to locomotion gave a fresh impetus to progress; in 1817 the first steamer appeared on the Mersey, and in 1830 crossed the Atlantic; in 1830 the Liverpool and Manchester Railway was opened.

Wonderful is the change the last century has wrought; seven miles of docks now confront the traveller, and every day sees the arrival or departure from the Prince's Landing-stage of some of the finest steamers in the world. The streets have been widened, and when the traveller leaves the railway terminus in Lime Street he sees before him a magnificent series of buildings, such as few towns can show: St. George's Hall, the Walker Art Gallery, the Picton Reading Room, the William Brown Free Library and Museum, the County Sessions Court and the Technical Instruction Centre. Then in Water Street and Chapel Street are the Town Hall and Exchange, in the latter, of course, being concentrated the vast commercial life of Liverpool.

Of the great Liverpool families I may mention a few: the Moores, who first appeared in the thirteenth century, and lived in the Old Hall, Oldhall Street, and afterwards in the Bank Hall, Kirkdale; Edward Moore, the author of the "Rental" was created baronet in 1675. The Stanleys were the ancestors of the present Earls of Derby; they lived in the Tower in Water Street, which was pulled down in 1819; during the eighteenth century the chair of chief magistrate was filled nine times either by the Earl of Derby or a member of the family. The Bootle family were the ancestors of the Earls of Lathom; Thomas Bootle, K.C., was M.P. for Liverpool from 1727 to 1735, Mayor in 1726, knighted in 1743, he then purchased the Lathom estates and built the present mansion. Other names still remain which have been prominent in the mercantile world for two centuries, *e.g.*, Clayton and Cleveland, after whom the squares are named. John Gladstone's is a name much honoured; in 1798 he built a house on the west side of Rodney Street, in which on the 29th December his famous son, the Rt. Hon. W. E. Gladstone, was born. In 1829 he moved a resolution for the opening of China trade, and in 1829 for the removal of restrictions on India trade, both of which were successfully carried.

In 1880 Liverpool was created both a city and a bishopric; St. Peter's in Church Street was chosen as the Pro-Cathedral, but there is now rising on St. James' Mount, a splendid cathedral which when completed will be worthy of the great city in which it stands; the exquisite Lady chapel is already finished and open for worship.

EXETER

EXETER, the city on the Exe, is the capital not only of lovely, leafy Devon, but in reality of the whole of the West Country. It is set on a hill in the green valley of the Exe, with the river flowing at its feet, and all around the softly wooded heights of other hills. West Country folk love it with a love that neither time nor distance can alter ; it was enshrined in their hearts before the making of history, for it is the oldest city in Britain, and, in the words of Professor Freeman, " It is the one great English city which has, in a more marked way than any other, kept its unbroken being and its unbroken position throughout all ages." Before Christ was born it was " a city walled and suburb to the same, of the most reputation, worship, defence and defensible of all these parties." The earthworks on the Castle Hill were made by the ancient Britons ; the thousands of Roman coins dating back to Nero and Claudius, the pottery and other relics that have been dug up within its walls prove the city to have been the Isca Damnoniorum of the Romans ; and its importance as the key to the West Country may be gathered from the fact recorded in the quaint old chronicles of Izaacke :—

> " In midst of Devon, Exeter city, seated
> Hath with ten sieges grievously been straitned."

The first of these sieges was in A.D. 634. It was twice besieged by the Danes in the reign of Alfred the Great, and he came anxiously to its assistance. An earthwork north of the city, dating from this period, is still known as Danes' Castle. Athelstan surrounded it with walls and towers and bestowed upon it in 926 the monastery of St. Peter, the minster church of which was the beginning of its great cathedral, and is said to have stood on the site of the present Lady chapel. In Ethelred's reign the Danes made two more attempts to take the city; on the second occasion, led by Sweyn, they succeeded, and in revenge for the brave resistance of the towns-folk they pillaged and burned it to the ground. Not long after, however, Canute, the Christian Dane, rebuilt the minster church, and it was the scene of a grand and imposing festival in the reign of Edward the Confessor. When transformed into the cathedral of the new see of Devon and Cornwall, it received Leofric, the King's Chancellor, as its first Bishop. There he stood before the high altar, robed in splendid vestments, in full view of the assembled multitude, the King holding his right hand and the Queen his left, while the two Archbishops invoked "blessings upon all who might increase the See," and a "fearful and execrable curse upon all who should diminish or take aught therefrom." Leofric was a good and great Bishop, reverenced even by the Normans, and he was left undisturbed in his diocese until his death in 1072. Meanwhile there had been stirring doings in the city, for Exeter held out long and valiantly against the Conqueror, and two years after the battle of

EXETER. The Corner of Frog Street.

Hastings was still unsubdued. At last the new King came in person to demand submission, but he found the gates fast barred, and all the answer made by the townsfolk to his threatenings was, "We will neither take any oath to the King, nor allow him to enter our city, but the tribute which, following ancient custom, we were wont to give formerly, the same we will give to him." In great anger William caused a hostage to be brought forth, and his eyes put out in view of those upon the walls, but they remained obdurate. Then he brought to bear upon the town all his great military skill and many devices quite unknown to the Devonians; for eighteen days they held out, and then when, already weak with hunger, they beheld their walls crumbling around them, they bowed their proud heads, and came forth to beg for mercy. William, whose policy was mercy to the conquered, received them graciously, and suffered them to return to their homes in full security, but he took the precaution to replace the Saxon buildings upon the Red Mount with a strong Norman castle, and to man it with a sufficient garrison to keep the town in check.

Neither Leofric nor the Norman bishops who succeeded him touched the Saxon fabric of the cathedral, but with William of Warelwast, in Rufus's time, the rebuilding began which was to continue for four centuries, and to transform the simple minster, in the words of Mr. Bumpus, into "one of the finest examples of symmetrical decorated Gothic in existence." Warelwast's two vast towers still stand, serving as transepts, and distinguishing Exeter Cathedral from every other church in the kingdom. Nearly every bishop who followed him added something towards its perfecting, many expending vast sums and infinite pains upon it. Bishop Marshall added the Lady chapel, Bruere, in the first half of the thirteenth century, built the chapter house and carved the beautiful misereres—the earliest now existing in this country ; Grandisson completed the nave, Brantyngham the wonderful west front with its niched statues of prophets, apostles, martyrs, saints and kings. These have survived the effects of weather and west country superstition remarkably well, considering that even now some of the country folk will surreptitiously chip off a fragment to pound into a " Peter plaster " for a sore that will not heal. The choir screen and the splendid episcopal throne, with its great carved canopy, were the work of Bishop Stapleton, founder of Exeter College, Oxford. These are only a few out of the many who embellished the ancient fane, and by 1320 it was completed much as we see it now. Many of these early Bishops of Exeter were men of great note : two were Lord High Chancellors, two Lord High Treasurers, one Lord High Privy Seal, three were founders of colleges at Oxford and Cambridge, and one helped in the translation of the Bible.

One of the chief beauties of Exeter Cathedral is the tracery of its windows, no two of which are alike, and another is its pillars. The vaulting has been declared to represent " the high-water mark of English vaulting." In the nave is the picturesque minstrels' gallery, from which singers and players were wont to greet with sweet music the entry of any members of the royal family, as when the Black Prince, passing through Exeter on his way to London, visited the Cathedral with his captives, the French King and the Dauphin; and in this gallery the seven best boys were stationed to sing, "All glory, laud and honour," during the procession on Palm Sunday. The beautiful pulpit in the nave was designed by Sir Gilbert Scott in memory of Bishop Patteson, of Melanesia, who was killed by savages on a South Pacific island twenty-two years after his ordination as deacon in Exeter Cathedral; one of the three principal compartments represents the dead body of the bishop, wrapped in palm leaves, being borne to a canoe.

To go back to the history of the town. When Matilda strove to wrest the throne of England from Stephen, it was in Exeter she centred her hopes. Baldwin, the Governor, was her strong partisan, and cared so little for the city which had been entrusted to his charge that, failing to move the townsfolk from their loyalty, he began to burn and destroy; but a relieving force from Stephen quickly put a stop to such proceedings, and Baldwin and his men were forced to take refuge in the castle, which they held for three months, thirst ultimately driving them to surrender, and thus ended all hope for Matilda in the west.

Edward I. and his Queen spent a Christmas at Exeter, on which occasion the Bishop and Chapter were granted the right to enclose the ecclesiastical precincts with a wall. During the same visit the King interested himself in a change in the city's ground-plan. The principal thoroughfares no longer conformed to those of the Romans, the present High Street being formed, and the older streets becoming of secondary importance. Eleven years later Edward was again in the city. In consequence of these visits a strange story was circulated many years afterwards by the son of a tanner in the town, who claimed the crown on the plea that he was the true son of King Edward and Queen Eleanor, having been changed at birth with the present holder of the throne. His tale received no credit, and he was promptly hanged, after a confession had been extorted from him that it was all a falsehood, his excuse being that a familiar spirit who attended him in the shape of a cat had put it into his head.

In the Wars of the Roses the town remained staunch to the Lancastrians; Henry VI. was entertained for a week "with the best the church and city could afford, clergy and citizens sharing the cost"; and for twelve months the town sustained a siege before it finally surrendered to the Yorkists.

Exeter played a large part in the conspiracy of Perkin Warbeck; he marched for it immediately after landing in Cornwall, but his undisciplined mob of followers were no match for the armed and sturdy townsfolk, and were driven off before they effected any mischief beyond setting fire to the gates. Exeter, however, had not seen the last of them, but next time they came as captives, and were conducted into the presence of the King in the Cathedral Close, "bareheaded, in their shirts, with halters about their necks"; the King, happening to be in a forgiving mood, "graciously pardoned them, choosing rather to wash his hands in milk by forgiving than in blood by destroying them."

Richard III. visited Exeter for the purpose of chastising certain rebels, and when this had been accomplished he gave his attention to the town. The Castle met with his entire approval until he heard its name, Rougemont, also pronounced Richmond, whereupon he was, in the words of an ancient chronicler, "suddenly fallen into a great dump and as it were a man amazed," for, as Shakespeare makes him say—

> "Richmond! when I was last at Exeter
> The Mayor in courtesy showed me the castle
> And called it Rougemont—at which name I started;
> Because a bard of Ireland told me once
> I should not live long after I saw Richmond."

Nor did he long survive.

In the time of the Western Rebellion, soon after the Reformation, when the men of the West Country uprose in violent protest against the compulsory substitution of the Prayer Book service for their beloved mass, Exeter was the stronghold they immediately tried to secure. Ten thousand rebels marched upon the town and called upon it to surrender. Among them was Welch, the vicar of Saint Thomas by Exeter, who was "in this rebellion an arch-captain and a principal doer." He was evidently a formidable fighter, for we are told: "He was a very good wrestler, shot well both in the long bow and also in the cross bow; he handled his hand gun and piece very well; he was a very good woodman and a hardy, and such a one as would not give his head for the polling, nor his beard for the washing. . . ." But the men of Exeter kept their gates shut and stood firm, and the siege began. After a few weeks their supply of food became so low that the "bakers and householders were driven to seek up their old store of puffins and bran, wherewith they in times past were wont to make horsebread and to feed their swine and poultry; and this they moulded up in cloths, for otherwise it would not hold together, and so did bake it up, and the people were well contented therewith . . . In the end, for want they were fed on horseflesh, which they liked, and were well contented withal." But they were at length delivered by Lord John Russell with an armed force, and so great was their relief and thankfulness that it was determined the anniversary of the day "in memorial for ever to endure was (to be) kept for a high and holy feast." Most of the ringleaders of the rising were sent to London for trial and execution, but the vicar of St. Thomas was hanged in full canonicals on his own church.

The staple industry of Exeter in ancient days was the manufacture of a famous woollen cloth, merchants coming from every part of England to traffic in it. Their meeting-place was in a finely plastered chamber, still in existence, in what was once the "New Inn," and is now a draper's shop, in the High Street, and while they deliberated in the stately chamber above, the courtyard beneath was alive with the bustle of the continual coming and going of the carriers, who brought in the cloth not only from the neighbouring towns and villages, but also from the lonely farmsteads and cottages on the moors where it had been woven by the peasants during the long winter evenings. The trade was greatly developed by the "Society of Marchantes Adventurers of the Citie of Excestre, trafiquing the Realms of Fraunce and the Dominions of the French King," to whom Elizabeth granted a charter; it grew to such an extent that goods to the value of half a million were sent every year to Spain, Portugal, Italy, Germany and Holland, and to facilitate their export the Exeter Canal was constructed, thus enabling vessels to come right up to the city quays. It was one of the first canals to be opened in the kingdom, and so eager were all the members of the community for its completion that even the parish churches contributed a quantity of plate towards the expense. As years went by the merchant adventurers extended their trading overseas, to the Indies, the New World, they went with Adrian Gilbert to discover China, and helped Sir Humphrey Gilbert on his last expedition. These merchants were widely travelled men, versed in the speech of many lands; their "Society" reached the zenith of its prosperity in the reign of James I., but the Civil War of his son's reign checked all enterprise for many a year. When the war first began the Roundheads took possession of the town, but it was easily wrested from them by the Cavaliers, with whom the townsfolk were in sympathy, and it was then looked upon as one of the chief Cavalier strongholds in the kingdom.

Charles I. took up his abode for some time at Bedford House together with his queen, and it was there that on the 16th June, 1644, Princess Henrietta

Anne was born; on the 3rd July she was baptized in the cathedral at the font which stands in the bay at the south side of the nave, and was used for the purpose for the first time. The princess's portrait by Sir Peter Lely hangs in the Guildhall, having been presented to the city by Charles II. at his Restoration in recognition of its kindness to his sister. The days of the Commonwealth were sad ones for Exeter Cathedral; the Roundheads, in the course of their usual work of destruction, "brake down the organs and taking two or three hundred pipes with them, in a most scornefull, contemptuous manner, went up and downe the streets piping with them; and meeting with some of the choristers of the church, whose surplices they had stolne before and imployed them to base servile offices, scoffingly told them, 'Boyes, we have spoyled your trade, you must goe and synge, "hot pudding pyes."'" The present organ was put up at the Restoration, when every church was busy repairing the damage wrought, but it has since been rebuilt. No city in the west welcomed Charles II. more eagerly than Exeter, but its loyalty met with scant reward, and as time went on its feeling changed, so that when William of Orange came into Exeter four days after his landing at Brixham, he was heartily welcomed by a cheering multitude, in spite of the torrents of rain that poured down upon them; the Bishop and the Dean alone refused to acknowledge the usurper, and left the town. The Prince thereupon took up his residence in the deanery. An immense crowd gathered in the cathedral to listen to the Te Deum sung in celebration of his arrival in England, while he took his seat upon the bishop's throne. Then the Declaration was read, which set forth the reasons for his invasion; at the first words all the clergy left the building, but the crowd which remained endorsed it with a loud "Amen." William stayed some time in Exeter and received recruits from all parts of the country, and when he left the town his success was practically assured. This was the last great historical event which took place in Exeter.

Though much that was old in the town has, of course, been swept away, there still remain some fine old timbered houses with elaborately carved gables, among them the Guildhall, dating from 1466, the front alone being late Elizabethan; it has a fine projecting porch. Many parts of the town walls still remain, but all the gates have gone.

To mention three out of Exeter's many famous sons: Archbishop Langton, framer of the Magna Charta; Sir Thomas Bodley, born here in 1544; and Matthew Baring, who in 1717 came to Exeter to learn the serge manufacture, and marrying the daughter of a rich grocer, was enabled to set up a factory, which was the beginning of the great mercantile fortunes of his family.

NEWCASTLE

WHEN any one wishes to express the superfluity of a gift, he says, "Why, it's like carrying coals to Newcastle," and indeed Newcastle is so much identified nowadays with coal that its name calls up a vision of mines and collieries and the town's romantic past is in danger of being forgotten. Modern Newcastle with its tall grimy houses, pall of smoke and rough mining population, does not date back more than a century and a half, having come into being with the development of the coal fields in the south-east corner of Northumberland; but old Newcastle, a fortress on the Border, that historic fighting ground of Englishman and Scot, has a history that goes back to the days of the ancient Britons.

In prehistoric times, possibly three or four centuries B.C., a series of ditches and mounds, of which a considerable number is still intact and known as the Four Dykes, stretched from the Tyne to the Solway, and formed the boundary line between Britain and Caledonia. When the Romans came they strengthened this boundary by building to the north of it a stone wall, eight feet wide and sixteen feet high, with forts at every mile, and extending between what are now Wallsend and Bowness. One of these forts, called the Pons Aelius, from the bridge across the Tyne which it commanded, was the first

NEWCASTLE. The Interior of the Cathedral.

beginning of the ancient town of Newcastle. A stone slab, broken in half, which was found in the old church at Jarrow, records that "troops stationed in the province of Britain in forts between the two shores of ocean, were commended by Hadrian for having under circumstances that tried the faith and loyalty of all, preserved intact the boundaries of the Republic, being only restrained by dire necessity from subduing the furthermost limits of the known world." In early days, therefore, Newcastle stood on the Border line, in the thick of the never-ending frays between English and Scots, but up to the time of the Conquest it was merely a fort, and sometimes a neglected one, for neither Britons, Saxons nor Danes, as in turn they occupied the country, were capable of the systematic defence practised by the Romans, although gradually they pushed the boundary line a little to the north.

A sturdy, independent race the men of bleak Northumberland were in those days, impatient of control, lovers of a fair fight, haters of shams and double-dealing, swift to avenge a wrong fancied or real, and loyal, chivalrous, even romantic to the core, characteristics which time has hardly obliterated. They were among the first to obey the call of Christianity, and the abbey church on the Isle of Lindisfarne, that retreat of St. Aidan and St. Cuthbert, was for many years the most venerated shrine in Britain, the mother-church of more than half England and Germany. They were always the last to submit to any usurper, and William the Conqueror, in his efforts to subdue them, laid waste the country from the Humber to the Tweed, turning it into a desert in which for nine years no attempt at cultivation was made.

It was William's son, Robert, who made a later campaign famous by building the New Castle upon the site of the old Pons Aelius, his practised eye having at once perceived the advantages of its position. Round the castle a town quickly grew up, which soon came to be regarded as one of the chief Border strongholds, and consequently of particular value to the English kings. William Rufus enclosed it with walls, strengthened the castle, and provided a permanent garrison in the shape of twelve Barons with their retainers, whose services he rewarded with the grant of certain lands. The old church, dedicated to St. Nicholas, patron saint of those "who go down to the sea in ships, and occupy their business in great waters," was built in his reign, and became the chief sanctuary for Border fugitives; it was entirely rebuilt in the fourteenth century, and the only remnant of the ancient fabric that has come to light is a shaft and capital.

Henry II. built the square keep to the castle as a further measure for defence, but he managed throughout his reign to maintain friendly relations with the Scots, and, in consequence, Northumberland prospered until "right down to the Pyrenees there was no country so well provided with the necessaries of life, nor inhabited by a race more universally respected." In the early part of Stephen's reign, David of Scotland, following the invariable custom of the Scotch kings when trouble in England or war abroad drew off the troops, advanced over the Border, and forced the harassed King to create his son Earl of Northumberland. Stephen tried hard to retain Newcastle, but David promptly took possession of the town. He made no attempt, however, to curb the independent spirit of the burghers, but admiring their method of government, caused it to be adopted in the various burghs he founded north of the Tweed, and thus Newcastle came to be regarded as the civic authority for Scotland. With the death of the Scotch prince Northumberland again lapsed to England.

Richard Cœur-de-Lion, when in urgent need of money for the Crusades, tried to sell Northumberland, but the negotiations fell through because he would not part with Newcastle. Henry III. built the Black Gate as main entrance to the castle, and the ruin in Heaton Park is a remnant of one of the great battlemented houses he encouraged his northern nobles to build for the protection of the Border.

During the reigns of the first three Edwards there was a continuous series of Scotch wars; for years Northumberland lay waste, no one daring to live outside the walls of town or castle, and when Richard II. came to the throne the famous feud between Percies and Douglases, celebrated by Border minstrels in the ballads of "Chevy Chace" and the "Battle of Otterburn," was at its height. One encounter took place before the gates of Newcastle, young Henry Percy, surnamed Hotspur, the Earl of Northumberland's impetuous heir, meeting the Earl of Douglas in single combat, amidst the Scots who were besieging the town. Douglas was the victor, and as he triumphantly bore away the gauntlets, embroidered in pearls with the arms of the Percies, which Hotspur had carried as a pennon at his lance point, he shouted: "This much of your finery, Henry, I will carry back with me to Scotland, and set on the highest point of my castle at Dalkeith, that it may be seen the farther." "Par Dieu, Earl of Douglas," the undaunted Hotspur replied, "Never shall you carry it out of Northumberland, be sure of that." True words, for before the Scots had crossed the Border the English were upon them, and in the bloody battle of Otterburn which followed the Douglas lost his life.

In the Wars of the Roses the men of Northumberland were faithful to the unfortunate Henry VI. to the very end, affording him and his Queen and the little Prince their last refuge on English soil.

When all the country had turned Protestant the Northumbrians still clung to their old faith, and despite the persecution their steadfastness brought upon them, flaunted it openly in the sight of men. At the death of one well-known Roman Catholic, who had built a house dedicated to Saint Anthony on the banks of the river and called every room in it after some saint, her remains were brought on a barge into Newcastle at night, the streets illuminated so brightly that "it was as light as if it had been noon," and magistrates and aldermen assembled on the landing-stage to meet the coffin and convey it in solemn procession to the church. Even when Elizabeth had reigned several years, there were, it is said, not three Protestant gentlemen to be found in the whole of the East Marches, and the Northumbrians' love for their ancient belief, coupled

with the chivalry aroused in their breasts by the beauty and sorrows of Mary Queen of Scots, impelled them to make an attempt to free her from Bolton Castle and place her on the English throne; but the rising ended in disaster, disgrace and death were the portion of the Earl of Northumberland, and Mary was removed to a safer prison in the South. This was the beginning of the whole-souled devotion to the Stuarts which characterised the Northumbrians, many of whom willingly sacrificed everything in their cause, and reverenced their memory long after the rest of the country had practically forgotten them. Chief and most unfortunate among these staunch adherents were the Radcliffes, Earls of Derwentwater, who remained faithful to the end, losing their lives and the whole of their estates, the last young earl dying a hero's death on Tower Hill. Mary's son, when he entered Newcastle as the first King of Great Britain, was received with such enthusiastic joy that he is said to have remarked :—
"By ma saul, they are enough to spoil a gude king." Charles I., when discontent was stirring in the country, and he was obliged to proceed against the rebellious Scots with an army, was "magnificently entertained at Newcastle, and the town seemed unanimous for him," in spite of the fact that Parliament had forbidden any to trade with it, an injunction which had speedily to be revoked, as lack of coal caused distress all over the country. Twice in the following year Newcastle was besieged by the Roundheads. On the first occasion, when the mayor, Sir John Marley, and his councillors were called upon to surrender the town, they made answer that

they would not " betray the trust reposed in them, or forfeit their allegiance to his Majesty for whose honour and preservation, together with the Religion and Lawes of the Kingdome, they intended to hazard their Lives and Fortunes." On the second occasion Sir John Marley, with a garrison of 1600 men, half of whom were volunteers, having strengthened the fortifications with the utmost care and ingenuity, proceeded to conduct the defence with extraordinary spirit. The enemy encamped round the town in such fashion that no provisions could be received by the besieged from the outside, and proceeded to direct their batteries upon it. The upper stage of the Carpenter's Tower was first to go, then part of the wall near St. Andrew's Church was " brashed down " and a breach made through which ten men might have entered abreast had it not at once been filled up with timber and rubbish. St. Andrew's Church suffered considerably, and the beautiful spire of St. Nicholas would certainly have been demolished if the burghers had not discreetly placed their captives in the lantern. A sharp look-out was kept for the mines which the enemy persistently laid beneath the walls, and all one night the church-bells rang to celebrate the discovery and destruction of three large ones. The siege dragged on until Marley sent a messenger to enquire politely if the Scotch general were dead, as he had not been seen for some days, and the angry Scots determined to storm the town. Their preparations were rather lengthy and were watched derisively from the ramparts by the besieged, who repeatedly urged them to come on. All being at length in readiness the batteries commenced their deadly work and four great breaches were made in the walls, but so furious was the fire kept up by Marley and his garrison that it was two hours before the Scots managed to effect an entry, and three times they were driven forth again. The defenders of Pilgrim Street gate did not give in until they were attacked in the rear, and Sir John Marley with a small but resolute following retreated to the castle, which they held for yet another three days. Then the sack of the town began and lasted for a never-to-be-forgotten day and night. At the Restoration, in memory of this gallant resistance, Newcastle adopted as her motto the words, "Fortiter Defendendo Triumphat" (she glories in her brave defence), afterwards altered to "Fortiter Defendit Triumphans." Two years after the siege Charles I. was brought a prisoner to Newcastle and lodged at Anderson Place. With the aid of friends he managed to escape in disguise, but was discovered and brought back, and his one recreation, that of playing golf on the Shieldfield, was stopped. That he had many sympathisers in the town is evident from the fact that on one occasion when he was attending Divine service in St. Nicholas', and a Scotch minister pointedly gave out the fifty-second Psalm: "Why dost thou, tyrant, boast thyself, Thy wicked works to praise," the congregation, at the King's instigation sang instead the fifty-sixth:—"Have mercy, Lord, on me, I pray, For men would me devour." At length the Scotch, having sold him to the English Parliament, evacuated the town and returned home. Long after the Stuarts had for the second time been driven from the kingdom the North remained secretly faithful and in every Jacobite rising Newcastle men played a part. As late as 1750, five years after the battle of Culloden had extinguished the last hopes of the ill-fated family, the keelmen, going out on strike, proclaimed Charles Edward king, in Elswick fields; and the northern squires for years and years had a rose and an oak-leaf engraved on their Venetian wineglasses so that they might drink to the King " over the water " and " under the rose." With the failure of the last Jacobite conspiracy Border warfare came to an end. Northumberland was no longer a fighting ground and Newcastle became a quiet country town. Then came the great development of the coal-mines, and a rush into the town on the part of the rural population, and Newcastle grew and grew until it merged into Gateshead and stretched down to the mouth of the Tyne, a dense mass of houses. They rise up, tier above tier, on the hill crowned by the beautiful spire, upborne on flying buttresses, of what is now the cathedral church of St. Nicholas; that spire which is " justly the pride of the inhabitants," the only ancient landmark left untouched by the hands of the ruthless utilitarians of the eighteenth century. These zealots, in the first rush of modern progress, forgot the historic past and set about re-modelling the town in such reckless fashion as to give rise to the following satire:

> " Their foolish pride there's none to stop,
> Improvement's all the go;
> Unseemly's everything that's old
> So all that's old's laid low."

They carried the East Coast railway right through

the castle, and after advertising the ancient Norman keep as suitable for a mill, and failing to dispose of it, conceived the ingenious idea of utilising it as a signal box, and were proceeding to carry out the necessary alterations when the Society of Antiquaries fortunately stepped in and took it off their hands. The Society also rescued the Black Gate, and after judicious restoration, placed therein the splendid collection of Roman altars and other "treasures of the wall," which had long been lost to sight in the dungeons of the castle. The utilitarians meantime were busy, pulling down the great town wall along the quay, destroying the monuments in St. Nicholas, demolishing All Saints, one of the most interesting of the old churches, depriving the Guildhall of its ancient features, and removing the gates of the town. But amidst the work of devastation an improved Newcastle has gradually grown up, with many modern buildings and thoroughfares of which it may well be proud. To cite one or two: Grey Street is one of the "finest streets in the kingdom," the markets are of unusually excellent design, and the portico of the Central Station an admirable piece of architecture.

ST. ALBANS

THE neighbourhood of St. Albans is singularly rich in associations of ancient history. It is close upon two thousand years since the gleaming cohorts of Julius Cæsar, penetrating the country, vanquished the brave British Prince Cassivelaunus upon the south slope of the valley of the Ver, where they subsequently proceeded to build the town of Verulam. Before long, Watling Street, the Romans' Great North Road, connected Verulam with the south, and along it came long trains of merchants, traders, artificers and workers of all kinds, eager to participate in the prosperity diffused by the conquerors, and Verulam with its wide streets, temples, luxurious villas, public buildings, and theatre—the only one of which remains have as yet been discovered in this country—became the splendid southern capital of England. Here Christianity was preached for the first time in Britain, persecution following hard upon it, and many a Christian being hunted to death in the days of the Emperor Diocletian. One priest sought refuge in the house of Albanus, a young patrician, and so powerfully moved him that when the Roman guard came to seize the Christian, Albanus yielded himself up instead and suffered the first martyrdom in Britain upon the hill on the opposite side of the

ST. ALBANS. The Market Place.

stream. A wooden chapel marked the spot for a few years, and then all traces of the martyr's grave disappeared. The Romans left the country, and Verulam the magnificent sank into decay, hastened by fire, which left it nothing but a desolate mass of ruins. Three centuries elapsed and then the Saxon king Offa, tormented by the memory of many crimes, declared that in expiation he would search for the martyr's bones and build an abbey over them. Accompanied by a band of chiefs he set forth upon his quest; at the summit of Holmhurst Hill a flash of lightning struck the ground at their feet, and digging eagerly they came upon the sainted relics. Offa conveyed the joyful news to the Pope, who canonized Albanus, and gave the King authority to found an abbey with whose privileges none could interfere except the Holy Father himself. A gathering of the noblest in the land witnessed the laying of the first stone of the abbey, which was destined to become the most magnificent, except Westminster, in the kingdom.

Of the thirteen abbots who ruled over it from its foundation to the Conquest, many were of royal birth. The sixth, Ulsinus, encouraged the building of a town round the walls, bringing in folk from the country-side to live in it, and erecting for their benefit three parish churches at the three principal entrances, which he dedicated to St. Michael, first among the angels, St. Stephen, the first martyr, and St. Peter, the first of the Apostles. He is also said to have been the founder of the Grammar School, the oldest in England, which by the end of the eleventh century was a large and flourishing one, ruled by the abbot. Indeed, the abbot was lord of the town; it was mentioned in the Domesday survey as a part of his possessions, and the forty-six burgesses were termed "the demesne men of the abbot."

By this time the property of the abbey had grown to such an extent that the Conqueror, fearing its power, distributed some of its lands among his nobles, and the Saxon abbot protesting, took the opportunity to depose him, appointing in his stead Paul de Caen. A wise and fortunate choice, for this Norman abbot was strong alike in intellect, character and piety. His first care was to restore the Benedictine discipline that had grown lax under his weaker predecessors, and his next, to rebuild Offa's church, with tiles from ruined Verulam, in a style that earned for it a name for being "the vastest and sternest structure" of that age; it was an edifice of rigid simplicity, massive construction and enormous size, so solidly built that even now Paul de Caen's transepts and central tower and twelve bays of his nave may still be seen. Probably he utilised some of Offa's work, for part of the columns in the transepts are evidently Saxon.

The first change in the austere Norman structure was begun in 1195 by Abbot John de Cella. He was a man of intense spirituality and asceticism, whose one great aim was to make his beloved church the most beautiful in Christendom. He began with the west front, but lack of money prevented the realization of his lifelong dreams, and all he completed was three portals which must have been perfect of their kind, but unfortunately were

ST. ALBANS.
The " Fighting Cocks."

obliterated in the restorations of recent years. Yet his dreams were not wholly futile, for his example fired his successors with an enthusiastic desire to make their abbey more and more magnificent. William de Trumpington (1215-1235), achieved most ; he rebuilt the first nine bays at the west end of the nave in the beautiful Early English style, but each of those who followed helped on the work, extending the aisles and chapels, enriching the architecture, adorning the church with lovely paintings, raising the magnificent reredos, of which the central feature—the great crucifix—was cut from a single block of stone weighing seventeen tons, and heightening the splendour of the gorgeous ceremonial. It was not only the example of those who had preceded them which inspired these later abbots, for during the fourteenth century, when there was the most wonderful revival of art and learning that the world has ever seen, an immense impetus was given to ecclesiastical architecture, and all over the country Early English churches were growing up, whose beauty has never been equalled. By the end of the century St. Albans possessed an eastern end " which is one of the most perfect pieces of complete Gothic in the country," and a Lady chapel, which is a dream of Decorated work and exquisite window tracery. But while they thus strove to render their church magnificent, the abbots, preoccupied, allowed the reins of monastic discipline to slacken, and, moreover, alienated the affections of the townsfolk, as enormous sums of money being required for all the building and beautifying that was going on, and the funds of the abbey, though very large, not sufficing, they cast about for some new method to supply their needs, and squeezed money out of their tenants in the town. They set up mills for fulling cloth and grinding corn, and compelled all and sundry to bring their cloth to be fulled and their corn to be ground, charging them high prices. The townsfolk grumbled and at length rebelled, and set up mills of their own; the abbot tried force, but they were desperate and carried their complaint to Westminster. "An appeal from the decision of their spiritual lord to a secular judge appeared to the monks no better than sacrilege. They tolled the great bell. They walked in procession, singing their penitential psalms and invoking the aid of the blessed Alban." Westminster supported them, and the monks, emboldened, went further still, enclosing woods and preserving fish streams hitherto open to all. The people grumbled more than ever, but waited: in the downfall of Edward II. they saw opportunity, and again appealed to Westminster. This time the decision was in their favour and, "mad with delight the boys dashed off with their nets and lines to the ponds. The men rushed to the woods, tore down the fences, and marched back to the town in procession, carrying branches of the trees as a symbol of their victory." It was short-lived. They had only had to deal with an old abbot, bowed down by debts and worn with care, who died soon after his humiliation at their hands. The next abbot, Richard of Wallingford, was of far sterner stuff, son of a blacksmith, who by sheer force of character had risen to the position he occupied. He restored discipline among

ST. ALBANS. The Cathedral.

the monks, and watched for an opportunity to subdue the townsfolk to his will. Arrogant in their new freedom, it was not long before the wilder spirits among them outraged the law, and then the abbot, backed up by the civil authorities, compelled the restitution of all the privileges they had wrested from his predecessor, and as an object lesson he seized the millstones they had set up to grind their own corn, and used them for the paving of the abbey "parlor." During the next few reigns the sullen, enforced submission of the townsfolk continued, but all the time the gulf between abbey and town was widening, and at last, in the reign of Richard II., when the whole country seethed with revolt and the peasants' wars broke out, the townsmen, taking courage from the example of Wat Tyler and Jack Straw, marched in a body to the abbey, forced their way in, compelled the abbot to sign a parchment restoring all their privileges, and celebrated the occasion by tearing up the millstones from the "parlor" floor, and breaking them up, distributed the fragments around the town as memorials of their triumph. But again it was short-lived. Richard calmed rebellion by agreeing to all claims, but when the insurgents had returned to their homes and the danger was over, he determined to teach them a lesson. In every part where risings had taken place assizes were held in turn, and the ringleaders tried and hanged. Hearing this the burgesses of St. Albans, in great alarm, came to the abbot and begged him to intercede for them, resigning their newly-won privileges, replacing the broken millstones in the "parlor" floor, and even offering him gold. But all in vain. The King came in person to St. Albans, and held an eight days' court in which he sentenced fifteen of the leading townsfolk to be hanged in his presence. When he had left the town their sorrowing relatives took the bodies down and buried them, but word of this reaching the King, he sent an order back post haste that the bodies were to be dug up and replaced upon the gallows. Thus ended the town's second attempt at freedom.

The first battle in the Wars of the Roses took place at St. Albans; both sides fought bravely, but the Lancastrians were put to flight, and Henry VI. had to take refuge in a baker's shop, where he was discovered and conveyed a prisoner to the Tower. Later on a second battle was fought at St. Albans, the Yorkists now being in possession of the town and Henry a prisoner in their hands. They were taken unawares by a large Lancastrian force, driven back upon the market-place, and finally as night came on, they fled precipitately. The victorious Lancastrians, led by the exulting Margaret, took the King from his guards, and placing him at their head proceeded to the abbey, at the door of which they were met by the abbot and his monks, chanting hymns of thanksgiving for the King's safe restoration, and a solemn service was held. But that night Margaret's triumphing army sacked the town, in spite of all the abbot's earnest entreaties, for the Queen could not control the rabble of forces she had raised. This was fatal to the cause; it hardened the hearts of the Londoners against them, and soon Margaret's brief triumph ended in despairing exile.

Cardinal Wolsey was the thirty-eighth abbot of St. Albans. There is no record of his ever having come down to take possession, but his influence was exerted at least in one direction, and that was in the stoppage of the printing press which had been brought to the town by Caxton, who issued from it the first historical work printed in this country. Wolsey declared that if the clergy did not suppress the art it would be the ruin of the Church.

The freedom for which the townsfolk of St. Albans had striven so long was at length secured them by Henry VIII.'s suppression of the monasteries, and the constitution of the town "a free borough corporate in deed, fact and name for ever." But though they had won their freedom, they had lost the abbey, under whose protection their town had come into being, and which had been their pride and glory for eight hundred years, second only to Westminster in dignity and magnificence, whose monks had visited them in sickness, relieved them in poverty, administered to them the rites of the Church throughout their lives, and taught them in youth; for with the fall of the abbey the Grammar School ceased to be. The abbey church, too, would have been swept away had not the townsfolk begged to be allowed to purchase it for use as their parish church, and on payment of four hundred pounds it was handed over to them. Now that the gorgeous ceremonial of Roman Catholicism was abolished the church contained a great deal more space than was needed for the services, therefore the beautiful eastern chapels were turned into a schoolhouse, and a passage-way was cut through the venerable walls, dividing the fine old church into two parts. This arrangement was continued up to comparatively modern times, when the abbey church was transformed into a cathedral, and the school was removed to the great gatehouse, a picturesque old place, sole remnant of the magnificent abbey buildings which had once covered the hill on the south side of the church, stretching down to the river.

One of the best known patrons of the original Grammar School was Sir Nicholas Bacon, father of the famous Sir Francis. His country seat was at Gorhambury, and he took great interest in the school, used his considerable influence with Elizabeth to obtain a grant for it, and drew up a set of rules for its governance. When Sir Francis succeeded to the estate at Gorhambury he spent much of his time there, particularly after he had fallen into disgrace. His will contained the following clause: "For my burial I desire it may be in St. Michael's Church, St. Albans; there was my mother buried, and it is the parish church of my mansion house of Gorhambury, and it is the only Christian church within the walls of ancient Verulam." His wishes were carried out. The monument to his memory, which was erected in St. Michael's, is a most exquisitely executed white marble one, representing the philosopher sitting in a high-backed chair, arrayed in his Chancellor's gown and apparently meditating. After a eulogy of his virtues and attainments, the Latin epitaph, translated, reads thus: "Of such a man that the memory might remain, Thomas Meautys, living his attendant, dead his admirer, placed this monument."

The new diocese of St. Albans was created in 1877, and during the seventies the great church, which is one of the largest and most interesting in England, was restored in a manner which caused considerable controversy. At the same time a wonderful archæological triumph was achieved in the almost complete reconstruction of the shrine of St. Alban; two collections of fragments having been discovered by accident, it was pieced together with the utmost pains, and now stands behind the great reredos, on the spot it had occupied for many centuries close by the old watching gallery, from which the shrine which then contained the martyr's relics had been watched night and day in unbroken succession by the monks of the abbey. South of the shrine is the chantry, which was erected in memory of Humphrey, the good Duke of Gloucester.

Of ancient Verulam, whose tiles form so large a portion of the fabric of the cathedral, nothing can now be seen except two remnants of a Roman wall in a field near the river.

PLYMOUTH

FROM the broad walk that runs along the top of the famous hill known as the Hoe, standing between Plymouth and the sea, a view is obtained which "has no rival in England." In front, three miles away, is the great breakwater which, at the cost of a million and a half, was built across the mouth of the Sound at the beginning of the nineteenth century, converting it into one of the finest natural harbours in the kingdom. On the right are the green slopes of Mount Edgecumbe, crowned by the Earl's mansion, the wide and shining Hamoaze into which the Tamar empties its waters, and, beyond, glimpses of the Cornish shore. Beneath, in the centre of the Sound, Drake's Island, named after Plymouth's hero, Sir Francis, bristles with fortifications, on the left lie outspread the broad Catwater and the downs of Staddon, while fourteen miles out in the channel rises the Eddystone lighthouse.

The Hoe is of very ancient fame indeed; here, as Spenser tells us in his "Faerie Queene," the giant Cormoran, or Corineus, afterwards done to death by Jack the Giant-killer, slew the giant Gogmagog, or Goemot :—

> "The Western Hogh besprinkled with the gore
> Of mighty Goemot, who in stout fray
> Corineus conquered and cruelly did slay."

Gogmagog's jawbones with the teeth still in them are said to have been dug up when the foundations of the citadel at the eastern end of the Hoe were being laid in the time of Charles II., and in Spenser's time figures of the two giants were cut out of the turf, an item of 8d. " for new cutting of the Gogmagoge on the Howe," being entered in the town accounts.

It is to some Augustinian monks in the far-off days of King Edgar, or possibly even earlier, that we owe the beginnings of the present flourishing seaport. They lived in Plympton Priory, and it was on some land of theirs in Sutton that a few fisher folk and small traders, encouraged by their kindly aid, began to build the hamlet which by the thirteenth century had developed into the town of Plymouth and begun to play a part in the history of England.

One of the most romantic figures connected with the town in early days is that boyhood's hero, the Black Prince ; from Plymouth he set sail with a fleet of three hundred ships to invade France, and here he landed in the full flush of his victory, both at Crecy and Poictiers, bringing with him not only the flower of the French nobility, but King John and his youngest son, hostages for the observance of the treaty of Bretigny. He treated his royal captives with all the chivalry that has made his name famous. At the banquet given by the town in his honour he " stood at the French King's back . . . constantly refused to take a place at table, and declared that, being a subject, he was too well acquainted with the distance between his own rank and that of royal majesty to assume such freedom." His fourth visit to the town fourteen years later was a sad contrast; his chivalrous expedition into Spain to restore the ungrateful Pedro to his throne had cost him his health, and he was returning home to die, saddened by news from France that England was losing all he had fought for there. He was too ill to continue his journey at once, and lingered at the priory until he was able to bear the journey to London, where he died soon after, leaving behind him "a character illustrious for every eminent virtue, and from his earliest youth till the hour he expired, unstained by any blemish."

Plymouth had now become the fourth largest town in England, and as the French had twice descended upon and sacked it, the citizens, urged by the Prior of Plympton, decided on fortification and built "a strong castle quadrate, having at each corner a great round tower" on a rocky point at the east end of the Hoe, commanding the Catwater and Sutton Pool. Except for the remains of a tower in the outworks of the citadel, and some fragments of a gateway in Lambhay Street, Plymouth Castle has long since disappeared, the name Barbican alone preserving its memory. But it was in the days of good Queen Bess that the town reached the height of its glory and produced the long series of heroes the fame of whose exploits made the name of England resound in every quarter of the globe. "In the latter part of the sixteenth century Devonshire was the foremost county in England and Plymouth its foremost town. Elizabeth called the men of

Devonshire her right hand." "If any person desired to see her English worthies, Plymouth was the likeliest place to seek them. All were in some fashion associated with the old town. "Per mare, per terram," was the motto of Elizabeth's true-born Englishmen, and familiar and dear to them was Plymouth with its narrow streets, its dwarfish quays, its broad waters and its glorious Hoe." On the roll of Plymouth's illustrious men the Hawkins family figures largely: "For three generations in succession they were the master spirits of Plymouth in its most illustrious days; its leading merchants, its bravest sailors, serving oft and well in the civic chair and in the Commons House of Parliament. For three generations they were in the van of English seamanship, founders of England's commerce in South, West and East, stout in fight, of quenchless spirit in adventure—a family of merchant statesmen and heroes to whom our country affords no parallel." In 1573 Sir John Hawkins was chosen by the Queen "as the fittest person in her dominions to manage her naval affairs," and for twenty-one years he served her faithfully as Comptroller of the Navy, turning out her ships in such taut and trim condition that "they had no match in the world."

Never was such pleasant bustle as at Plymouth in those days. The very air seemed full of the spirit of enterprise and adventure, and all the gossip ran upon the strange countries overseas, the wonders to be beheld there, and the vast riches waiting only to be gathered. Now it was Sir Richard Hawkins, nephew of stout Sir John, off to the South Seas with five ships; and now Sir Humphrey Gilbert bound for the New World with the "first European settlers of Northern America"; or Sir Walter Raleigh in search of new land to add to his Queen's possessions; or Grenville, Frobisher, Cox and countless others; or, prime favourite of all, Francis Drake, starting out on his wonderful voyage round the world. When he returned in triumph the whole town turned out to welcome him, and the bells were set a-ringing in his honour; with one voice the pleased burgesses elected him mayor, and the Queen commanded him to bring round his ship to Greenwich in order that she might knight him on board.

Then one day came news of a great Spanish fleet, named vaingloriously the "Invincible Armada" setting sail from the Tagus to avenge a long series of harassments by Hawkins and Drake, and all the English ships that could be mustered assembled in Plymouth harbour, eager for the fray. There they waited and waited, day after day, and the captains and officers beguiled the time with games of bowls upon the Hoe. They were in the midst of one of these when word was at length brought by a Scottish privateer that the Armada, ranged up in the form of "a crescent, of which the horns were seven miles asunder" had appeared off the Lizard. At once all was ardour and bustle; only the imperturbable Drake remained cool and wanted "to finish the game and beat the Spaniards afterwards," but for once he was overruled, and all embarked. The history of that day is well known; how, with the aid of fireships and tempest and their own skilful manœuvring and brave right hands, the English soon sent the Spaniards flying, and it was a very battered Armada, shorn of ninety-nine ships and many thousands of men, that returned sadly to Corrunna. And this is not all that Drake did for Plymouth; he it was who set on foot the great work for which the town could never be too grateful, the bringing of an efficient water supply, by means of an artificial channel, though the poorer folk believed he did it by magic, from Dartmoor right into the town. On the back of his portrait in the Guildhall the burgesses recorded their gratitude as follows :—

" Great Drake, whose shippe about the world's wide waste
In three years did a golden girdle cast;
Who with fresh streams refresht this towne that first
Though kist with waters, yet did pine with thirst:
Who both a Pilot and a Magistrate
Steered in his turne the Shippe of Plymouthe's state."

In 1592 Drake was elected M.P. for Plymouth; no wonder the town was proud of him. A splendid bronze statue of the hero, by Sir Edgar Boehm, stands on the Hoe, and also a tercentenary monument in memory of the Armada. Drake's Island too commemorates the great man.

Now we come to the Pilgrim Fathers; they were a company of Independents who had sought refuge for a time in Holland from religious persecution, and in 1620, having heard much talk of Raleigh's discovery, Virginia, had resolved to begin a new life there. Returning to England they embarked at Southampton in two vessels, the "Mayflower" and the smaller "Speedwell"; countless were the delays and difficulties, chiefly caused by the poverty of their resources, before they were really off, but at length, in the words of Nicholas Bradford, afterwards their first governor in the New World, "with good hopes they put to sea, conceiving they should go comfortably on, but it fell out otherwise, for after they were gone to sea again, about 100 leagues without the Land's End, holding company together all this while, the captain of the small ship complained his ship was so leaky that he must bear up or sink at sea, for they could scarce free her with much pumping. So they came to consultation again and resolved both ships should bear back again and put into Plymouth, which accordingly was done." They landed at the Barbican and were so "kindly entertained and courteously used by divers friends there dwelling," that afterwards in grateful remembrance when they landed in Massachusetts they gave the name of New Plymouth to their settlement. While they were in Plymouth "no special leak could be found, but it was judged to be the general weakness of the ship and that she would not prove sufficient for the voyage. Upon which it was resolved to dismiss her and part of the companie, and proceed with the other ship. The which, though it was grievous and caused great discouragement, was put in execution. So after they had taken out such provisions as the other ship could bestow, and concluded both what number and what persons to send back they made another sad parting, the one ship going back to London and the other proceeded on her voyage."

Three times Plymouth, which was a Puritan stronghold, was besieged by the troops of Charles I., and three times it successfully withstood them; on the first occasion the Puritans might well think that the Lord was on their side, for when they were on the verge of starvation a shoal of pilchards suddenly appeared in the harbour and Sutton Pool in such quantities that the besieged were able to dip buckets into the water and draw them out.

Admiral Blake, another of our great naval heroes, died as he was entering Plymouth Sound on his return from a successful expedition against the Spaniards at Teneriffe, and though his body was interred in Westminster Abbey, his heart, at the earnest wish of the people of Plymouth, was buried in St. Andrew's Church " by the door of the Mayor's pew." Blake was one of the staunchest, bravest and best of England's many naval heroes; he had his work to do and he did it, regardless of any man's opinion. " It is not for us to mind State matters," he said, " but to keep foreigners from fooling us." His despatches were a marvel of brevity; the following being a typical example: " Please your honours and glory, yesterday met with the French fleet, beat, killed, took, sunk and burned as per margin." It is to him we owe the long pennon that floats from the mainmast of our men-of-war. Van Tromp adopted a broom as a token that he would sweep the sea, Blake retorted by hoisting a horsewhip, which we have borne ever since.

One event in Plymouth at the beginning of the nineteenth century excited the most extraordinary interest, and that was Napoleon's arrival as a prisoner on the " Bellerophon " on his way to St. Helena. " The Sound was covered by one entire mass of boats filled with people. Every boat that could swim was there, from the splendid barge to the little cockleshell, and so closely were they wedged together that no sea could be seen." This historic event was the occasion of a young native of Plymouth springing into fame. Charles Eastlake, later to be President of the Royal Academy, took the sketch from which he afterwards painted his great picture "Napoleon standing on the gangway of H.M.S. 'Bellerophon.'" Napoleon, who heard what the young artist had done, courteously sent him the clothes he had been wearing to enable him to complete his picture. Another great artist connected with Plymouth is Sir Joshua Reynolds, who was born at Plympton in a house which is still standing, as is also the old Grammar School where he received his first lessons. In the Plymouth Library are three portraits he painted, one of himself and the other two of his father and youngest sister. James Northcote, Samuel Prout, Haydon and Cook were also natives of Plymouth.

Old Plymouth is almost a thing of the past, and has to be searched for in odd corners; the present town is supremely modern with many Government buildings, and all the hustle and bustle of modern days, for Plymouth is the place of call for all the great lines of steamships sailing from London or Southampton for the east or south, and *vice versa*. Next to it, so close as to appear from the water all one town, have, almost within the last century, grown up Stonehouse, with its Naval Hospital, Marine Barracks and Naval Victualling Yard, the largest in the kingdom, and Devonport with its dockyard, seventy acres in extent and employing 3,000 men, which turns out every single requisite for the building of the largest battleship. They are known as the Three Towns, and each has its separate governing body; a line of fortifications, consisting of sixteen forts, protect them, stretching from Staddon Heights on the east to Tregantle on the west, besides which there is a great iron fort just within the Breakwater, to say nothing of Drake's Island, which is practically covered by batteries, and would form a very strong protection against any attack from abroad.

On the Hoe may be seen a relic of great interest, the tower of Smeaton's lighthouse, the third erected upon the dangerous rocks upon which the fourth Eddystone now stands. The story is a strange one. The rocks, which are covered at high water, had been the cause of so many wrecks and loss of life that Mr. Winstanley, a wealthy gentleman with a hobby for mechanics, designed and erected a lighthouse which he frequently boasted would stand the strongest gale that ever blew, adding he only wished he might have the opportunity of being in at the time. His wish was granted with tragic results; one day, while he was in it superintending some repairs, a storm came on of such extraordinary violence that in London alone 800 houses were destroyed, 315 ships were wrecked, and in Kent 50,000 trees blown down. When it was over no trace remained of Winstanley, the men who had been with him, or the lighthouse. Three years later a London silk merchant named Rudyerd made another attempt; his structure also was made of wood, but circular instead of polygonal, like Winstanley's. For fifty years it successfully weathered every storm, and then in 1755 it caught fire; the three keepers tried in vain to extinguish the flames, but the lead with which it was roofed spouted off in molten streams, and they had to take refuge in a hole in the rock, but not before one of them in looking up had received a quantity down his throat; he died twelve days afterwards. One of his companions, when rescuers appeared to take them off the rock, went raving mad, and breaking away flung himself into the sea. Twelve months later Mr. Smeaton began to build a third lighthouse, made of stone. We were at war with France at the time, and a privateer carried off the workmen engaged upon it to a French prison. When news of their capture reached Louis XV. he was exceedingly angry: "I am at war with England, but not with all mankind," he said, and releasing the workmen with a handsome present he placed their captors in prison instead. This lighthouse might have lasted to the present day but for the undermining by the waves of the rock on which it stood; so 123 years after its first erection it was removed to the Hoe, and the present structure put up in its stead at a cost of £80,000.

Plymouth still ranks as one of the most important towns in England, and it may have an even greater future before it, if the men of Devon, with the enterprise which distinguished them in the reign of good Queen Bess, profit by the natural advantages of the town, and erect docks which might easily rival those of Southampton or even Liverpool.

WARWICK

"NOTHING," says one chronicler, "can well be imagined more happily chosen than the situation of Warwick"; "in which," adds another, "this town may justly glory beyond any other." It stands on a gentle hill in the beautiful valley of the Avon, its four main streets climbing up to the fine old church of St. Mary's, which towers above the surrounding houses. Lower down, yet rising high above the river, stands the splendid castle, "one of the greatest and by far the most famous in the Midlands, famous not only for its early strength and later magnificence, but for the long line of powerful earls, culminating in the Kingmaker, who possessed it and bore its name." It is one of the very few Norman castles now used as a residence, and the earl holds it, just as he did in Saxon days when it consisted of a mere timber keep, erected by Ethelfleda the warlike daughter of Alfred the Great, and surrounded by a deep fosse or ditch.

Warwick is one of the oldest towns in England; its early history is partly legendary, but Rous, a chantry priest at the chapel at Guy's Cliff in the fifteenth century, the most learned of its first historians, declares it was founded by an early British king, used as a military station by the Romans, created a bishop's see by St. Dubritius, and regarded as of such importance that it was six times destroyed by invading enemies and as often rebuilt by the surviving inhabitants before the Conquest. The device of a bear and ragged staff, which has been borne by the Earls of Warwick for many centuries, and meets the eye continually in church and town, is said to have had its origin in the name of one British earl, Arthal, signifying a bear, and the exploit of another British earl who vanquished a giant with a young tree he had plucked up by the roots.

Evidently there was a royal mint at Warwick in the time of Harthacanute, for a genuine Saxon penny still exists bearing his name and that of the town. Rous gives a list of eight Saxon earls and recites at great length the romantic history of the famous Guy of Warwick, whose humble birth had been attended by remarkable portents, and who dared to fall in love with the fair proud Phyllis, daughter of Earl Rohand; but he had to perform many marvellous feats before he won her, the chief of which was the slaying of a monstrous dun cow, the terror of the countryside. Married bliss and high estate, however, could not long content him, and he returned to the wars, where he soon became known as the most valiant of warriors, and the slayer of a mighty Saracen giant. Years passed and

"At length to Warwick I did come,
  Like Pilgrim poor and was not known;
And then I lived a Hermit life
  A mile and more out of the town (at Guy's Cliff).

And daily came to beg my bread
  Of Philis at my Castle gate
Not known unto my loving wife,
  Who daily mourned for her mate

Till at the last I fell sore sicke,
  Yes, sick so sore that I must die.
I sent to her a ringe of golde
  By which she knew me presentlye.

Then she repairing to the Cave
  Before that I gave up the Ghost,
Herself closed up my dying eyes,
  My Philis fair whom I lov'd most."

Various relics of this doughty champion are still preserved and shown to visitors at the castle, such as his porridge pot, meat fork and sword, and in the courtyard Felyce's Well is still a feature.

At the time of the Domesday Survey Warwick was evidently considered a town of considerable importance and strength ; it contained two hundred and sixty-one houses and two churches, St. Mary's and one on the site of the present St. Nicholas'. The earl was a Saxon named Turchill, afterwards known as the "Traitor Earl," because he submitted to the Conqueror, and was in consequence allowed to retain possession of his estates on condition that he fortified the town. This he did by surrounding it with strong walls and a ditch, and rebuilding the castle. When he died, the Conqueror bestowed the earldom upon his favourite, Henry de Newburgh.

In 1268 the title passed by marriage into the Beauchamp family, in whose time the present castle was built, and the importance and prosperity of the town were steadily in the ascendant, as may be judged from the fact that in Edward III.'s reign it contained at least eight churches. The second of the Beauchamp earls was that Guy of Warwick, who, among Edward II.'s proud barons, was the most incensed by the weak King's preference for the upstart Piers Gaveston. When he heard that the favourite had mockingly nicknamed him "the black hound of Ardern," he exclaimed, "Let him call me hound, one day the hound will bite him," and true enough, when the barons did conspire against Gaveston, it was the earl who headed them and seized the wretched man, imprisoning him for a night in a dungeon in Warwick Castle, the entrance to which is still shown, and the next day leading him out to Blacklow Hill, where they smote off his head. The name of Piers Gaveston and the date of his death may still be seen cut in the rock on the brow of the hill. Soon after the earl mysteriously died. His breastplate and shield are in the armoury of the castle. He began the fortifications.

His son Thomas, who succeeded him, became Earl Marshal of England, and took a very prominent part in the French wars of Edward III., displaying remarkable valour; he led the van of the English army in the battle of Crecy and greatly distinguished himself at Poictiers. A piece of the Black Prince's armour, relic of those days, is in the castle armoury. This earl rebuilt the walls of the castle, erected the fine tower in the N.E. corner named after the Saxon Guy, added strong gates, fortified the entrance with embattled towers, and built the choir of St. Mary's, in the centre of which he lies, under a tomb bearing his effigy and that of his countess, beautifully carved in white marble. His son Thomas, the next earl, was governor to Richard II. during his minority. He built Cæsar's Tower, which is considered one of the strongest and most graceful in England. He was buried with his countess in the south part of

St. Mary's, and their portraits, engraven on brass, are still there.

His son Richard, who followed next, was one of the most famous personages of his time, not only in his own country but on the Continent. The German Emperor declared "That no Christian Prince hath such another knight for Wisdom, Nurture and Manhood, and that if all Courtesie were lost it might be found again in him," and thus he came to be known as "the Prince of Courtesie." He was concerned in all the principal transactions of the reign, acted as governor to Henry VI. during his minority, and as Regent of France after the Duke of Bedford. To him Warwick owes the exquisite Beauchamp chapel, a building only surpassed by Henry VII.'s chapel at Westminster, and one of the most perfect examples of Perpendicular architecture in the kingdom. In the centre of it is his beautiful tomb, bearing his effigy in brass gilt, larger than life and in full armour, around which are carved fourteen figures of mourning relatives, all belonging to the noblest families in England. Opening out of the chapel is a small chamber called the Oratory, remarkable for its fine fan tracery roof. This earl also rebuilt the chapel of St. Mary Magdalene at Guy's Cliff, established a chantry there, of which Rous, the historian, was priest, and erected the statue of the Saxon Guy which is still there. His son Henry was only fourteen when he succeeded, yet before he died at the early age of twenty-two he had received from the King all the honours royalty had to bestow and was even declared and crownėd King of the Isle of Wight. His brother-in-law

Richard Neville, the greatest of all the earls of Warwick, and called the Kingmaker, because he played with kings as if they were pawns, was the next earl. "He was the greatest as well as the last of those mighty barons who formerly overawed the crown, and rendered the people incapable of any system of government." It was in the Wars of the Roses that he played his game of kings; first he sided with the Yorkists and himself offered the crown to Edward IV.; afterwards connecting himself still more closely with the new King by marrying his two daughters to Edward's brothers, the Duke of Clarence and the Duke of York, later Richard III. Then at some fancied slight he veered completely round, and joining the Lancastrians captured Edward IV. and kept him prisoner for a month, part of the time at Warwick Castle. His next step was to restore Henry VI. to the throne, but eventually his plans failed and he was defeated and killed at the battle of Barnet. A mace and other relics of him are preserved at the castle. His son-in-law, the Duke of Clarence, next took the title, but he soon incurred the royal suspicion and was sent to the Tower, where he was secretly murdered, tradition says, in a butt of malmsey wine. The story of his little son and heir is most pathetic; when only nine years old he was shut up in the Tower by Henry VII., for fear of his claims to the crown. There he languished in secret for years, once or twice when impostors, such as Lambert Simnel, personated him, being paraded through the streets of London. Finally, on the excuse that he was concerned in the conspiracy of Perkin Warbeck, the unhappy young man was beheaded on Tower Hill.

The Dudleys were the next earls; John Dudley, who was Duke of Northumberland as well as Earl of Warwick, rivalled his predecessor, the Kingmaker, by endeavouring to make a queen of his daughter-in-law, Lady Jane Grey; an attempt that ended in disaster and brought about his downfall and execution. His son Ambrose, who was forgiven his share in the conspiracy by reason of the gallantry of the Dudleys in the foreign wars, was known as the "good Earl of Warwick," and became a great favourite with Elizabeth. One of the most interesting incidents in his life was a magnificent reception he gave her in 1572, when there were the greatest rejoicings and festivities, and "it pleased the Queen to have the country people resorting to see the dance in the court of the castle, the Queen beholding them out of her chamber window," the evening ending with "a show of fireworks prepared for that purpose in the Temple Fields." Warwick is specially interesting as containing enough old houses to show one what the town was like in Elizabethan days. The East Gate with St. Peter's Chapel and the West Gate with St. James's Chapel, the beautiful chancel of St. Mary's, the vestry, the chapter house and the Beauchamp Chapel are all untouched. Mill Street is full of ancient half-timbered houses, and at the bottom of it are the picturesque remains of the Great Bridge over which the Queen rode, when she entered Warwick. Then to the north of the town there is the Priory, built by a man named Fisher in the time of Henry VIII. on the site of the ancient Priory of St. Sepulchre, which was founded by the first of the Norman earls, and of which two galleries are included in the newer building, while the ruined chapel is still standing. Queen Elizabeth herself visited this house on the occasion of her second visit to Warwick and honoured the family by sitting down to supper with them. Fisher's large fortune was entirely self-made, his father having been a fish seller in the market-place of Warwick, and when he died his riches were speedily dissipated by his son, who perished miserably in the Fleet prison. Last but perhaps the most interesting of all is the Leicester Hospital, a very old building at the top of the High Street, and a perfect example of a half-timbered house. The chapel and gateway date from the reign of Henry I., the tower and hall from that of Richard II. The place having passed into the possession of Ambrose Dudley's younger brother Robert, the famous Earl of Leicester, lover of Queen Elizabeth, he founded therein a hospital for a master and twelve brethren, and it is still maintained as such, the brethren wearing the dress of the order as commanded by the founder, a blue gown with a silver badge of the bear and ragged staff on the left sleeve; the present badges are the identical ones worn by the first brethren, and bear their names on the back and the date 1571. The Earl of Leicester was a great figure in Warwick in his day and accounted a considerable benefactor by the people. He has a splendid tomb against the north wall in the Beauchamp Chapel, with statues of himself and his Countess Letitia, successor of the unhappy Amy Robsart; and against the south wall near the altar is a monument to his son Sir Robert

Dudley, "The Noble Impe," a very remarkable personage, who was never able properly to establish his legitimacy and spent the greater part of his life in Florence.

The Dudley family having died out, the title passed into the self-made family of Rich, while the castle was granted by James I. to Sir Fulke Greville, whom he also created Lord Brooke. The castle at the time was terribly dilapidated, and Sir Fulke repaired and adorned it at a cost of £20,000. Sir Fulke was one of the most accomplished men of his day and the lifelong friend of Sir Philip Sidney, with whom he was at school. He was one of the pall bearers at Sir Philip's funeral at St. Paul's Cathedral, and wrote his life, and a portrait of Sir Philip hangs in the castle. Sir Fulke's end was a tragic one; he was murdered by a servant, who immediately afterwards committed suicide. He was buried in the chapter-house north of the choir, where his monument, erected by himself, may still be seen.

Warwick Castle underwent a great siege in the Civil War, when Sir Fulke's cousin, an ardent Roundhead, had succeeded to the title :—" Lord Brooke had gone, leaving it to be defended by Sir Edward Peyto, who was twice summoned to surrender by an army under Lord Northampton but refused; after two days Sir Edward ordered all to leave the town and a red flag floated out from Guy's Tower; the strong massive walls of the castle were proof against all attack and the besiegers tried to starve them out; then Sir Edward hoisted the quaint device of a Bible and winding sheet, implying that as he put his faith in the one, he was not afraid of the other. At last the Cavaliers in despair raised the siege and joined the King's forces."

In 1759 the title of Earl of Warwick passed into the Greville family and is still borne by them.

A great fire in 1694 destroyed a large portion of the town, as well as the nave of St. Mary's Church, but it was very carefully rebuilt, subscriptions coming in from all parts of the country. In the days of Catholic superstition St. Mary's possessed a remarkable number of holy relics—*e.g.*, part of the chair of the patriarch Abraham, part of the burning bush of Moses, part of the hair of the Blessed Virgin, part of the manger in which the infant Jesus was laid, part of the pillar to which He was fastened when scourged, part of the crown of thorns, part of the cross, part of the towel in which His body was wrapped by Nicodemus, part of the hair of Mary Magdalene and part of the face of Stephen.

In 1871 there was a terrible fire at the castle which destroyed all the private apartments and many treasures; but it still contains a very large number of valuable and interesting objects, such as the beautiful portrait of Charles I. on horseback by Vandyke, a helmet studded with brass worn by Oliver Cromwell, a magnificent table known as the Grimani, inlaid with precious stones and worth £10,000, a set of bedroom furniture which belonged to Queen Anne; portraits by Holbein of Henry VIII., Martin Luther, and Anne Boleyn; the beautiful white marble vase known as the Warwick Vase, five and a half feet high, which was found in the Vale of Tempe by Sir William Hamilton in 1770 and presented by him to the Earl of Warwick; it stands on a high pedestal in a glass house in the gardens overlooking the park. Izaak Walton's marriage chest is another treasure, and a travelling trunk which belonged to Queen Anne, etc., etc., etc.

BOSTON

Boston, the humble and primitive mother of the great city in the U.S.A., has a curious history, reaching back to Roman times, though such Roman remains as have been found in the neighbourhood are scanty, and sometimes doubtful. The Romans probably had some sort of defensive post here to defend the builders of their sea-wall.

Founded by a saint, and ruined by a quarrelsome brawler, it has recovered through the efforts of its Corporation. In the middle of the last century it was so decayed that the American driver in "Martin Chuzzlewit" was able to say: "It brought Old (New) York home to him quite wivid, on account of it being so exactly unlike in every respect." At one time, not more than a century ago, no vessel of more than 150 tons could reach the town, and matters had been even worse; now the docks have quayside accommodation for vessels of 3,000 tons' burden.

Of its origin, Bede informs us that St. Botolph, patron saint of mariners, founded a small monastery at Icanhoe, which Leland and others take to have been on the site of the present city. From its foundation in A.D. 654, it continued until the Danish invasion of 870. A village seems to have grown up beside the convent, to be included in the survey of Skirbeck by the compilers of Domesday Book. The Chronicles of Croyland state that after the terrible conflagration which destroyed that abbey, Fergus, a brazier, of Botolphstone, gave two skillets to make good the loss of their bells and tower. This was in 1091, only five years after the compilation of the great survey; we must suppose that the two towns were returned under the name of Skirbeck, which is mentioned as having two churches, two priests, two fishgarths, and the equivalent of forty acres of meadow.

Alan Rufus, Earl of Brittany, later of Britain and Richmond, became the feudal lord.

The rise of the port under its early Norman lords must have been extremely rapid, for in 1204 we hear of the men of Boston paying £100 and two palfreys in order that no sheriff or bailiffs should interfere with them, but that they should choose a bailiff among themselves. Already, vague as history is as to the growth of the port, it had come to be of the greatest importance; for in this very year of 1204 the *quinzaine*, or tax of one-fifteenth, was nearly as high as that of London, being no less than £780, as against £836; moreover, it was no poor community that was in those days ready to pay £100 for the privileges of a primitive charter.

In the reign of Edward I. the first blow was struck at the port's early prosperity. One Robert Chamberlain, gentleman, with a number of followers, came to the annual fair at Boston disguised as monks and canons, and set fire to the town. While the people were fighting the fire the conspirators plundered the fair ; and even after the raid the fair was so rich, and the fire so fierce, that gold and silver ran melted in the street. Chamberlain was hanged, but resolutely refused to betray his accomplices. Soon afterwards—in 1285—there was a disastrous flood. But prosperous years succeeded, the town was rebuilt, and the staple for wool, felt, leather and lead was fixed at Boston. Then followed the great days of the port. The Hansa merchants—the "Esterlings," as the men of the Baltic provinces were called—settled in great numbers, and formed their guild or "steelyard." In 1336, Boston sent members to Parliament, and continued to do so until 1352.

Despite these advantages, it was natural for Boston to suffer by the rise of other ports, for the estuary was swift and awkward to navigate, with constantly shifting channels.

But before speaking of decay we must mention the great glory of Boston, and one of its greatest assets—the church of St. Botolph. It was not at first the parish church, but its size and beauty, together with the numerous religious houses and guilds founded and flourishing in the town, brought many pilgrims and religious thither, Boston offering the devout Catholic very superior facilities.

In 1309 "the foundation of Boston steeple on the next Monday after Palm Sunday was begun to be digged by many miners, and so continued till the midsummer following, at which time they were deeper than the haven by five foot. . . . Upon the Monday . . . was laid the first stone by Dame Margery Tilney, and thereupon she laid £5 sterling,

Sir John Truesdale, then parson of Boston, gave also £5, and Richard Stephenson . . . gave £5 more. These were all the great gifts at that time." For a time the tower made slow progress, but the rest of the church rose quickly: about 1450 the chancel was lengthened, and early in the fifteenth century the beautiful tower and lantern were completed. Leland tells us that originally St. Botolph's "was but a chapel to" St. John's. "But now it is so risen and adornid that it is the chiefest of the toune, . . and so served with singging, and that of cunning men, as no paroche is in all England. . . The society and bretherhodde longging to this chirch hath caussid this."

Leland is speaking of the guild of the Blessed Virgin. He relates a curious anecdote of one enterprise of theirs. It must be understood that the attractions of religion were well nigh as profitable as the famous fairs. In the year 1510 (Leland quotes from Fox's "Acts and Monuments") it happened "that the town of Boston thought good to send up to Rome for renewing of their two pardons, one called the great, the other called the lesser pardon. Which thing, although it should stand them in great expences of money (for the Pope's merchandize is always deare ware), yet notwithstanding such sweetnesse they had felt thereof, and such gain come to their towne by that Roman merchandize," that, to cut a long story short, they sent "one Geffrey Chambers with another champion," supplied with money and all that was fitting, "who coming to Antwerp, and misdoubting to be too weak for the compassing of such a weighty piece of work, conferred and perswaded with Thomas Cromwell . . . to assist him"—to wit, in making an easy bargain. Cromwell, despite his apprehensions of "the unreasonable expences of those greedy cormorants," consented, and the three travelled together to Rome. Pope Julius II., that wily diplomat and downright old soldier, was on the throne. How circumvent him? Cromwell inquired and meditated, having already discovered what served him so well in later life, that great men are to be managed through their weaknesses. At length, "having knowledge that the Pope's holy tooth greatly delighted in new-fangled, strange delicates and dainty dishes of gelly," and that his "greedy humour must needs be served with some present or other (for without rewards there is no doing at Rome)" he waited until a day when Julius returned from the chase to his pavilion, hot and famished; when he and his companions approached with divers confections of the "gelly" nature, "with a three-man's song." "The Pope suddenly marvelling at the strangenesse of the song, and understanding that they were Englishmen, and that they came not empty-handed, willed them to be called in. Cromwell there shewing his obedience and offering his gelly junkets, "such as kings and princes only," said he, "did vie to eat in England," and which he and his fellows, poor suitors, had brought as a novelty meet for his recreation, etc.," the Pope, after prudently getting a cardinal "to take the assay," presently ate of them himself, with the result that the astute Cromwell made a very much better bargain than was usual in that city of "cormorants," getting both the "jolly pardons of the towne of Boston" stamped in return for the recipes of his "gelly junkets."

The pardons were curious documents, giving the brethren and sisters of the guild of Our Lady in St. Botolph's Church many privileges and facilities, especially in respect of carrying a portable altar and having masses said in any place and at any time, and enabling them to bestow 500 years of pardon upon any one who subscribed to the guild, while a visit to the chapel of the guild on certain days was equivalent to a visit to all the stations of Rome. All members of the guild, moreover, might receive full remission *a pœna et culpa* once in life or at the hour of death.

Such privileges as these were swept away by the Reformation, and their loss accelerated the already apparent decline of the town. Let us hear Leland as to its condition before that change:—

"Al the buildings (east of the river) of this side of the towne is fair, and marchaunts dwelle yn it; and a staple of wulle is used there. . . . A gentleman . . . told me that syns that Boston of old tyme at the great famose fair there kept was brent, that scant syns it ever came to the old glory and riches that it had; yet syns hath it beene manyfold richer than it is now.

"The Staple and the Stiliard houses yet there remayne but the stiliard is little or nothing at all occupied."

He tells us further of all the rich foundations of friars; and that there were "IIII colleges of Freres Marchaunts cumming by all parts by Este were wont greatly to haunt Boston; and the Grey Freres toke them in a manner for founders of their house, and many Esterlinges were buried there." The Black Friars had a house there since before the year 1288, in which one of the house of Huntingfield lay buried, and on being exhumed was found to have "a leaden Bulle of *Innocentius*, Bishop of Rome, about his nek." This house the Duke of Suffolk obtained at the Reformation. The White Friars were founded about 1300, and their property was granted to the Mayor and Corporation; the same fate befell the Augustines, founded by Edward II., and the Grey Friars, founded in the reign of Edward III. There were other smaller establishments, mostly founded by the Tilneys, who had a manor-house in Boston. Many of these communities were in reality wealthy corporations of farmers and wool-merchants.

In the hope of recovering some of their former greatness the Mayor and Corporation applied to Henry VIII. for an enlarged charter; but all in vain; they obtained the charter, but not the results they hoped for, in spite of other charters and the institution of a Court of Admiralty. But before the Dissolution the end was in sight.

In the reign of Edward IV., one Humphry Littlebury stabbed "an Esterling," *i.e.*, a merchant of the powerful Hansa league, "whereupon rose so much controversy that the Esterlinges left their course of marchandise to Boston." Before very long Boston was a mere fishing village, its harbour silted up, its wharves deserted. Not until the time of George III. did the trade begin to return; then the harbour was improved and the town largely rebuilt, so that it again became the richest port of Lincolnshire. But the port has grown to its present dimensions only since 1882, when a new dock was built, of seven acres area, admitting ships of 3,000 tons to the quayside. The river was deepened and a new channel cut, giving a depth of 27 feet; the railway was brought across the river to the dock by means of a swing bridge, and building and repairing slips were laid down. Now Boston is a model of a modern fishing and trading port, having a fleet of deep-sea trawlers and other fishing vessels, with fishmarkets at the dock, granaries, warehouses, timber-yards, and all the usual facilities. The trade is largely in Baltic produce—grain, timber, pitch, linseed, hemp, cotton, etc. It increased eightfold in the first twelve years after the improvements were instituted. Oil-cake and tobacco are local manufactures; other industries are the making of sail-cloth, ropes, sacking, engineering and light foundry-work, etc.

The church—to speak of such monuments of old Boston as remain—is of unusual size, with a light and spacious interior. The roof perhaps is a fault, being an elaborate imitation of stone vaulting in oak; as usual, when the natural genius of a material is violated, the result is not satisfactory to a cultured eye. There is evidence that an open timber roof was intended. The tower—now open within to the great height of 160 feet, and 288 feet in height externally—is visible far out at sea, and is a well-known landmark; with its lantern and flying buttresses it strongly resembles the tower of

Antwerp. Its truncated appearance from a distance has earned it the name of "Boston Stump."

The finest old houses remain in Spain Lane—named after the great trading family, the De Spaynes; on the wall of a house in Spain Court is the monumental slab of one Wisselus de Smalenburg, an "Esterling," showing a figure of a man with his feet resting on a dog; it is dated 1340, and was dug up near the Grammar School, on the site of the Grey Friars.

The house of the Guild of the Virgin is still extant, serving now as the Guildhall; it is a fine red-brick building of the fifteenth century. The window in the west wall has some remains of the original stained glass. Near by is the Grammar School, dating from 1567, also of red brick, with modern glass; behind it is the Hussey Tower, part of the dwelling of the Lord Hussey who joined the Lincolnshire Catholic rebellion in 1537, and was beheaded. Near by are the public gardens and baths, and behind them the docks. By the iron bridge—a single arch, by Rennie (1803), is the market-place, affording an excellent view of the church. In one corner stands a much-restored timbered house—Shodfriars Hall—and, by the river, the fish-market.

The famous chimes of Boston, played on thirty-six carillons, are now disused, having a poor tone; they were set up in 1867. There is included in the full list of chimes a tune known as "The Brides of Mavis Enderby"; but at the time when Miss Ingelow wrote her well-known poem, "The High Tide on the Coast of Lincolnshire," no such tune existed; the tune included among the chimes is a modern fabrication. There is also a peal of eight bells; there used to be an unusually large clock bell, covered with curious rhyming inscriptions, but it was broken in 1710, and no record kept of the inscriptions.

A certain amount of misapprehension has existed in England as to the founding and naming of the American Boston; the facts, which are perhaps not yet quite generally known, are briefly these: Governor John Winthrop, with his followers, sailed from England in the "Arbella," with the King's charter to establish a government, in the year 1630. They settled temporarily at Charleston, on the Charles. The present site of Boston appeared to them across the water as a hill with three summits, which they named Tremont, or Trimountain—hence Tremont Street. The one summit of the three to-day remaining appeared to have been used as a signal-station, and became Beacon Hill. It seemed that a pestilence had removed the aboriginal inhabitants; the hill was tenanted by one white man, the Rev. William Blaxton, one of a few isolated settlers about the capes and islands of the Charles; he had been there some seven years. He invited the new settlers to cross over, the water being good. A court was held at Charleston on September 17th (N.S.), at which it was ordered "that Trimountaine should be called Boston." Associated with Winthrop in the settlement was Isaac Johnson, of Boston, with his wife, Lady Arbella, daughter of the Earl of Lincoln; Atherton Hough, ex-mayor, and Thomas Leverett, ex-alderman of Boston.

Isaac Johnson died in September, his wife having predeceased him. In October or thereabouts the settlers crossed to the peninsula of Boston; Blaxton, not liking their company, departed in search of fresh fields. The first pastor was the Rev. John Wilson, of Sudbury; Cotton, attacked on account of Nonconformity and administering the sacrament to persons seated, arrived in the "Griffin" three years later, accompanied by Bellingham, afterwards governor. A memorial of Cotton will be found in St. Botolph's in the "Cotton Chapel," a Decorated structure now used as vestry and morning chapel; formerly it sheltered a fire-engine, but the citizens of Boston, Mass., descendants of John Cotton and members of his American church, subscribed toward its restoration, as a memorial tablet in the chapel relates, Edward Everett, then United States Minister at the Court of St. James, being responsible for the inscription. The restoration was commenced in 1856.

Certain of the Pilgrim Fathers and other "Puritan Separatists" of Scrooby and Gainsborough had an extremely unpleasant experience at Boston, some years before the sailing of the "Mayflower." In 1608 two parties of these worthies, intending to sail for Holland, repaired to Boston and the Humber respectively, the Boston party including Bradford and Brewster. Just as their vessel was on the point of sailing the captain betrayed them to the Boston magistrates, with the result that they were at once taken ashore, "not without circumstances of contumely," which seem to have included the plundering of their personal effects. By whose authority the arrest was made is not clear; however, the emigrants were "put into ward" and the Lords in Council informed. After a month's detention, robbed of their goods, they were sent back to their homes, there to "endure the rigours of ecclesiastical discipline"; seven were kept in prison and bound over to the assizes. Brewster seems to to have been the chief sufferer. Of the party who were to have sailed from the Humber half were served in a similar manner. Before the lapse of many months, however, the majority of the Scrooby "separatists" seem to have arrived safely in Leyden, from which town the "Mayflower" party set out some twelve years later, on the first stage of their memorable journey.

ELY

Ely is best approached by rail; the finest view of the city dawning on the approaching traveller. Like Venice it rose from an inland sea, of waving cornfields now, but once a vast reedy lagoon, subject to tide and flood, the haunt of beast and fowl and fish, and the last eastern refuge of the ancient British race.

Much of the fertile plain, sprinkled with hamlets that mark the islands of an ancient archipelago, is below the level of the sea; it is drained by pumps which pour the water into "lodes" discharging into the New Bedford river. The stupendous task of draining the fens was commenced by a company promoted by the Earl of Bedford, the engineer being Cornelius Vermuyden, a Dutchman. The scheme first saw the light in the reign of Charles I., but Cromwell, who opposed it, preferred to flood land rather than drain it, if by so doing he could annoy the King and his tenants; for Charles had bought up the company. When Lord Protector Cromwell changed his tactics, and the New Bedford river was cut, the drainage of the fens meant ruin and a total change of life to the fenmen, but their expostulations, after many riots and much breaking of sluices, were overcome by the presence of troops; and the work was cheaply executed

ELY. The Cathedral.

ELY. The Interior of the Cathedral.

by such Dutch and Scottish prisoners of war as Cromwell did not sell to the slave-owners of the West Indies or the galleys of Venice. Windmills at first supplied the motive power, but are now superseded by steam. The whole scheme was not fully completed until late in the nineteenth century.

The old fenmen, racked with ague and steeped in opium, are gone; and gone, too, is the last corner of primeval England. All but treeless now, the fens were once a vast forest of oak and beech, willow and alder, forming part of the great continent now severed by the North Sea, where elephant and rhinoceros, elk and bison, lion and bear roamed at will.

Even in Roman days the fens, though subsiding, were still mainly forest; but the Roman dykes gave way, the land continued to sink, the streams of the forest delta became choked, and the country was gradually changed into a labyrinth of sluggish channels, reedy broads, and impenetrable bogs. Here, during the Saxon invasion, the British, elsewhere exterminated, or absorbed, or driven into the west, found a refuge, and lived a life of their own until the Conquest. They were known as the Girvii (Welsh, *gwryw*, manly or brave), and Ely itself is derived from the Welsh *helig* (willow), though the Venerable Bede naively suggested that the derivation of the word might be found in the fact that the waters of the district were *eely*. Another Welsh word—basket—has passed into the English as it did into the Latin tongue. As early as 100 B.C. the baskets of the fen district were known to Europe. Posidonius, the Rhodian, mentions them as an article of export; Strabo tells us they were used in granaries, and Martial speaks of a gift contained in

"A basket rude, from painted Britons brought."

Here we may picture a British, then a Romano-British people, busied in snaring fish and fowl, in hunting game, in growing corn on the uplands, and in their special industry of basket-making, driven by Saxon invasion into the fastnesses of the fens, but still surviving as a separate people when the Normans came upon the scene.

The nucleus of the present city was the work of Etheldreda, daughter of Anna, a Christian Saxon king, who fell defending his country against Penda the heathen. Etheldreda, who was one of four sisters, all queens and saints, was strongly influenced by Hilda, her aunt, who founded Whitby, and that bold and somewhat officious prelate, Wilfrid. Married to Tonbert, a lord of Mercia, she refused him the usual privileges of a husband, and when a widow, and remarried to Egfrid, king of Northumbria, she treated that prince in the same way. At Wilfrid's instance she eventually left him, and fled to her own domains, Egfrid in hot pursuit. We are told that he would have caught her, but that the waters, in defence of her virginity, rose suddenly and divided them, which so impressed her husband that he departed.

At Ely she founded a religious house for monks and nuns; Peterborough, Thorney, Crowland and Ramsey were contemporary.

Etheldreda died of a quinsy; not unnaturally, as she used to pray from midnight until daybreak.

She regarded the affliction as a special punishment for the wearing of a necklace in the past. It is curious that so austere a lady should be immortalised in such a word as *tawdry*, but so it is; the popular form of her name is St. Audrey, and St. Audrey's fair, at which all kinds of showy and inferior trinkets and stuffs were sold to the primitive fen-folk, gained such a name for the cheap and nasty that the word tawdry resulted as a natural corruption of the saint's name used as an adjective (S't Awdrey—a "s't'awdrey stuff.")

Saxon England appeared to be quieting down when in 787, "first there came three ships out of Haeretha-land"—Norway. In a few years fire, pillage, and massacre followed Dane and Northman from end to end of England. In the Wash their ships lay snug, their wives and families often aboard, while they raided inland, after a time horsing themselves for their greater raids. Cambridge was soon part of the Danelagh, abbeys and convents, and monkish learning were all swept away.

Not until 912 did Edward the Elder, in conjunction with his sister, Ethelfleda, commence the re-conquest of the Danelagh. He brought up fighters from all parts of England.

Alfred re-established a small religious foundation at Ely, which prospered awhile; but in 982 the Danish raids recommenced. Brithnoth, a patron of Ely, headed the heroic defence, but fell in battle in 991, as the "Lay of Maldon" tells us. Only his headless corpse was recovered. The body, with a ball of wax in place of the head, was buried in the abbey church, to be discovered rather more than a century ago. The Danes, though victorious, were so discomfited that they sailed away. But then came Sweyn, and finally Canute; the Danes now fighting on horseback. Ely, however, escaped, Canute being a Christian; indeed, he became a notable benefactor, and paid frequent visits to the Abbey. An old tradition states that it was the singing of the monks which first brought him to the spot, and an old ballad says:

> "Merrily sang the monks at Ely
> When Cnut the king he rowed thereby;
> Row to the shore, men, said the king,
> And let us hear these monks to sing."

In his days the Abbot of Ely was chancellor of the kingdom for four months in each year; this was in the winter, and most of Canute's visits fell in that season. A tradition tells of his coming on a sledge, with the heaviest man to be found—one Pudding—skating ahead to prove the ice.

Emma, his wife, and widow of Ethelred the Unready, gave hangings for the church and shrine; and here Edward the Confessor, her younger son by Ethelred, was educated. Edward, when he came to the throne, confirmed the charters of the abbey and made extensive grants of land. In his reign there was not in all Cambridgeshire one gentle family of English blood left, and no free churls. But Ely still prospered.

In 1069 the Danes made their last invasion in the hope of placing Sweyn, nephew of Canute, on the throne of England. After raiding Yorkshire they came south to Ely; Christian, the bishop, Earl

Osbjorn, and the Danish house-carles (Royal Guard). The remnant of the English flocked to their standard, in the hope of expelling the Normans; the fenmen came in under the leadership of Hereward the Wake. We learn that Hereward led the Danish fleet to Peterborough, then held by the Normans, and ruled by a Norman abbot, in order to rescue it from alien hands. The rescue took the shape of pillage and fire, after which the Danes, whose object had been pillage as much as the hope of establishing Sweyn, sailed away, leaving Hereward to be excommunicated. It is possible that Hereward acted thus to get the Danes away from Ely, which he regarded as defensible; at all events, at Ely he established himself as leader, in spite of the ban of the Church, with the intention of defying the Conqueror. At this time no causeway existed, and the game, fish, and fowl of the fens—stags, roes, goats, hares, eels, pike, perch, roach, burbot, lamprey, salmon, and sturgeon, and more birds than we can mention—would have nourished the garrison indefinitely. Morkere of Northumbria broke prison at Winchester to join Hereward; the Bishop of Durham left the safety of the Scottish Court, and lesser nobles and leaders flocked thither by the score, and monks and soldiers crowded the abbey halls.

This was a serious matter, that called for the presence of William himself. He at once came down to Cambridge. His plan of attack was to harry one side of the island with his fleet, while building a causeway to the opposite side. When the causeway, made of logs, bavins, sacks of earth and bundles of rushes, was all but completed,

Hereward fired the reeds, and destroyed a column of the enemy.

No general rising of the English supported the garrison of Ely, so one by one the leaders surrendered, to be rewarded by imprisonment for life. Not so Hereward the "strenuissimus," but at length the monks betrayed him; William threatening to confiscate all the property of the abbey outside Ely, they guided the Normans across the Ouse. Hereward escaped, and later obtained lands from William; his followers were brutally mutilated. The monks, despite their treachery, were fined 700 marks of silver. The moneyers who minted their plate for William at Cambridge were fraudulent, so the fine was increased to 1000 marks, or 8000 ounces-worth, £20,000 of our money.

William left a garrison of forty knights quartered on the monks; one on each monk. In the cathedral is a most interesting relic, the "Tabula Eliensis," on which are painted (it is a Tudor copy of the original) the portraits, names, and arms of the forty knights, and the names of their unwilling hosts. This table is valuable as demonstrating the immense variety and splendid organisation of William's army; there were cavalry and infantry, archers and spearmen, sappers, seamen, marines, commissariat men, ambulance men, and scouts. A few extracts may interest the reader:

1. Opsalus, Miles, Ballistarum Dux (artillery captain, the artillery consisting of catapults or slings hurling great masses of stone or ponderous javelins), cum Godfrido Monacho.

5. Hastingus, Miles Nauttic, Exercitus (of the marines), cum Nigello Monacho.

9. Bryan de Clare, Veteranus, cum Clitone Monacho.

Of these the first was probably a Swede, and the ninth, the veteran, an Irish soldier of fortune. Among the monks' names are Donald, Duff, Owen, and David, all Celtic names.

The cathedral, as we know it, was commenced by the first Norman abbot, Simeon, who erected the greater part of the nave; it was completed by Bishop Ridel in 1189. We owe its continued existence to a squabble; for as a result of a dispute as to the right of nomination to the post of abbot, the crown was appealed to, and the see of Ely instituted. But for this the Reformation would have swept it away with many another noble fabric.

Henceforth the history of Ely is the history of the cathedral. Much of it is written in the stone for all to read. The Bishop of Ely was a Bishop Palatine; that is, he had the prerogatives of a sovereign in the Isle, appointing his own justices and police. His London palace was in Holborn. Richard III. refers to the garden:

> "My Lord of Ely, when I was last in Holborn
> I saw fine strawberries in your garden there."

Ely Place, being part of his dominions, was long a sanctuary to debtors, the King's writ not running there. This condition of things only ceased in the nineteenth century. All that is left of the Palace is St. Etheldreda's Chapel. Ely Place still has its own local government of commissioners, and a day and a night watchman take the place of the police. The later palace was in Dover Street; it was built in 1775, and is now the Albemarle Club. The bishop's mitre may be seen on the façade.

Having admired the vast fabric of the cathedral from the railway, the visitor leaves the station, and proceeds, passing a row of old thatched cottages, to the iron gate of the Cathedral Park. Here, in the midst of sixteen acres of undulating ground, beyond which the cathedral rises, as a modern writer has noted, like a ship from the waves, is an artificial mound, thickly wooded, now surmounted by a monument to Bentham, the historian of Ely, but of old by the abbey windmill. This mill was known as one of the four marvels of Alan de Walsingham, the others being the octagon with its lantern, the Lady chapel, and the abbey vineyard. Near the Walpole Gate (commenced in 1396 and completed by Prior Walpole) is the abbey tithe-barn, one of the largest known examples, with its tiled roof; a relic of the days when rents were paid in kind.

The Walpole Gate, or "Ely Porta," is worth attention; it bears the arms of Edward the Confessor and those of the see, for the upper chamber (used in the past as a chapel, a prison, and part of a brewery) is now the schoolroom of the famous choir school, at which Edward received his education.

Near by, but without the gate, is the beautiful little building known as Prior Crauden's Chapel, built, like so much of what is best at Ely, by Alan de Walsingham. Prior Crauden "ruled the convent as a peaceable shepherd, and was beloved by God and man." He was elected Bishop of Ely by the monks, but the Pope refused to confirm the election. This chapel he built for private prayer and meditation. It measures only fifteen feet by thirty. It is a beautiful example of the Decorated style; there is a mosaic pavement of Adam and Eve, and on one wall the remains of a fresco of trefoil and daisies. This beautiful little chamber is approached by a spiral staircase; a vaulted chamber is below. The chapel is now part of the King's Grammar School, and is in daily use.

Next to the chapel is the priory, now the canon's residence. Here Crauden once entertained Queen Philippa, wife of Edward III. Next we come to the deanery, once the dining-hall of the abbey, and then to the fair-hall, meant for large assemblies, now the residence of the head-master of King's School.

Returning to the gate, passing through, and turning to the right, we find ourselves in a street known as the Gallery, from an overhead gallery or covered bridge which once connected the palace and cathedral, spanning the roadway. Opposite the gateway is Hereward Hall, a modern adjunct to the King's School. On the left is the wall of the palace garden, with its magnificent old plane-tree, planted in 1639.

The palace was built by Bishop Alcock, late in the fifteenth century; it is of red brick, faced with stone. Note the punning coat of arms, *all cocks*, or rather their heads, and the arms of the see, and the empty canopied niches. Goodrich added the west gallery with its oriel window. On the stonework of the window are inscribed Bishop Goodrich's "Duties," the germ of the catechism; they are much defaced by time. They end with the phrase so often misquoted by the smug in criticism of the discontented poor, "in ye state of lyfe it plese God to call us on to." It is interesting to note that the original, like the Catechism, expresses the idea of progress and uncertainty, which is lacking in the popular misquotation—"to which it has pleased God to call them."

We have now reached the cathedral. Across the road is the beautiful Galilee Porch—nearly removed by Essex, the fashionable "restorer" of the time of George III., as "neither useful nor ornamental." Its date is probably about 1200. It acts as a buttress to the great tower. The tower was originally surmounted by a spire; it was proposed to remove this in 1748, but the inhabitants protesting it was left thirty years longer, when it was demolished as unsafe. This spire crowned the octagonal lantern, which, with four turrets, forms the upper portion of the tower.

The splendid Norman nave is one of the most impressive features of the interior. The great timber roof is now hidden by a vaulted ceiling, which was beautifully decorated in the last century by two amateurs; the subject of the decorations is the Root of Jesse. The dignity and harmony of the grave Norman arches of the supporting tier, the triforium, and the clerestory, the massive lower piers being alternately clustered and circular, produce an impression of restful simplicity and majesty.

The most remarkable feature of the building is the famous octagon tower and lantern, erected by Alan de Walsingham to replace the great Norman tower, which fell in 1322, crushing the Norman choir. The stonework of this daring structure was completed in six years; the woodwork took sixteen. To provide the eight gigantic balks of oak that support the roof, they are sixty-eight feet in length, was a matter of no small difficulty; and even in our times, when timber was needed for repairs, the transport of such enormous beams proved a most formidable difficulty.

The windows contain modern glass; but there are ancient portrait-heads in the mouldings of the arches, and a series of corbels depicts incidents in the life of St. Etheldreda. It is believed that the builder lies here, under a much-worn slab, at the commencement of the nave.

The transepts are earlier than the nave, being the work of the first Norman abbot. The presbytery of Bishop Northwold, with its three orders of windows, is an unusually fine example of the late Decorated style. The beautiful Lady chapel is another example of the same style. It measures about 100 feet by 50, and has a vaulted roof of a single span. Canopied niches divide a stone bench which runs round the walls like so much mediæval and ancient sculpture, the richly decorated canopies were originally painted; traces of blue, green, red and gold still remaining. The statues are of course gone; and of the stained glass only a few fragments are left.

John of Wisbech built this chapel, to the designs

of Alan of Walsingham. When he was ready to begin the actual work of erection there was a dearth of funds. Brother John took to prayer, called some monks and lay brethren to help him, and commenced to dig the foundations by night. While digging, John found a pot of ancient silver coins, but said nothing at the time; all night they dug, until "a small rain came on." John hid the money secretly under his bed, and cleaned the coins a few at a time, and with them paid the workmen as long as the money lasted. John finished the chapel, and a few months later fell a victim to the Black Death.

The cloisters, alas! are no more; their site is now the deanery garden. They played a dominant part in the old corporate life of the abbey, being schoolroom, study, atelier, office and library in one. Here the clerical, artistic, literary and educational work of the community was performed, as far as possible in silence, and not always interrupted by the cold of winter. Many reference books were kept in the cloister, and here were compiled the famous Liber Eliensis, containing the history of the abbey from its foundation till the end of the twelfth century, the episcopal rolls and registers, the account rolls—nearly 300 in number—the cellerarius rolls, containing all the details of housekeeping, and many others—now in the cathedral library, or at Lambeth, or in the British Museum. From these records we find that the monk, who was a gentleman by position and usually by birth, cost the community the equivalent of £4 of our money weekly in food and clothing; so that apart from discomforts incidental to the age—such as the lack of windows and chimneys—he lived in comfort and dignity.

We find in the outfit of the monk such articles as cowls, frocks, winter and summer coats, wool-lined cassocks, furred tunics, blankets, counterpanes, day and night boots, gaiters, and "willcocks"—a species of headgear to defy the wind, and possibly the progenitor of the modern "billy-cock." Novices carried pencils and tablets on which to note breaches of the rule, to be referred to at confession. As for the pleasures of the table, we do not find the diet ascetic. Five kinds of bread and beer were supplied, beef, mutton, venison, fowls and fish—and of these the variety would be endless—rice, sugar, milk, and vast quantities of eggs, seem to have formed the staple diet. The vineyard produced vinegar only, but foreign wines were consumed on special occasions.

The rule of the Benedictines was fairly strict. The monk rose at two in the morning—it is only fair to say that he had had seven hours in bed—and attended matins; at four he returned to bed for another hour. Then came prime and tirce; then the Chapter met to apportion tasks for the day; then came low and high mass. At ten the monk broke his fast, while a brother read the scriptures. Then came study or scholastic or clerical work in the cloisters, lasting till 3 p.m.; then vespers, and at 5 supper, compline, and bed. At certain seasons games were allowed. Once in six weeks each monk was bled, so faithfully as to necessitate a week in the infirmary.

All this came to an end in 1539. Members of

communities that made "voluntary surrender" were modestly provided for. The abbey became a chapter of dean and canons.

Returning to the cathedral, we should especially note Bishop West's chapel, despoiled by his successor, Goodrich, who was bishop at the time of the Dissolution. It is a rich example of the finest Perpendicular style. Over two hundred stone canopies once held statuettes, broken by Goodrich, the last bishop to be abbot. Alcock's chapel is earlier, but of the same period in style, and contains some wonderful carving of grape-vine ornament; a curious boss seen from one point of view becomes a grinning demon. The bishop's coat-of-arms is a frequent motive.

The shrines of the four saints and queens were long ago despoiled. The shrine of Etheldreda was once rich in silver and pearls, emeralds and onyx, with crystal lions and ivory angels. One Bishop Nigel robbed it, but others enriched it again. The coffin was a Roman sarcophagus, found soon after her death by a party of monks on the ravaged site of the Roman city of Grantchester, Cambridge. The monument, by Alan de Walsingham, still survives, but the coffin was broken up at the time of the Reformation, and the dust within it scattered.

The body of another Queen—Witburga—was stolen from Dereham, to make the collection complete. The abbot held a Court of Justice at Dereham and afterwards feasted the inhabitants royally; in the night he secretly dug up the body of the saint, and by horse litter and boat conveyed it to Ely, the men of Dereham in vain pursuit. Ely was forced on appeal to give up the spoil, but revenged herself by saying that she had surrendered only a worthless skeleton, and still possessed the true relics. An inquiry forced the monks of Ely to confess that this was a trick ; Dereham had her saint again.

In Bishop West's chapel lie the remains of Brithnoth. His widow gave a " curtain " depicting his deeds, possibly the Bayeux tapestry was suggested by this.

Before leaving the cathedral the visitor should climb the tower, whence a magnificent view may be obtained of the fertile plain, the villages marking the situation of the islands of old. Peterborough and the spires of Cambridge are visible on the horizon.

Leaving the cathedral and passing the palace we come to St. Mary's Church, an interesting combination of Norman and Early English architecture. Near it is the present vicarage. This was once the tithe house, attached to the tithe barn, and the residence of the hereditary steward. Steward indeed became the family name, and when the last of the male line died in 1636 Oliver Cromwell, who was his grandson, stepped into his office. Here he lived for ten years, becoming in time Governor of the Isle of Ely. Here he drilled the levies that formed the nucleus of his Ironsides ; and from this house he crossed to the cathedral, in January, 1643, while Canon Hitch was conducting the choir service after having received and ignored a letter from Cromwell requiring him to discontinue that " so unedifying and offensive " service. Sword in hand, hat on head, he requested the canon to " leave his fooling and come down," and drove the people from the building. In 1648 the cathedral had a narrow escape. Parliament made an order that it should be examined with a view to pulling it down and using the material for a hospital for sick and wounded soldiers. It was then in a somewhat ruinous condition.

Not far away is the modern Theological College. St. John's Farm should be visited,—the remains of a thirteenth century hostel for such monks as were not of the foundation. To the south of Ely is the water tower. Before the water supply was established water for brewing and washing was brought from the river in great leather bags, slung one on either side of a horse; an arrangement that made a livelihood "for many industrious poor." The industrious poor are now largely occupied in fruit-picking, jam-making, farming, and the making of the classic basket.

CHICHESTER

IF to be happy is to have no history, Chichester should be accounted fortunate, for it very nearly fulfils that condition. A quiet agricultural market-town, once one of the towns of the Staple and later the home of the needle-making industry, its existence has for the most part been prosperous and uneventful and it has given few hostages to fortune in the shape of eminent sons.

In one respect, however, Chichester is in the proud position of being unique among English towns; there is good reason to believe that two of its early inhabitants are mentioned in the Bible.

Chichester is ancient as English towns go. Below it lie the remains of the Roman Regnum, capital of the Regni, a British people friendly and subject to Rome from an early date. In the time of Claudius, Plautius was commissioned to subdue the Sussex coast, and the local British ruler, Cogidubnus, became king and imperial legate. Of all Roman relics found in Chichester the most interesting is a slab of Purbeck marble now at Goodwood, which contains the dedicatory inscription of a temple erected in the time of Cogidubnus—who, as the custom was, took the name of his Roman suzerain —which reads as follows :

" The temple of Neptune and Minerva, erected

for the preservation of the Imperial house, by the authority of Tiberius Claudius Cogidubnus, the king and legate of the empire. The college of artificers (the guild, probably, of shipwrights) and those who were desirous of supplying materials defrayed the expense; Pudens the son of Pudentinus gave the site."

Now there are fairly good reasons for believing that this Pudens, and Claudia, the daughter of Cogidubnus, are the Pudens and Claudia mentioned not only by Martial, but by St. Paul in the second epistle to Timothy; they having eventually, like so many influential Britons of the time, visited Rome and embraced Christianity. Cogidubnus is mentioned also by Tacitus.

The church of Roman Chichester was evidently on the site of the present St. Olave's, both tiles and urns having been found in the walls; and one small doorway is probably actually of Roman construction.

Under Roman rule Chichester was evidently a place of considerable importance. The walls followed the line of the present city walls, indeed the latter are largely Roman, and the town itself has retained the general plan of the Roman city. Not only was Chichester a stronghold, but a considerable garrison seems to have been maintained without the walls, as the lands known as the Broyle (Latin *bruillum,* coppice) show the remains of a military station. Relics of the Roman city have been found in abundance, and the church and churchyard of St. Andrew conceal a large tesselated pavement, which lies at a depth of four or five feet, so that the coffins in the churchyard actually rest upon it.

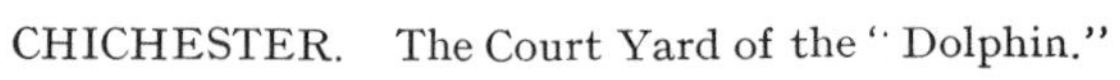
CHICHESTER. The Court Yard of the "Dolphin."

The end of the Roman Regnum came in the year 480. Ella, the first of the Saxons to invade Sussex, had landed three years previously, and in the year after his landing had sent for reinforcements. When the city was finally taken there was the usual scene of fire and pillage. Cissa, who succeeded Ella as king of the South Saxons, rebuilt the town on the old ground-plan and gave it the name of Cissa's ceaster or camp—Chichester. He ruled about seven years.

Chichester remained pagan until the year 650. Then Adelwalch, king of Sussex, taken prisoner by the Christian king of Mercia, became a convert and was released. On returning to his city he founded, according to Bede, the church which was the predecessor of the cathedral and also the monastery and see of Selsea. Another tradition, however, makes Caedwalla the founder of Selsea; but Bede and William of Malmesbury state that Adelwalch was the founder, Caedwalla being an unruly person who slew Adelwach and obtained the throne of Wessex, but was driven out of Sussex.

However this may be, it is clear that Wilfrid, after being previously wrecked on the Frisian coast, was with other Northumbrians shipwrecked on the Sussex coast, on his way back from Rome, and reached Selsea, the "island of seals" at a time when the Saxons, driven frantic by a three years' drought followed by famine and pestilence, were chaining themselves together in batches and casting themselves into the sea. As soon as Wilfrid landed rain fell abundantly, and he was credited with a miracle. He founded a monastery and an episcopal see, and is said to have taught the inhabitants to fish. After sojourning there some five years he returned to the north, "and while yet living did not cease to perform miracles." His church now lies beneath the sea, and the anchorage off Selsey, known even to-day as the Park, was in the time of Henry VIII. a stretch of forest full of deer.

Thanks to Athelwulf, son of Egbert, Chichester seems to have escaped the common fate of ravage by the Danes, who, sailing up the muddy Sussex rivers, devastated so many other towns; now and again, however, coming off second best, as is proved in one instance by fragments of the skin of a flayed pirate still adhering under the nail-heads of a church door. In the time of Alfred the Danes, returning from the sack of Exeter, put in to a neighbouring harbour, but the men of Chichester fared forth and slew them in hundreds, taking or sinking several vessels of the fleet.

Just before the Conquest Chichester was a town of some importance for those days, containing 283 houses, and paying a yearly rental of £15, £10 going to the King and 100 shillings to the earl (Godwin, father of Harold). At the time of the Conquest the rental was £35, and Domesday Book informs us that one Humphry Flamen possessed a house of 10s. value—perhaps the old Saxon castle. The Saxon town was divided into ten wards, each having two constables, and the whole presided over by two head-boroughs, each of whom officiated for six months in the year. In the year 992 a mint was erected here. We may picture the town as four streets of wooden houses, or houses of timber framing filled with clay stiffened with twigs or reeds, and thatched roofs; probably only the castle and the abbey were of stone. Each house had its garden, either beside it or within the walls, and a corresponding piece of pasture without the walls.

William the Conqueror gave the town to Roger de Belesme or Montgomery, together with the city of Shrewsbury and 157 manors. He also removed the see of Selsea to Chichester. Probably the church of St. Peter's Abbey served as the early cathedral.

Roger had two sons; Hugh, the younger, inherited the English manors; Robert de Belesme, of whom we shall hear in connection with Shrewsbury, the elder, the Norman estates. Hugh tried to dethrone Rufus and had to pay a fine of £3,000; he died in repelling a raid of Magnus of Norway upon Anglesea and the north-west of Wales. Robert then inherited; on the death of Rufus, when Robert of Normandy was in Palestine, and Henry II. usurped the throne, Belesme conspired to obtain the crown for his sovereign. Robert eventually "sold out" his claim, on the understanding that his supporters were to be reinstated; Henry broke his word. Belesme fortified Arundel, and Henry besieged him; he fled to Bridgenorth, and was taken and expelled the country. The lordship of Chichester and the earldom of Arundel were then granted to William de Albini.

The feudal lord residing at Arundel or elsewhere, Chichester was singularly free of the usual feudal squabbles, having always been a quiet agricultural centre rather than the stronghold of a few powerful families.

The first cathedral built as such was the work of Ralph Luffa, and was completed in 1108, only to be destroyed by fire in 1114. It was a wooden building, and the succeeding fabric was partly of wood. In the year 1180 another fire destroyed the greater part of the cathedral, and Seffrid, then Bishop, built the cathedral very much as we see it to-day. Ralph II., who followed him, built the great central tower and broadened the nave by adding chantries. Bishop Gilbert of St. Leofard added the Lady chapel, and John of Langton (1305-37) the cloisters. Bishop Sherborne (1508-36) added screen and stalls, and employed three Italians of the name of Bernardi who embellished roofs and walls; one of these was responsible for the curious pictures of English kings and saints, Henry VIII. appearing both as himself and as Caedwalla, and Sherborne figuring as himself and as Wilfrid. Much of the Bernardis' lace-like decoration was whitewashed by a vandal dean in 1817, but was to some extent rescued some twenty years later.

The most exciting events in the history of the cathedral were the irruption of the Parliament men in 1643, when Sir William Waller besieged and took the city, and the fall of the great tower. "Although it rained heavily half an hour after the town was taken, no rain had fallen while the besiegers were lying abroad," so the troops were well, and in excellent humour for the cheerful work of destruction. They "pulled down the idolatrous images from the market-cross; they brake down the organ in the cathedral, and dashed the pipes with their poleaxes, crying in scoff 'Hark how the organs goe!'" and after the thanksgiving service, held appropriately in the cathedral, they " ran up and down with their swords drawn, defacing the monuments of the dead and hacking the seats and stalls."

On February 21, 1861, a terrible gale did much destruction in the southern counties. The cathedral was undergoing extensive repairs at the time. The four great piers of the tower, Norman rubble-work cased in stone, were known to be insecure, and the superincumbent arches were shored with timber. Suddenly cracks appeared in the piers, the dry rubble within began to pour out like sand, a fissure was seen to run up the spire, and suddenly tower, spire and all collapsed and sank, slowly and in a dignified manner, like a telescope shutting of its own weight. Singularly little damage was done to the rest of the building, and a new tower and spire were soon commenced.

Of notable bishops of Chichester we may mention St. Richard (1245-53) whose relics were translated hither in the presence of Edward I. and his Queen in the year 1276; and now lie in a much-restored tomb in the choir; Bishop Sherborne, to whom the cathedral owes much indeed, and his successor, the infamous Christopherson, who was jointly with Bonner responsible for the burning alive of twenty-seven people, ten in one fire at Lewes, none of whom were arrested upon a proper writ, but were burned two or three days only after their arrest. Bishop Lake is famous as one of the seven bishops who protested against James II.'s declaration of the liberty of conscience, and was therefore imprisoned, but released, to the joy of the populace. He was deprived on the accession of William III., as he refused the oath of allegiance.

It was said of Christopherson, who had translated Eusebius, the historian of the martyrs of the early Church, that he behaved "as if he had studied the arts of cruelty in the school of the heathens." Fortunately he was not long bishop, being installed only a year before Mary's death. He was succeeded by William Barlow, Bishop of St. Asaph's under Henry VIII., then of St. David's, then of Bath and Wells. Barlow was deprived by Mary, and fled to Germany, but returned upon the accession of Elizabeth, and was sent to Chichester. He had five daughters who married five bishops; his wife's tomb (in Hampshire) bears the following epitaph:

> Hic Agatha tumulus Barloi Praesulis inde
> Exulis inde; iterum Praesulis, Uxor erat;
> Prole beata fuit, plura annis, quinque suarum
> Praesulibus vidit, Praesulis ipsa, datas.

> "The tomb of Agatha, of Barlow, sometime a Bishop,
> Sometime an exile, then Bishop again, the wife;
> Full of years and of blessings, five of her daughters
> Saw she to Bishops, herself to a Bishop, given."

The visitor to Chichester will obtain a handbook of the cathedral. Here it suffices to mention that the building is best seen from East Street looking west. Its central spire and flying buttresses give it a graceful pyramidal outline. Entering through the west porch, the five-aisled nave displays a wonderful effect of light and shade. In the nave are ten monuments by Flaxman; one of the poet Collins, who was born in Chichester on Christmas Day, 1719, and died in a house near the cloisters in 1759. He is buried in St. Andrew's.

The pictures by Bernardi the elder are at the back of the stalls in the south transept, and in the north transept, which for a long time was in use as the parish church of St. Peter. In the latter are portraits of all the Bishops of Selsea and Chichester from the foundation of the see to the Reformation; the companion portraits of the Kings of England have not all survived. The loss may be regarded as less in that they all have a very strong family resemblance. In the south transept is a picture representing Caedwalla bestowing the monastery of Selsea on Wilfrid, and Henry VIII. confirming the grant to Bishop Sherborne.

The Lady chapel gives an unusual length to the cathedral; it is a prolongation of the retro-choir. The latter contains some splendid Norman and pointed arches, with Purbeck marble shafts and foliated capitals; the Lady chapel is largely Decorated.

On the whole the cathedral is Norman, with Early English and Decorated additions. An unusual feature is the separate campanile—a squat tower some 120 feet in height. The stone of which it is built came from the Isle of Wight, and was intended by one Rimare, of Appledram, for the material of his castle, but his sovereign—Edward II.—forbade the erection of any such building, and the stone was sold to Bishop Langton.

Collins, the poet, has been mentioned as a native of Chichester. He was not its only poet. A historian, writing of the city early in the nineteenth century, speaks warmly of one Daniel Foot; like Collins, the son of a Chichester tradesman, who during his minority wrote and published, "Poems on Various Occasions, and Three Letters on Moral Subjects," which subjects, we must suppose, did not include prudence or moderation, since the unfortunate young man died at the age of twenty-three "from a surfeit of hedge-picks" consumed during a country walk.

A more eminent native was Bishop Juxon, perhaps the best known of Chichester's sons. From Merchant Taylors' he went to St. John's, Oxford, and followed Laud as president. He became Dean of Worcester, Prebendary of Chichester, Dean of the Chapel Royal, Bishop of London, and Lord High Treasurer—the first Churchman to hold the office since the reign of Henry VIII. He advised Charles I. to refuse his assent to the bill which sealed the fate of Strafford, "seeing that he knew his lordship to be innocent." It was he, as all will remember, who attended Charles on the scaffold. During the Commonwealth he kept a pack of hounds in Gloucestershire. Charles II. created him Archbishop of Canterbury.

The bishop's palace has been in part rebuilt, but the dining-room ceiling is decorated with heraldic devices by Bernardi. The chapel is Early English, and contains a curious old fresco. The palace stands at the west end of the cloisters of the cathedral; at the south-east corner is the chantry of St. Faith, founded in the fourteenth century, but now a dwelling-house.

An interesting old building is St. Mary's Hospital, which still supports eight poor people. It was founded as a convent about the middle of the twelfth century, by a dean of Chichester, but was suppressed in 1229, and the endowments applied to the support of thirteen decayed persons and a warden. It is entered from the street by an arched doorway. A long refectory ends in a chapel, which is separated from it by an open oak screen. The roof is very wide in span, and is supported by wooden standards; the aisles at the side contain the inmates' apartments, which consist each of two rooms. The timber roof comes to within six feet of the ground on either side.

St. Olave's Church has already been mentioned; it stands in North Street. Near the end of the same street is the Guildhall, once the chapel of the Grey Friars. It is Early English, and has a very fine window of five lancets; the sedilia behind the magistrates' bench are also fine. The garden, now a cricket-club ground, contains a mound which is probably the site of the old castle keep.

St. Andrew's Church, mentioned in connection with its underground Roman pavement and the tomb of Collins, contains also the monument of John Cawley, father of Cawley the "regicide." This Cawley founded almshouses for the poor, but the endowments have been vested in the Corporation and go towards the upkeep of the workhouse. The almshouses were intended to support twelve poor tradesmen. In 1772 a tobacconist of Fleet Street left his estate "to ease the inhabitants in their poor-rates for ever."

The Canon Gate, opening from the close into South Street, was probably erected by Sherborne, as it bears his arms; the same street contains the museum, in which an excellent collection of local antiquities may be seen. A curious exhibit is a vast lantern, known as the moon, which used to be borne in front of the Mayor when he went abroad at night. South Street also contains some interesting old houses, some of which are attributed to Wren. Opening out of South Street is the Pallant—*i.e.*, the Palatinate or " Archbishop's peculiar." It forms a miniature city in itself, with four main streets.

In Canon Lane is the hall of the old Vicars' College, founded for the vicars choral in the fourteenth century. It contains the ancient lavatorium and pulpit. It is now used by the Theological Training College.

The old city walls are fairly intact, with their semicircular bastions ; in parts they form the boundaries of the gardens of the dignitaries of the cathedral ; in several places they have been laid out as public promenades. They are mostly of Roman flint. The gates are not extant. They last played a part in the defence of the town during the civil war. After Edgehill, when the King lay at Reading, the gentlemen of Sussex sent thither to ask his authority to raise the south. They assembled at Chichester, but the south failed to rise. Sussex is a phlegmatic county. Recruits were few, and the citizens none too friendly. However, they repaired the walls, and razed two churches that hampered their artillery ; but Waller had them ready to surrender at the end of ten days, with no great damage to either side.

Chichester has been mentioned as one of the towns of the Staple. The Staple was instituted for the furtherance of trade—and incidentally the filling of the king's exchequer—by Edward III. The object of the Staple was to collect all the chief exportable produce of the realm—wool, felt, lead, and tin—and to store it in certain towns, from which it could be exported against goods or bullion, and to which foreign merchants could resort. The company of merchants of the Staple formed an independent commonwealth within the State ; there was a mayor and a constable of the Staple in each Staple town, and six mediators—two Germans, two Lombards, and two Englishmen. It is obvious that such an arrangement greatly reduced the cost and difficulty of collecting taxes on produce and exports, and was also of assistance to commerce. The towns of the Staple were originally Chichester, London, York, Canterbury, Winchester, Bristol, and Exeter. The Brotherhood of St. Thomas à Becket, which was a kind of wool trust, founded in the reign of Henry IV., did much to injure the merchants of the Staple. The organisation of the Staple did not prove successful, and from 1360 to 1558 the Staple for wool—that is, the trading-town for English wool—was usually fixed at Calais. This organisation hardly affected Chichester as the market-town of a wool-producing country.

Chichester was once famous for its needles, and also for its malt. The malt was exported chiefly to Ireland (the port of Chichester is a little to the west of the town) but the quality of the malt fell off, and the trade decayed. The needle industry for some reason never recovered from the effects of the civil war. It was carried on chiefly in the suburb of St. Pancras without the gates, and both church and suburb were destroyed to clear the ground adjacent to the walls.

A notable monument not yet described is the market cross. It was built by Bishop Story, about 1500, who left an estate of £25 to pay for its upkeep. Originally the niches above each arch contained figures, but Waller's troops destroyed them. The clock was given by Dame Elizabeth Farrington in 1733. The bronze bust of Charles I. on the east side is probably by Le Soeur or perhaps Farrelli. The whole structure forms a sort of open arcade being octagonal in form, with buttressed angles and a central pillar supporting a groined roof. The arches were long filled in with iron railings; the stone seats are recent. The lantern surmounting the structure is a doubtful "improvement"; the original finial was probably a cross. Bishop Story was the founder of the Grammar School, whose scholars wear upon their caps a representation of Prester John, the Bishop's heraldic cognisance.

A good example of a mediæval moated dwelling-house, though now modernised, is Kingsham House, now a farmhouse, on the south side of the railway, in St. Pancras' parish.

NORTHAMPTON

For centuries the town of Northampton occupied a position, both geographical and political, of peculiar importance. It is almost exactly in the centre of England, " so that travellers from the remotest parts of the land may be said to meet by the town " ; it was the natural meeting-place for north and south, east and west. Its surrounding forests, rich in all kinds of game, attracted monarchs and their courts, with the result that many councils and parliaments were convened here.

There is no very good evidence of its existence during British or Roman times, unless we may accept the evidence of its name in Saxon times, Hamtune, which would appear to be a tautological compound of the British and Saxon words for town—somewhat analogous to such names as Wickham, Berwick, Hamboro, Burton. As Southampton rose in importance the northern town naturally became Northampton.

The county was extensively settled by the Romans and was crossed by Watling Street and Ermine Street. The town was an important centre of the Middle Angles. In the ninth century it was, like so many English county towns, taken and occupied by the Danes, but in 921 it submitted to Edward the Elder as he made his famous advance upon the Danelagh. In 1010, however, the Danes returned and burned the town, "and took thereabout as much as they would"; this was in the harrying that preceded the conquest of Sweyn. In 1063, when Northumbria deposed Tostig, his successor Morkere marched south to Northampton, raising the country as he went, and made his headquarters in the town; and thence, with his brother Edwin, he ravaged the country round about, "slew men, burned houses, corn, took cattle," and departed with a number of slaves, after the lively fashion of the day. Then a great "gemote" was convened in the town by Harold—perhaps its earliest Parliament—at which Morkere and Edward the Confessor settled various points of difference. The earldom of Northampton was severed from that of Northumbria—Siward had held both—and given to Siward's son, Waltheof. Waltheof married Judith, niece to William the Conqueror. He was beheaded at Winchester in 1076, and his daughter brought the earldom in marriage to Simon of Senlis, the first of the three Norman earls of that name. He it was that built the castle on the bank of the Nene, and in all probability the Church of the Holy Sepulchre, of which more anon.

The "Saxon Chronicle" speaks of sixty burgesses and sixty houses, but at the time of the Conquest fourteen of these were waste. Domesday Book mentions forty burgesses.

With the third Simon, the earldom became extinct, and the castle reverted to the Crown, in 1184. The second Simon built the abbey of Delapré, of which nothing now remains.

From the time of Henry I. onwards we find the Kings of England constantly visiting the town for

NORTHAMPTON. Cromwell's House.

sport or sterner reasons. Here Henry kept Easter with his court in 1123; here in 1131 he called the barons together to swear fealty to his daughter Maud or Matilda, wife of Geoffrey of Anjou, and later of the Emperor Charles V. Here the barons reassembled to do the same for Stephen. In 1144 Stephen held his court here; and twenty years later Northampton was the scene of the famous Council of Northampton, when the Constitutions of Clarendon, subjecting the Church to the Crown, were ratified. Becket had agreed at last to the proposed provisions, but he retracted his promise, and came to Northampton in a mood of defiance. Taking his archiepiscopal cross from Alexander, the Welshman, he swept into the presence of the assembly, protested against the claim of the nobles to judge him, and appealed to the Pope. He was followed, as he left, by cries of "Traitor!" Henry, sulking in an inner chamber, would not see him. "A fool he was and ever will be," was his comment upon Becket's somewhat theatrical appearance. Becket fled that night in the dress of a monk, and the quarrel commenced which ended in his assassination.

Ten years later Henry's sons were in arms against him. Anketil Mallory, supporting Prince Henry, defeated the loyalists of the town, plundered it, and returned to Leicester with booty and 200 prisoners.

Ten years later still the famous Assize of Northampton was held. Barons, prelates, knights and burgesses were called to form a Parliament, which was the first in England to unite the three estates of the realm, and so may be regarded in a sense as the parent of the English Parliament, although many assemblies were held subsequently which did not represent the Commons. This assembly confirmed the Constitutions of Clarendon, and divided the kingdom into six circuits for the administration of justice, thus subordinating both the Church and the Law to the control of the Crown, and admitting the right of the Commons to advise the Crown. The King and clergy of Scotland were present, for the purpose of making submission to the English Church.

In 1199 we find one Geoffry Fitzwalter paying a fine of 40s. to be discharged from the inspection of the coinage, which proves that the town possessed a mint at that time; it is mentioned in the records of the two subsequent reigns. In 1184 Richard granted a charter which gave the burgesses the right of choosing a portreeve and of "holding the town"—always a somewhat expensive privilege. Kings were accustomed to sell charters when impoverished, and if there were none to sell would "resume" a charter and charge a substantial sum for its restoration.

In the same year, Richard being dead, the nobles of the realm again assembled, and were prevailed upon to accept John.

John was a frequent visitor to the city. Even before his time Northampton was famous for its boots, and an old record exists to the effect that King John bought a pair of single-soled boots here—"8 tari botarum singularum"—at a cost of twelve pence.

In 1209, John having a difference with the

burgesses of London, Northampton was honoured by the removal of the Royal Exchequer thither. In 1212 he met the Papal nuncios, Pandulph and Durand, who came to demand the restoration of property confiscated from the clergy, and upon his refusal excommunicated him.

Henry III. also was a frequent visitor. In the Barons' War both sides took and lost the town. We read that he was here when the news of Fulke de Breauté's rebellion reached him, and his council granted a subsidy for the manufacture of machines to be used in the reduction of Bedford, the forests close at hand supplying abundant timber for such a purpose; hides too, a staple article of commerce in Northampton, were largely used in the construction of mediæval scaling towers, catapults, and so forth. We read that he confirmed the charter granted by Henry II. for a fee of 200 marks, in return for which considerable sum he gave it new liberties as ample as those of London.

In 1234 the disputes between "town and gown" at Oxford became acute, with the ultimate result that the majority of the students of the University removed to Northampton. A similar migration occurred from Cambridge, and Northampton bade fair at one time to become the great university town of England. However, the scholars did not confine themselves to the gentle paths of learning. Despite the fact that in 1261 Henry bade the mayor and bailiffs and other good men afford the scholars every facility and protection, they sided with the barons in the war, and in 1264, fighting under their own banner, "did more with their slings and longbows and crossbows to vex and gall the king's men than all the forces of the barons besides." "Henry swore to hang them, but in the end he only packed them back to Oxford, making an enactment prohibiting Northampton from ever becoming a university town." On this occasion the King's men, who were led by Prince Edward, entered the town by undermining the wall of St. Andrew's convent. Simon de Montfort, the younger, had twice beaten off the attack, but the third time was taken prisoner "with all honour." The town was sacked. Simon retook it, and held a tournament, inviting the knights and barons of England "to give proof of their manhood."

By this time, as in most cities of England, there was a large and wealthy Jewish community. For a long period the Jews, as almost the only bankers, were protected by the Crown, but now greed regarded persecution as a more profitable policy. In 1278 no less than 300 Jews were hanged for clipping money, and in 1279 the old cry was raised, just as to-day it is from time to time raised in Russia—the Jews were accused, on Good Friday, of sacrificing a Christian child. Thirty were dragged behind horses and afterwards hanged. Ten years later Edward I. expelled all the Jews from the country, confiscating their property.

Edward I. was a constant visitor. In his reign letters patent were issued permitting the burgesses to keep dogs—previously forbidden, perhaps, by reason of the nearness of the royal hunting-grounds. An old tapestry shows some five or six different breeds of dogs used in venery; a long-coated deerhound, greyhounds or whippets, something like a setter, a sort of spaniel, and a dog strongly resembling the modern bull-dog; these latter are in leash, evidently to be slipped at the last to pull down the quarry.

In the year of Edward's death a Parliament met to arrange for his burial, and the marriage and coronation of his successor, in whose reign one John Poydras, the son of an Exeter tanner, was examined by a Parliament on account of his claim that he was the true son of Edward I., the King being the child of a carter. As he failed to bring forward any proofs he was hanged. In 1328 the Statute of Northampton confirmed the great constitutional charters and amended the laws. In 1338 the Corporation obtained permission to hold an annual fair of twenty-eight days. In 1380 the second Statute of Northampton was enacted, taxing foreign wines. The Parliament responsible for this measure did not meet in the castle; it is doubtful if any did so after the year 1323, when the great hall was destroyed by fire, but in the priory of St. Andrew. The last Parliament held here was in 1381, when the poll-tax was imposed that led to the rebellion of Wat Tyler. In the reign of Edward III. Thomas Wake, sheriff, claimed the castle as appertaining to the county; thenceforward it was held by the sheriffs, and later was used as a prison.

So far the history of the castle has been the history of the town. The next hostilities of note in which the castle was concerned were the Wars of the Roses. In 1410 the Battle of Northampton was fought on the meadows belonging to the abbey of Delapré. Margaret fled to Scotland and Henry VI. fell a prisoner into the hands of York. In this year the borough was finally incorporated.

Northampton boasted of many guilds at this period. When precisely the boot and shoe industry was first established we do not know ; but it existed, as we have seen, in the twelfth century, and probably centuries earlier. Northampton supplied Cromwell's army, the army sent to Ireland by Charles I., the English army in the Crimea, and the French army in the Franco-Prussian War. Spencer Perceval, who is chiefly famous for having been assassinated in the lobby of the House of Commons in 1812, was member for the borough, and obtained valuable Government contracts for the town. The old leather fair was and is of great importance. The "leather bottel" was a local product.

Northampton used to be an open borough—that is, every householder paying "scot and lot" could vote. In the eighteenth century the contests were as spirited as they were corrupt. Pennant ingenuously remarks that the householder's vote "was a cruel privilege" to such provincial magnates as "were ambitious of recommending their own representatives"—in coarser language, of buying the seat. Such ambitious gentry certainly found the privilege a very costly one for them. In 1768 the Earls of Halifax and Northampton, and Spencer tried each to return his own member, and materially impoverished themselves in the process, Spencer paying £100,000, and the other two £150,000 apiece. This for 1000 voters ; many of whom, by the way, voted twice, in which case they presumably sold themselves more than once. A wide-awake tradesman, in those days, might easily make a thousand pounds at election time. Reform must have been a sad blow to such.

To return for a moment to the castle, and the Wars of the Roses, we read that the unfortunate Earl Rivers, father of Elizabeth, Queen of Edward IV., and Constable of England, was seized and beheaded in Northampton in 1469. During the Civil War the castle was seized by Lord Brooke, and a Parliamentary garrison left in charge. The battle of Naseby was fought only twelve miles away. In 1662 the demolition of the castle was ordered, and the ruins were used as a quarry.

Charles II. seems to have been the last king to resume and regrant the charter of the Corporation. The plague visited the town in his reign, and in 1678 a great fire destroyed 600 to 700 houses. For the rebuilding of the town it is curious to note that £20,000 was publicly subscribed, but for the rebuilding of London after the Great Fire only £18,000.

One of the finest views of the town may be obtained from the well-known Eleanor Cross, one of the many similar monuments erected in commemoration of the sad journey of the court from Harby in Notts to Westminster. Each night, when the bier was set down before bearing it into the church or religious house that was to give it shelter, " the King's chancellor and the great men " fixed upon a suitable site for such a memorial. Two of the three remaining crosses are in Northamptonshire.

The Northampton cross, actually a mile south of the town, is in very fair preservation, and has on the whole been respected by the restorers. It consists of an octagonal base, a lower stage of canopied panels and shields of arms, a second stage containing four statues of Queen Eleanor, under richly carved canopies, and a final tier which presumably was once surmounted by a cross, but which now supports a broken shaft. Near by is a causeway from the town built at a cost of £20 " for the soul of the Queen." The accounts of the payments made to the sculptors and stonecutters engaged on the work are still extant.

Beloved as she was, Eleanor had some surprising characteristics. She acquired lands which the Jews had extorted from Christians, and to such an extent that Archbishop Peckham informed her that her " illicit and damned gain " had become " a scandal and byword," and refused her absolution. Carpets were introduced into England by Eleanor ; daughter of the King of Castile, she would have seen them at her father's court, to which the Spanish Moors introduced them.

The popular tradition that her presence of mind saved her husband's life in Palestine, appears to be a myth. Knighton says that when the wound had to be dressed the King had to order her to be carried shrieking from the room. But of Edward's passionate devotion to her there can be no doubt.

From the cross the city is seen to cover a ridge by the banks of the Nene. Delapré Abbey, a modern dwelling, may be seen on the right.

The town contains no very ancient houses, probably as a result of the great fire. There are four principal streets, and a market square, which lies off the Drapery. Here is the Corn Exchange, a somewhat unlovely building.

Of the old churches the most curious is that of the Holy Sepulchre, built, in all probability, by the first of the Norman earls. It is one of four English churches, built after the model of the Church of the Holy Sepulchre in Jerusalem. The other three are the Temple Church in London, and the churches at Cambridge and Maplestead in Essex. The nave is circular. The font in the centre is modern. The windows are late Decorated. The building was restored by Scott in 1860. The tiled floor and sepulchral inscriptions are worth noting. The Perpendicular tower has curious and unusual buttresses.

St. Peter's Church was probably built by the grandson of the first earl; the date is about 1160, being late Norman with Perpendicular alterations. The north gate, the corbels under the roof, and the tower buttresses, are interesting. John Smith, the mezzotintist, is buried here, and Dr. William Smith, the "father of English geology," whose observation of fossil remains peculiar to different strata was an epoch-making discovery.

All Saints' Church, in the Drapery, was burned down in 1675. Charles II., whose statue may be seen over the portico, gave "1000 tun of timber" for the rebuilding of the church and the town. The tower and lantern are old, in the Decorated style.

The annual bills of mortality kept in this parish are famous as being the basis of Dr. Price's "Northampton Tables," on which all life insurance calculations are founded. These bills used to be posted at the end of each year, with a suitable "copy of verses" attached. Cowper, in a letter to Lady Hesketh, tells us that the clerk of All Saints walked over to Weston Underwood to speak to him, explaining that "the verses had been supplied by a gentleman of so much reading that the people of our town cannot understand him," and begged that Cowper would undertake the matter; which he did, for seven years.

St. Giles (enlarged 1857) has a Norman west door, but is chiefly Perpendicular; a chapel contains a tomb of the Gobion family.

Northampton contains many new churches in various styles, including a Roman Catholic cathedral and church.

Of the old priory of St. Andrew nothing is left; of the abbey of St. James a wall remains.

Another old foundation was a college of sixteen priests, founded by Henry VI. to pray for the souls of Margaret of Anjou and Prince Edward. St. Thomas's Hospital, founded in 1450, the Bluecoat School, and the Free Grammar School still exist. Other institutions are an orphanage, an infirmary, an asylum, a corn exchange, two jails, a barracks, a theatre, and an opera-house.

Of modern buildings the town-hall is worth a visit. On the façade are statues of English kings, incidents in the history of the town, and carvings illustrative of the trades of the town. The great hall and committee room are good; there is a stained glass window on the staircase, and in the council chamber Chantrey's statue of Perceval.

The county-hall (seventeenth century) contains

some royal portraits and two fine ceilings in high relief. The museum and free library were enlarged on the fabric of the old jail.

Northampton had a notable citizen in Laurence Washington, the ancestor of George. He came of the branch of the family settled in Lancashire, was a member of Gray's Inn, and established himself in Northampton, where he was mayor in 1533 and 1546. He married a cousin of Spencer of Althorp. At the dissolution of the monasteries he received the manor of Sulgrave, and removed thither; part of the house still stands. He migrated later to Brington, to a house still standing. His great grandson, Lawrence, was the father of the John and Laurence Washington who emigrated to Virginia, and the great grandfather of George. Lawrence was buried at Sulgrave in 1584.

The American Northampton (Mass., co. Hampshire) on the Connecticut was founded in 1654 on lands bought from the Indians the preceding year. Jonathan Edwards was pastor there from 1727 to 1750.

TAMWORTH

TAMWORTH is a pleasant, prosperous town, partly dependent on the rich grazing grounds and market gardens that surround it, and partly on the numerous local industries; it has a goodly number of citizens in comfortable circumstances, and therefore a wealth of respectable houses and suburbs. Nearly half way between Birmingham and Burton-on-Trent, built on both banks of the Teme at the confluence of the Anker, it stands partly in Staffordshire and partly in Warwickshire, the two halves of the town being connected by several bridges. The inhabitants have rights of pasture over two large tracts of common land, known respectively as the Stafford and Warwick "moors."

The surrounding country is mainly level meadowland to the south, rising a little and more enclosed to the north. Coal, fireclay, blue and red brick clay are found in the district, and vegetables are grown for the market; the industries are various, including textile printing and weaving, brewing, paper-making, etc.; Tamworth used to be famous for its superfine narrow woollen cloth.

Leland the invaluable, describing the town as it was in the Tudor period, states that it "was all well builded of tymber," which usually meant what we call a "frame" house. "The town of

TAMWORTH. The Entrance to the Castle.

Tamworth having a celebrated market is of ancient memory, and after the Danes had razed and defaced it, Ethelthleda, lady of the Merches, and sister of King Edward, sen., repayred it. . . . I saw but three notable thinges, the paroch-church, the castle, and the bridge." To go back to the earliest times we find that Watling Street ran near by, but Tamworth was not a Roman settlement. Precisely when it was founded we do not know, but we may judge that it was of importance at a very early period, for numerous charters signed by the Saxon Kings of Mercia in their palace of Tamworth prove that it was long a favourite residence of the Mercian house. The whole town was then surrounded by a great moat as to three of its sides, the river protecting the fourth; this moat, of which traces still remain, and which is known as the King's Dyke, was 45 feet in width. Possibly it was from this circumstance that Tamworth or Tamanweorthe—the island of the Tame—derived its name.

One such charter, granted to the monks of Worcester, bears the name of Offa, and the date 781. At the invasion of Mercia by the Danes the town was completely destroyed, but the celebrated Governess of Mercia, Ethelfleda, daughter to Alfred, rebuilt it in 913, after she had expelled the invaders. On the site of the present castle she raised a fortress and watch-tower, and until her death in 920 was frequently in the town.

The form of military service instituted by Alfred is well known; the land was divided into military districts, each five hides sending an armed man at the summons of the King, and sustaining him during his service. The army so constituted—all of freemen—was divided into two parts, one of which took the field while the other served as garrison. The eastern half of Mercia was now the "Five Boroughs" of the Danes: Derby, Lincoln, Stamford, Nottingham and Leicester being linked in a loose confederacy, each ruled by an earl and having an army of its own, with twelve "lawmen" to administer justice—which they found no easy task—and a supreme federal court over all. It was not leisure alone that brought Ethelfleda to Tamworth; as a stronghold it played a part in her plan of conquest. Her tactics were to lay siege and to build forts. At Tamworth, Stafford and Warwick she built castles, securing the lines of the Trent and the Avon; then, closing the approach to Wales, she moved upon Derby and Leicester, taking each in succession. Before her triumph was complete she died; but in the year 922 Tamworth saw the submission of all the tribes of Mercia and the Prince of Wales to Edward, her brother, who, attacking the five boroughs from the south, reduced the Fens, the Ouse, and the Nene, and annexed Wessex to his dominions. Then the north suddenly owned his lordship, and for a few years the whole country was at peace.

From the time of Edward the Martyr to that of Rufus Tamworth was a royal mint. At the time of the Conquest it became a royal demesne, but after a while was leased to the lords of the castle. The castle itself, or the site thereof, William gave to Robert Marmion of Fontenoy, in whose family it remained until 1291, when a daughter of the house brought it to William Mortein; thence it passed to the Frevilles, and about 1400 to the Ferrers; thence to the Comptons, and in 1751 to the Townshend family. The present building, surrounded by massive walls and standing high on its mound, is chiefly Jacobean; by whom erected seems doubtful.

Leland says, " The bare court and the great wall is clean decayed, and the wall fallen downe. . . . The dungeon yet standeth and a great round tower of stone, wherein Mr. Ferrers dwelleth, and now repayreth it." We are told that Earl Leicester thought of residing here, and had Wyatt survey the fabric, but it was then considered too far decayed. In the early part of the nineteenth century it was used as a factory; it is now in private occupation. Two fine sitting-rooms are wainscoted and decorated with arms of the Ferrers family impaling the various marriages contracted. The hall has an open timber roof springing from very low walls; on one wall used to be visible an uncouth painting of Sir Launcelot of the Hall fighting Sir Tarquin, which incident occurred, so says a legend, in the meads without the town. There is a curious ivy-covered tower; from this or the leads of the roof a very fine view may be obtained.

To return to Robert of Marmion, who built the Norman castle, we are told that he confiscated all the property of Tamworth church and college; whereupon the spirit of St. Editha paid him a nocturnal visit, the result of which was that he not only returned the spoil, but endowed the church with several manors.

The church in question is dedicated to St. Editha,

who lies buried here; the shrine and image of the saint were destroyed at the Reformation. The Marmion foundation gave it a dean and six prebendaries, each having a vicar or substitute. As late as 1553 the incumbents drew pensions; but Elizabeth granted college and prebends to Edward Downing and Peter Ashton. In the eighteenth century the living was only a curacy, but was finally declared a vicarage by the House of Lords.

It is a building chiefly of the Decorated and Perpendicular periods, as the Norman church was burned in 1345; of this two fine arches, with zigzag mouldings, remain. There is a crypt full of human bones. The tower is a fine massive structure; of the spire only the base remains. The stairway leading both to the exterior and the interior of the upper portion of the tower is of a rare and curious type; it consists of two spiral staircases superimposed—in other words, of a double spiral, like a two-threaded worm or screw—so that the treads of one staircase form the ceil of the other. The chancel contains ancient monuments of Marmions, Frevilles, and others, and the tower a fine seventeenth century tomb with life-size kneeling figures of the two last Ferrers. It is said that the church was founded, in connection with a convent, by St. Editha herself; this is doubtful, but we know it was rebuilt and made collegiate by Edgar.

Tamworth town belonged to the Crown until the reign of Henry III. It was then declared a free corporation; but the charter was forfeited, and restored by Edward II. Edward III. granted a fair and other privileges. At some period the town decayed and lost the name of borough; but Elizabeth granted a charter by which it was incorporated with a high steward, two bailiffs, a recorder, a town clerk, and twenty-four burgesses. The Elizabethan charter was superseded by one granted by Charles II., which was in force until 1885, and until the latter date the town returned two members, all voting who paid "lot and scot."

The weekly market was by prescription from the days of the Kings of Mercia held on Saturdays; Tamworth also had five fairs: on the Monday before 25th January; on 4th May (St. George's day, old style); on St. Swithin's Day; on the 26th July; on the first Monday in September; and on the feast of Edward the Confessor—the 24th of October—and the four following days.

We have heard Leland; Michael Drayton, who was born on the banks of the Anker, apostrophises the stream and his mistress in a well-known passage:

> "Clear Anker, on whose silver-sanded shore
> My soul-shrined saint, my fair Idea lies:
> A blessed brook, whose milk-white swans adore
> The crystal stream refined by her eyes. . . .
> Where nightingales in Arden sit and sing
> Among the dainty dew-impearled flowers,
> Fair Arden, thou my Tempe art alone
> And thou, sweet Anker, art my Helicon."

The parish register contains some significant entries:

Mem. in 1563 and 1626 the plague in Tamworth.

Mem. in 1597 the blouddie flixe (epidemic dysentery) at which tyme the darthe of corne somewhat abated by reason of deathe.

1598. *Mem.* that the 30th day of this April Robert Earl of Essex went from Drayton Basset toward Ireland to make warre against the Earl of Tyroone, an Irishman.

"Blouddie warre," the scribe might well have said. Drayton Bassett, or rather Drayton Manor, once the seat of Hugh Lupus, Earl of Chester, who married a Bassett, passed to the Staffords and was forfeited; finally it became the residence of Lettice, Countess Essex, mother of Elizabeth's favourite, and was visited by Elizabeth. Lady Essex afterwards married Dudley, Earl of Leicester. After the death of her grandson it passed to the Thynnes, and the first Marquis of Bath sold it to the great Sir Robert Peel. The parliamentary interests of the borough of Tamworth were formerly divided between the Thynnes and the Townshend family; but now Sir Robert Peel became one of the members. At Fazely, about 1½ miles south of Tamworth, he erected cotton mills, and connected Fazely with the great inland waterway of the Midlands and the North. To a certain extent Tamworth lost by the introduction of the railways; of course, only relatively and for a time.

To return to the register: we find that during the Civil War the castle was taken and held by the Parliamentary troops. In 1677 the free Grammar School refounded by Edward VI. was rebuilt, as it was again in 1867.

The Hospital, or Guy's Almshouse, is interesting as having been founded in 1678 (for six men and six women) by Thomas Guy, the famous and wealthy bookseller of London, who founded Guy's Hospital in Southwark. Guy represented Tamworth in seven successive Parliaments. He also rebuilt the town-hall, in front of which is a bronze statue of Sir Robert Peel. The town also boasts of a swimming-bath, a boys' institute, etc., etc., and is in all ways a pleasant and well-governed type of the lesser industrial and market-town of the Midlands.

SHREWSBURY

SHREWSBURY, a city that " glads itself and beautifies the shire," to quote the city's poet, Churchyard, is built on one of two peninsulas formed by an S-shaped twist of the Severn, the neck of the peninsula being only some 300 yards wide. Oliver Mathews informs us that the site was chosen " before the incarnation of our Savioure Christe 438 years." Holinshed states that the " Brytaynes " assembled here to oppose the Romans in the year A.D. 28, and that Shrewsbury was then a town of importance.

Llywarch the Old, the great Welsh bard, who is said to have reached the age of 145 years—attributed the fortification of the town to Cyndelan—" the purple-bearer of Powis "—and in his many references to Pengwern—the city on the hill of alders—it figures as a border-town, for long the capital of the Princes of Powis. Uriconium (Wroxeter), a few miles distant, was a Roman city, but there was no Roman station at Shrewsbury. Uriconium was destroyed by fire about the year 570; nothing is left of it to-day but a few foundations, some trifles in a museum, and the names of Wroxeter and Wrekin. At its fall, it seems, the British took refuge on " the hill of the alders " ; the Severn then ran in many channels, and the site may have been chosen for its inaccessibility. However, the Saxon was not long in coming; Llywarch speaks of a raider in Powis by the name of Twrch, "the hog," and in another passage—either in lament or prophecy—calls on the maidens of Pengwern "to leave their dwellings and behold the habitation of Cyndelan, the royal palace of Pengwern, wrapped in flames;" in prophecy, perhaps, for despite Saxon raids Pengwern was long the capital of the Kings of Powis.

In the year 780 Offa, the Mercian conqueror, crossed the Severn, conquered a great part of Powis, drove its king from Shrewsbury, as the Saxons now called it (Scrobbesbyrig—the fenced town among the thickets), and built the great wall running from Dee to Wye known as Offa's Dyke to this day.

Shrewsbury was still a border-town, but henceforth in the hands of the invader. The British had long relapsed from the civilisation of the Romans; even their native civilisation, through ages of almost nomadic war, had notably decayed. It is probable that the Pengwern that fell into the hands of the Saxons was merely a collection of wattled huts with roofs of turf or thatch, the whole enclosed by a rough stockade. Probably the general appearance of the hill was much the same as when the Britons first took refuge there; the Saxons would hardly have been content with an exact translation of the name had it been inappropriate.

Under Saxon rule Shrewsbury soon became a town of some importance, and comparatively civilised in character. Alfred's daughter, Ethelfleda, a widow of the Ealderman of Mercia, succeeded in the government, and founded at Shrewsbury the collegiate church of St. Alcmund, while under Athelstan the town was of sufficient importance to become the seat of a mint, whose coins are still extant. This was after Athelstan's invasion of Scotland and conquest of Cornwall, as is shown by the fact that the superscription is *Rex. To. Brit.*—King of all Britain.

Edmund reformed St. Alcmund's and founded the abbey of St. Mary. Ethelred, pursued by the Danes, "passed over Thames into Scrobbesbyrigscire," and there spent Christmas with his court. By this time Shrewsbury was one of the larger English towns, and of increasing importance as a great centre of Welsh-English commerce.

About this time a curious incident gave rise to a still more curious custom. Edric, earl of Mercia, invited Alfhelm, a royal prince, to visit him at Shrewsbury, and after feasting him for four days took him hunting, when one Godwin Porkhund, who is variously stated to have been a butcher and master of the earl's boar-hounds, came out from a thicket and slew him, as instructed by his master. After this, whenever the King was in residence at Shrewsbury, the citizens had to keep watch over him, the duty being shared by twelve of their number; when he went hunting thirty-six had to stand around him; and when he left the town the sheriff had to supply him with twenty-four horses.

Domesday Book mentions 252 houses of burgesses in the time of Edward the Confessor; these paid an annual rent to the crown. A fine of 100s. was imposed for assault and 50s. for burglary. Perhaps these fines were intended to intimidate the Welsh inhabitants and visitors; they were of course enormous for the times. We also find marriage taxed for the benefit of the king. The area of the town, when assessed for the Danegeld, was 100 hides. "The bishop" had sixteen canons in the town, all exempt from Danegeld.

The area of the town at the end of the Saxon period cannot have been much less than at present; but in those days of frequent sieges, and especially in a border town, situated in a country infested by raiders, it was customary to shelter and often graze flocks and herds, and even to grow a considerable amount of corn, within the walls. As late as 1538 we read of an order that hedges of thorns should be removed from the streets, and many signs of agricultural life and relics of mediæval farms have been discovered.

At the time of the Conquest Briton and Saxon once more joined in revolt, laid siege to Scrobbesbyrig, and burned part of the town. William himself came down to the March, and having settled the country left Roger de Belesme, or Montgomery, earl of Shrewsbury; he was also lord of Chichester and Arundel, and possessor of many manors. He left his son-in-law, Warin the Bald, as governor of the town, and built the castle, which occupied the site of 51 houses, while 50 houses lay waste and 43 were held by Normans, yet Roger took £40 rent. The burgesses were ruled by a præpositus or provost, who did little but extort rent. Evidently Roger chose to treat Shrewsbury as a conquered town; like other cities, it had to win its municipal privileges gradually, and had as a rule to pay dearly for them.

This Roger, it will be remembered, supported Robert Curthose in his claim to the crown on the death of William, but eventually made his peace with the King; he died at Shrewsbury a few days after taking the cowl, in the monastery of his own foundation. The walls of the town were commenced by his son Robert, the third earl. Another son, it will be remembered—the second earl—was killed fighting Magnus Barefoot of Norway, Robert was taken by Henry I. and banished. The castle then reverted to the crown, William Fitzalan being steward.

We cannot suppose that either Welsh or English were sorry to see the last of the Belesmes. "Robert," says an old historian, "slew the Welsh like sheep, conquered them, enslaved them, and flayed them with nails of iron." All the March was a country of border baronies; Roger de Montgomery had subdued part of ancient Powis and given it his name; soldiers of fortune sought the royal licence, "to make conquest on the Welsh," English armies marched into the heart of Wales, often to retire discomfited. And at this very moment a new life seemed to be infused into the Welsh people; under the two Llewelyns a renaissance of literature and national feeling took place; strange prophecies were in the air; so persistent was a report that Arthur was living that Henry II. paid a visit to his grave at Glastonbury, to dispel the legend.

To go back to the reign of Henry I., we find Fitzalan steward of Shrewsbury, and afterwards seeking to hold it for Maud, but unsuccessfully. In the reign of John, who, like Henry, led a disastrous expedition into Wales, some trouble with the crown resulted in the hanging of ninety-four persons in the town. In the year 1215, though he had surrendered to John four years earlier, Llewelyn took Shrewsbury and regained the ancient kingdom of Powis. His triumph was not for long ; in the following year John retook the town. A heavy toll was imposed upon the Welsh—the Welsh bridge was long guarded by a strong gate-house—and the Welsh princes came in for the adjustment of various differences. A new charter was granted in 1226, which witnesses to the importance of the guilds of the city ; despite wars and border raids, Shrewsbury was the great mart for Welsh produce and Welsh necessities, and the burgesses seem to have prospered.

Then came the reign of Henry III. and the Barons' War, and the rise of the second Llewelyn. In 1264 Simon de Montfort took and held the town for a time. All through this war Llewelyn was supreme in Wales, but Edward at last, after returning from the Crusades, marched into Wales, captured Llewelyn, and built castles at Conway and Caernarvon. It was settled that the title of Prince of Wales should lapse at Llewelyn's death, and he was married at the English court to Eleanor de Montfort, daughter of Simon. Four years later his brother David, who had deserted the Welsh cause in the previous rising, and accepted an English lordship, persuaded him to revolt once more. An old prophecy of Merlin, that when money was round a Prince of Wales should be crowned in London, seemed near fulfilment, for copper coins were minted, and the people forbidden to cut or break the silver penny into halves and quarters as before. Edward again marched into Wales, bridged the Menai straits, and hemmed in the Welsh leader, who eventually fell in a petty raid. Six months later David was captured, and sent before a Parliament sitting in Shrewsbury for judgment. This Parliament is noteworthy as being the first in which knights and burgesses sat by legal authority. It sat, probably, in the abbey hall, the three estates in one assembly as yet. David was dragged by horses, hanged, disembowelled, and quartered. After this act of mediæval justice the Parliament adjourned to Acton Burnell, where it passed the statute of that name.

In the next reign we find the burgesses groaning under excessive taxation. The taxation roll of Edward II. vi. names 189 persons as subject to taxation, the tax being the value of one-fifteenth of all their movables, down to their malt and their spoons and the food in their larder. The following entries are of interest as giving us some idea of the standard of living; but we must remember that the burgesses would not precisely make a display of wealth before the assessor, so their possessions may not have been quite as modest as appears.

Wm. de Brugg (probably of Bridgenorth) tanner; hides, 20s.; bark, 5d.; cloth, 3d.; pledges, 3s.; quarter of wheat, 4s.; quarter of barley, 2s.; 4 pigs, 3s.; household utensils, 2d.

Prior of St. John's, 3 draught horses, 9s.; a cart and harness, 4s. 3d.; a quarter and a half of wheat, 6s.; a quarter of rye, 40d.; a quarter of oats, 6s., 3 bushels of pease, 9d.; utensils, 8d.

Roger le Parmenter; washed skins, 17s. 4d.; lamb, fox and rabbit skins, 13s. 4d.; furs, 20s.; malt, 6s.; wood, 4d.; utensils, 3d.

Six years later, on the execution of one Harcla for treachery, Shrewsbury was honoured by a whole quarter of the traitor. This was regarded as such a mark of royal favour that it encouraged the burgesses to petition the King. They begged that they might have cognisance of pleas, make engines to grind grain and malt, hold a fair, and use all liberties already granted, whether they had hitherto been used or not. Edward II. granted charters innumerable, and as he had pledged himself to levy no new taxes he took care to sell them at the highest prices he could obtain.

The reign of Edward III. was uneventful in the city; Wales was quiet. But in 1349, the year after the appearance of the Black Death, a pestilence visited Shrewsbury; the symptoms as recorded by local chroniclers appear to be those of pneumonic plague. So terrible was the devastation caused by this plague that the mill at Shrewsbury, which commonly took 30s. in the year, took only 6s. 8d. A murrain followed the plague—possibly the same disease—and in 1394 there was a disastrous fire.

In 1397 we find Parliament again sitting at Shrewsbury. Thither came "old John of Gaunt, time-honoured Lancaster," and Henry of Hereford, "his bad son," to make good "the boisterous late appeal" against the Duke of Norfolk. This of course meant the presence of Richard II. and his court. Two years later Henry IV. was welcomed by the city, as he entered it to hold the first Parliament of his reign.

Then once more Shrewsbury knew stirring days and nights. Glendower, who had been an esquire of the body to Richard, had commenced his predatory war, and Henry had promptly retaliated by a statute forbidding any Welshman to buy land or houses in any border county, or to enfranchise in any border city ; those that were enfranchised were to find sureties. Henry, marching north to subdue the Northumberland revolt, reached Shrewsbury on 19th July, 1403. The battle of Shrewsbury is familiar to all ; how Sir John Falstaff " fought a long hour by Shrewsbury clock " ; how Hotspur believed he had killed the King, and was himself slain ; how in the retreat Douglas fell and was taken ; how Glendower watched the fortune of battle from the boughs of an oak tree. An extraordinary scene took place before the battle. First Hotspur addressed his followers : " This day shall promote us all if we conquer, or deliver us from an usurper if we fall, and it is better to die in battle for the common good than after battle by sentence of the foe." Then two knights were sent forward to defy the King and charge him with a heavy list of crimes, among them the murder of Richard II. (who probably died of a hunger strike). Then follows an episode that reminds us of the death of Julian the Apostate, who, because it had been foretold that he should die in Phrygia, was so sure of victory against the Persians that he had burned his fleet upon the Tigris to prevent retreat ; and who, when he lay dying of a spear wound, asked where it was that he had fallen, and was told that the place was called Phrygia. Hotspur had asked for his sword, and was told that he had left it behind at Berwick. Now he knew that he had left it in the village where he had lain the previous night, so that this must be called Berwick, and remembered that it had been foretold that he should die at Berwick. " Now," he said, " I perceive that my plough is drawing to its last furrow, for a wizard told me that I should perish at Berwick, but I had thought it was Berwick-upon-Tweed."

Glendower, watching the tide of battle, did not come to the succour of the Northumbrians. Henry was thrice unhorsed by Douglas. Hotspur fell by an unknown hand. Most of the knights and squires of Cheshire were slain in this battle. The dead were buried in a great pit at the place now called Battlefield, and Henry founded a chapel with two priests to pray for the souls of the dead. Hotspur's body, rubbed in salt, was brought into the city, laid between two millstones, and cut into small pieces, which were distributed to the cities of England.

Later in this reign we hear of the burgesses complaining to the King that they had fought in all the raids into Wales—during the long Glendower revolt—and had borne all the heavy expenses of service, never receiving any fee. We hear of the town being watched all night; of a flood; of damaged walls, and heavy taxes and hard times—for a general Welsh rising always struck a blow at the trade of Shrewsbury—and at last of yet another new charter.

The first English Prince of Wales was often in Shrewsbury. We read of a pipe of wine at 23s., and bread to the value of 20s., being given as presents to the Prince—presumably to feed his followers.

Not many years later Richard III. was riding by Shrewsbury when he accidentally met the widowed Countess of Richmond. This seems to have opened his eyes to what was afoot. Buckingham was for a short time a prisoner in Shrewsbury. Later Richmond came to Shrewsbury gates, and was admitted. Here he was first proclaimed King, and here recruited his army.

Two years later Shrewsbury was again in the grip of pestilence—the sweating sickness, which was said to have first appeared in this city.

In the reign of Henry VIII. the great days of the castle were over. Leland says: "The castle hath beene a strong thing. It is now much in ruin." He mentions four churches: the hospital of St. Chad, the collegiate church of St. Mary, and three other monasteries. At the time of the Reformation the abbey was dissolved, and the Corporation obtained the grant of Abbey Foregate and the hamlet of Muryvale. The Reformation commenced in the year of Henry's death, and we hear of pictures of "Our Lady and Mary Mawdelen and St. Chadde" being burned in the corn-market. In 1551 the sweating sickness again visited the town.

Churchyard gives us a pleasant picture of his native town, speaking of the

> "buildings gay and gallant finely wrought. . .
> Some houses bare that seemed to be worth naught
> Were fat within that outward looked lean."

He speaks of the great numbers of gentlefolk and great families settled or having houses in the town, and is no less struck by the manners of the people than by their wealth:

> "These meeke folk that meetes you in the streete
> Will curchie (curtsey) make or shewes an humble spreete;
>
> . . . . .
>
> This argues well they have in Wales been bred
> Or well brought up and taught where now they dwell."

We read, too, of the aldermen going in scarlet on all "solemn daies," and learn that the town had its bull-ring, cockpit, and wrestling ground.

At the time of the Armada "many gentlemen" gave £25 for purposes of defence. In 1595 we hear of the plague once more, followed by a dearth. In the following year, dearth or no dearth, the town has to find £40 ship-money. In 1600 we hear of "a cryar for night-time"; in 1632 and 1634, of the plague. In 1642 Charles I. entered Shrewsbury, and with the Princes Maurice and Rupert stayed two days at the council house. Presently he returned, sent to Aberystwith for the mint that was there (the mines round about being rich in silver and lead), and commenced to coin the plate given by the Universities in order to pay his troops. Sometimes nearly £1000 of silver was coined in one week. He also built the Cadogan tower, and a press was set up for the printing of proclamations. He finally marched away, his army of 12,000 the richer by 200 foot and 60 dragoons levied by the Corporation, leaving two cannon behind him, and Sir Francis Ottley as governor of the castle. He was superseded by Sir Michael Earnley.

In the winter of 1644 came a Parliament force under Colonel Mytton to besiege the town. At four o'clock in the morning carpenters landed under the palisade in a quiet spot and made a breach—it was said by connivance of some within. By noon the castle surrendered, having made terms for themselves. The Irish among the garrison were not included in these terms by the gallant Cavaliers, and were one and all hanged; but such was the custom of the times. Eight knights and baronets, forty colonels, majors, and captains, and 200 privates were taken, with fourteen guns and much plunder.

In 1651 Captain Benbow, of a local family, joined Charles II. on his march south with the Covenanters. He was taken at the battle of Worcester. He had previously served under Charles I., and had then been concerned in the attack upon the town under Colonel Mytton. He was sent to Shrewsbury and shot.

About this time tokens were in common use, and a large collection has been preserved. They were prohibited in 1672, but there are Shrewsbury tokens dated 1794.

In 1684 the charter was surrendered to Charles II. A new charter had to be purchased. In 1687 the King visited the town. The next sovereign also paid Shrewsbury a visit, and while there spoke on his favourite subject of the liberty of the conscience.

The well-known play, "The Recruiting Officer," was written by Farquhar while stationed at Shrewsbury, and is highly topical, all the characters being portraits of local worthies. Farquhar was attached to an artillery regiment under Viscount Newport, which was sent to defend the town.

The first stage coach was seen in Shrewsbury in 1659. It did not run for long; there was then no coach until 1750. Pack-horses were the usual means of transport; but in the eighteenth century a stage-wagon drawn by eight horses plied to London. After a time, passengers wishing to make use of it, a great box was suspended within the wagon by means of chains, which was known as a "Gee-ho." This vehicle made the journey to London in nine days. It was superseded by a sort of caravan, with benches for twelve persons; this was drawn by six horses. At last the coach re-appeared, and in 1781 the Irish mails began to pass through the town.

For the preceding three centuries Shrewsbury had held a position of great importance as the market for Welsh flannels and woollens. Every Thursday saw a procession of ponies crossing the Welsh bridge to the woollen fair, led by straw halters and bearing each two bales of cloth, slung one on either flank; the Welshmen leading them dressed in their own blue cloth. From the fair drays took the bales to the warehouses. It was no uncommon sight to see 300 of these ponies cross the bridge in a morning, representing 600 pieces of web. The Welsh had long woven their homespun stuffs for their own use, and peaceful times and a knowledge of English civilization, together with an increasing need of money, had resulted in their producing a surplus for exchange against English commodities. As a matter of fact ready money was paid at these fairs, but it was mostly expended, before the ponies recrossed the bridge, on malt, groceries, and other necessities or luxuries. The fair began to decay after the year 1790; doubtless travellers by the Irish mail had watched the fair and found food for reflection therein; for very soon buyers began to travel through Wales, buying the cloth at the cottage door or on the loom; a course very welcome to the housewife, if less so to her husband, as not only was a long journey saved, and an additional profit, but less of the earnings were spent upon malt in a liquid state, and the temptation to scatter money inseparable from a fair day was gone.

A very great deal of old Shrewsbury is still standing. Perhaps no city in England is richer in beautiful old houses; timbered or half-timbered, with massive oak frames and projecting upper stories. Some of the old streets in which these houses stand have most curious names, which seem to argue a Welsh or Welsh-speaking population; Dogpole is a plausible corruption of Duck-pool, supposing the pool in question to have disappeared; but how, on English tongues, could Hill Top become Wyle Cop, or Soet Place, Shoplatch? Among the finest of the old houses may be mentioned the Market House, with its arcade and mullioned window (1596); Ireland's mansion, a half-timbered gabled house; Owen's House (1592); Butcher's Row, consisting of fifteenth century houses, where the dwellings of the chantry priests of St. Alcmund's are supposed to have stood; Jones' mansion, where the Duke of York and Prince Rupert stayed awhile; Lloyd's House (1570); Draper's Hall, Vaughan's Place, Rowley's Mansion, Whitehall, and many another. In Wyle Cop stands the house where Henry VII. stayed when Duke of Richmond, on his way to Bosworth Field. The Post Office is remarkable as covering the site of the Butter Market, where stood that high cross below which David ap Griffith was hanged, burned, and quartered.

A pleasanter monument of old Shrewsbury exists in the ale, cakes, and brawn for which the city has for centuries been famous. Shenstone refers to the cakes as "rendering through Britain's Isle Salopia's praises known," which, if sincere, speaks well for his digestion.

A notable date in the annals of Shrewsbury was the Monday after the first Sunday in Trinity, which was the day of the pageant or annual "show," when the guilds and Corporation went in gay procession to the suburb of Kingsland, where each guild had its arbour erected, and where the day was ended in sports and festivities.

There is little space to speak of the more notable buildings; but mention must be made of the castle, which stands in a conspicuous position on the isthmus. Not much of the old Norman fabric is left; indeed the building is modernized and habitable. Built of a deep red stone, with square keep and corner turrets, it is still imposing when seen from a distance. The turret in the garden was built by Telford, the famous engineer; below is the garden which saw the execution of Benbow. A magnificent view of the Welsh range, the Shropshire hills, and the Wrekin may be obtained from the castle walls.

St. Mary's Church is a noble example of Norman and Early English work, and contains some magnificent stained glass. Some of this is the original glass; some has been brought from Flanders and Cologne. The ceiling is a beautiful display of carved oak, and the old tombs—many dating from the thirteenth century—are numerous and interesting. There is a memorial in the tower which is unintentionally somewhat amusing: a tablet to the memory of a youth who in 1759 attempted to fly across the river. The tragedy of the rash inventor is simply told:

> "Who by an attempt to fly from this high spire
> Across the Sabrine stream he did acquire
> His fatal end. 'Twas not for want of skill
> Or courage to perform the task he fell.
> No, no, a faulty cord being drawn too tight
> Hurried his soul on high to take her flight,"

where we will hope no further constriction caused yet another hurried removal.

Near by is St. Alcmund's, founded as a collegiate church by Ethelfleda, the daughter of Alfred, and badly rebuilt, or rather destroyed, save for the tower, in 1794. Close by stood St. Julian's, a Norman building, also demolished in favour of a polite monstrosity of the eighteenth century.

St. Chad's, near the walls, was founded by a King of Mercia, about 780, on the site of the palace of the Princes of Powis. In 1293 it was damaged by fire, and in 1788 collapsed. The fire was due to a plumber, who fled in alarm, fell into the river, and was drowned. A small portion of the old church remains, mostly rebuilt in 1571, and contains the tombs of Captain Benbow and of many notable Shropshire families. New St. Chad's, close above the quarry, has a body formed by the intersection of two circles, and is a particularly unpleasing experiment; its date is 1792.

The abbey church, which was attached to the monastery of St. Peter, has survived only in part. It is a beautiful building of the red local stone. It was attached to the foundation of Roger de Belesme, who died here. It was supported by two manors, the grinding of the whole city, and a toll of wood. It was restored in 1814. There is a magnificent west window, filled with the arms of kings, nobles, and county families—the Dukes of Gloucester, York and Lancaster, the Earls of Chester, March, Suffolk, and many others. Relics of St. Winifred repose in a shrine removed in 1136 from Holywell. The tomb of Roger de Montgomery or de Belesme is in the south aisle, with many others. The monastery—the chapter house of which was the place of assembly of the great Parliament of 1283—has vanished; but the guest hall is believed to survive in the abbey house, and the wall of the refectory still stands, with a fine stone pulpit.

The church of St. Giles' is the oldest in the town, though greatly restored. It was built early in the twelfth century for the use of lepers.

In the market square is a statue of Lord Clive, three times member for the town, and whose descendants are the modern Earls of Powis. It is related of him that when rebuked in the House for spoiling the Indian princes, his rejoinder was, "Damme, Mr. Speaker, I wonder I did not take more!"

The town is well equipped with museum, library,

assize courts, music and assembly rooms, corn exchange, market, infirmary, etc., etc. Notable among the charitable foundations are the Drapers Almshouses, founded by Diggory Watur in 1461; and Millington's Hospital, for the maintenance of fifty boys and girls. Last but not least is Shrewsbury School, founded by Edward VI. in 1551, described in the seventeenth century as "a fair free schoole of which there are fowr maisters and thir are sometimes six hundred schollers," a disproportion not likely to obtain again. The school is now across the river from the Quarry gardens. Among the notable men here educated are Sir Philip Sidney, Judge Jefferies, Sir William Jenner, and, most famous of all, Charles Darwin, whose statue in bronze stands by the museum of Roman antiquities. It should not be forgotten that in his younger days Coleridge preached here in the Unitarian meeting-house, which building was once wrecked by an enthusiastic mob of muscular and outraged Christians, but by order of George III. was rebuilt.

The council house, where Charles I. was quartered with Prince Rupert, is known as Lord's Place, and has been converted into private dwellings. A fine gateway, dated 1620, leads into the courtyard. It was originally the hall of the Court of the Marches of Wales.

INDEX.